## REMOTE WORK AND LABOR INSTITUTIONS

This volume shows how remote work is regulated by a holistic set of arrangements that govern all forms of employment, weaving together labor institutions in complex ways that the book presents and explains. The scholarship assembled here examines the handling of remote work through institutional analysis cutting across national cases and focusing on both fundamental rights and regulatory challenges. The rights that are examined – by analyzing their interaction with employer powers – include privacy, equality and non-discrimination as well as collective rights and the distribution of responsibilities in the workplace. The book shows how the location of work interacts with new technologies redefining the universe of labor relations and the institutional system governing employment. This title is also available as open access on Cambridge Core.

Julia López López is Senior Researcher of Consolidated Group (GREDiTSS, UPF). Her main research topics are collective labor rights, fundamental labor rights, gender equality and social protection and solidarity. She is the author of numerous articles, book chapters and books including Inscribing Solidarity: Debates in Labor Law and Beyond (Cambridge University Press, 2022) and Collective Bargaining and Collective Action: Labour Agency and Governance in the 21st Century? (Hart, 2019).

# Remote Work and Labor Institutions

Edited by
**JULIA LÓPEZ LÓPEZ**
Universitat Pompeu Fabra (Barcelona)

CAMBRIDGE
UNIVERSITY PRESS

CAMBRIDGE
UNIVERSITY PRESS

Shaftesbury Road, Cambridge CB2 8EA, United Kingdom

One Liberty Plaza, 20th Floor, New York, NY 10006, USA

477 Williamstown Road, Port Melbourne, VIC 3207, Australia

314–321, 3rd Floor, Plot 3, Splendor Forum, Jasola District Centre, New Delhi – 110025, India

103 Penang Road, #05–06/07, Visioncrest Commercial, Singapore 238467

Cambridge University Press is part of Cambridge University Press & Assessment, a department of the University of Cambridge.

We share the University's mission to contribute to society through the pursuit of education, learning and research at the highest international levels of excellence.

www.cambridge.org
Information on this title: www.cambridge.org/9781009597043

DOI: 10.1017/9781009597029



First published 2026

Cover image: Triangular shaped tunnel. Digital generated image of multicoloured triangular shaped tunnel. Metaverse concept / Andriy Onufriyenko / Getty Images

*A catalogue record for this publication is available from the British Library*

*Library of Congress Cataloging-in-Publication Data*
NAMES: López López, Julia editor
TITLE: Remote work and labor institutions / edited by Julia López López, Universitat Pompeu Fabra (Barcelona).
DESCRIPTION: Cambridge, United Kingdom ; New York, NY, USA : Cambridge University Press, 2025. | Includes bibliographical references and index.
IDENTIFIERS: LCCN 2025025341 (print) | LCCN 2025025342 (ebook) | ISBN 9781009597043 hardback | ISBN 9781009597067 paperback | ISBN 9781009597029 epub
SUBJECTS: LCSH: Telecommuting | Flexible work arrangements
CLASSIFICATION: LCC HD2336.3 .R464 2025 (print) | LCC HD2336.3 (ebook)
LC record available at https://lccn.loc.gov/2025025341
LC ebook record available at https://lccn.loc.gov/2025025342

ISBN 978-1-009-59704-3 Hardback
ISBN 978-1-009-59706-7 Paperback

# Contents

*List of Figure* — *page* vii
*List of Contributors* — ix
*Acknowledgments* — xi
*List of Abbreviations* — xiii

**Introduction – Labor Institutions and Remote Work: An Interactive Perspective** — 1
Julia López López

1 **How Remote Work Redefines Labor Institutions: Applying an Interactive Approach** — 13
Julia López López

2 **The Sustainability of Remote Work: The Significance of International Institutions** — 26
Tonia Novitz

3 **The Societal Value of Workplace Ties and the Challenge of Remote Work** — 44
Cynthia Estlund

4 **Hybrid Action for a Hybrid World: Collective Freedoms and the Challenges of Digital Work Fragmentation** — 59
Fotis Vergis

5 **Telework in Japan: A Game Changer for the Employment System and Labor Law Policy** — 81
Takashi Araki

6 **Remote Working and Subordination** 98
Adalberto Perulli

7 **Cross-Border Remote Workers and the Virtual Place of Work: New Pressure on the Territorial Application of Labour Law** 116
Alexandre de le Court

8 **Remote Work and Redistribution of Responsibility: The Korean Case in Perspective** 133
Choi Sukhwan

9 **Telework and Digital Surveillance: Legal Challenges on the Interface of Labour and Data Protection Law** 148
Elias Felten

10 **Remote Work and Artificial Intelligence: Threat or Chance for Worker's Rights?** 162
Miguel Rodríguez-Piñero Royo and Eusebi Colàs-Neila

11 **Telework and Work–Life Balance: Best Practices Addressing Gender Inequalities** 183
Nuria Pumar Beltrán

12 **An International Perspective on Occupational Health and Safety Challenges for Remote Workers** 199
José Luis Goñi Sein, Beatriz Rodríguez Sanz de Galdeano, Julen Llorens Espada, and Uxue Del Río Ilincheta

*Index* 217

# Figure

Figure 11.1 Employed persons working from home as a percentage of the total employment *page* 184

# Contributors

**Takashi Araki**, Chairman, the Central Laour Relations Commission, Professor Emeritus, University of Tokyo

**Eusebi Colàs-Neila**, Associate Professor of Labour Law and Social Security Law, Pompeu Fabra University

**Alexandre de le Court**, Serra Hunter Fellow in Labor Law and Social Security, University of Barcelona

**Uxue Del Río Ilincheta**, PhD in Labour Law and Social Security Public, University of Navarre

**Cynthia Estlund**, Crystal Eastman Professor, New York University School of Law

**Elias Felten**, Full Professor for Labour Law and Social Security Law Paris Lodron, University of Salzburg

**José Luis Goñi Sein**, Full Professor of Labour and Social Security Law, Public University of Navarra

**Julia López López**, Full Professor of Labor law.Senior Researcher of Consolidated Group (GREDiTSS Agaur, UPF)

**Julen Llorens Espada**, Associate Professor in Labour Law and Social Security Public, University of Navarre

**Tonia Novitz**, Professor of Labour Law, University of Bristol Law School

**Adalberto Perulli**, Full Professor of Labour law, Ca' Foscari University of Venice

**Nuria Pumar Beltrán**, Associated Professor of Labour Law and Social Security, University of Barcelona

**Miguel Rodríguez-Piñero Royo**, Full Professor in Labour and Social Security Law, University of Seville

**Beatriz Rodríguez Sanz de Galdeano**, Associate Professor in Labour Law and Social Security Public, University of Navarre

**Choi Sukhwan**, Associate Professor of Labour and Employment Law School of Law, Seoul National University

**Fotis Vergis**, Lecturer and Fellow in Law at Gonville & Caius College, University of Cambridge

# Acknowledgments

I would like to thank the Catalan Research Agency (AGAUR) for financial support during 2021–2025 with a grant (2021-SGR 00919) that has been of critical importance in our work on this book.

**Julia López López**

# List of Abbreviations

| | |
|---|---|
| AI | Artificial Intelligence |
| CEEP | Centre of Employers and Enterprises providing Public Services |
| CFREU | Charter of Fundamental Rights of the European Union |
| CJEU | Court of Justice of the European Union |
| COVID-19 | Coronavirus Disease 2019 |
| DX | Digital Transformation |
| EC | European Commission |
| ECHR | European Convention of Human Rights |
| ECtHR | European Court of Human Rights |
| EFAs | European Framework Agreements |
| EPSCO | Employment, Social Policy, Health and Consumer Affairs Council configuration (European Council) |
| ESC | European Social Charter |
| ETUC | European Trade Union Confederation |
| EU | European Union |
| GDPR | General Data Protection Regulation |
| HLPF | High-Level Political Forum on Sustainable Development (United Nations) |
| ICT | Information and Communications Technology |
| ILO | International Labor Organization |
| INSST | Instituto Nacional de Seguridad y Salud en el Trabajo (Spanish National Institute for Occupational Safety and Health) |
| IT | Information Technology |
| ITSS | Inspección de Trabajo y Seguridad Social (Spanish Labour and Social Security Inspectorate) |

| | |
|---|---|
| LPRL | Ley de Prevención de Riesgos Laborales (Spanish Law on the Prevention of Occupational Risks) |
| LSA | Labor Standards Act (Korea) |
| MOEL | Ministry of Employment and Labor (Korea) |
| OECD | Organisation for Economic Co-operation and Development |
| PWD | Platform Work Directive |
| SDGs | Sustainable Development Goals |
| TEU | Treaty on European Union |
| TFEU | Treaty on the Functioning of the European Union |
| UN | United Nations |
| UNICE | Union of Industrial and Employers' Confederations of Europe |
| UEAPME | European Association of Craft, Small and Medium-Sized Enterprises |
| VNR | Voluntary National Review |

# Introduction

## *Labor Institutions and Remote Work: An Interactive Perspective*

*Julia López López*

This book analyzes remote work through a holistic approach. The combination of advancing technologies and transformations in the thinking about work location has interacted to provide the axes defining remote work and its treatment by regulatory systems. The upsurge of work at home and other versions of remote work has transformed the traditional basis for the operation of labor institutions not only as a direct result of this form of employment – and its regulatory challenges – but also because of more indirect ways in which the complete employment system has been transformed due to the influence of home-based work regulation. I argue that the impact and interactions of employment forms as viewed in a holistic approach offer a more accurate understanding than would the effort to examine remote work in some sort of analytical isolation from other conditioning and interacting factors. The fruitfulness of a holistic approach is tied to the fact that types of work and regulatory instruments initially designed for a specific type of work or work situation interact with one another in complex ways. I suggest that those interactions can fortify protections for workers by linking different rationales and logics of protection in an encompassing set of regulatory arrangements.

The configurational thinking of methodologist Charles Ragin[1] provides a very useful framework for carrying out institutional and case study analysis such as the work that we undertake in this volume. Ragin's work emphasizes the significance of context-based combinations and configurations of causal factors and dynamics. In this perspective, causally relevant conditions or dynamics are really interactions and intersections of forces and events that constitute "configurations" that should be understood holistically. Ragin rejects the view that the causal impact of a given factor can be understood in isolation from its context and the other factors with

[1] Ragin, C.C. (2008) *Redesigning Social Inquiry: Fuzzy Sets and Beyond*, University Chicago Press, p. 109.

which it interacts there. Cases[2], in this perspective, should be examined behaviorally through an analytical focus on "casing" that involves both practical and theoretical efforts to identify and understand the patterns of interaction that shape outcomes of interest. This approach is valuable for the study of institutions and their transformations – including the regulation of types of labor. The important work of Kathleen Thelen on institutional evolution and her theoretical elaboration with James Mahoney develop this theme, arguing that the interactions between features of political context and properties of institutions themselves are important to explain institutional changes[3]. According to Thelen[4] the world around institutions is changing and therefore their survival involves ongoing active adaption to transformations in the political and economic environment in which they are embedded. The insights of this literature as well as arguments on remote work suggest that the regulation of remote work cannot be usefully analyzed as an isolated case of employment relations. Instead, these new relations and the regulation of them involve interactions with other forms of employment and the labor institutions designed to regulate them. The overall set of factors that interact with remote work and its regulation is quite large, encompassing, for example, the regulation of working time, the use of technologies and entrepreneurial powers, the right of privacy, conciliation between life and work, mobility, and channels or systems of union representation. This overall set of interactions is new despite the existence of some earlier efforts to deal with partially related phenomena. For example, the regulation of remote work poses challenges that extend beyond the bounds of the arrangements promoted by the flexicurity model. The new set of technologies and work locations that have proliferated with the growth of home-based work introduces growing complexities for labor institutions, complexities that cannot be fully handled or summarized by earlier regulatory treatments of flexibility. I have argued that the evolution of legal regulation of home-based and remote work can contribute to such ends not only because of how it is handled as a specific matter but instead because of how it *interacts* with other types of work and their regulation. The overall legal structure of labor regulation provides strong grounds for fortifying the defense of worker rights through such interaction. This book is premised on the significance of analyzing labor regulation interactions between remote and "in presence" work for reading current debates on labor law. In reconstructing the entire frame of regulation of remote employment relations, it is crucial to focus not only on protections for workers based on their location of work but also on protections

[2] Ragin, C.C. and Becker, H.S. (eds.) (1992) *What Is the Case? Exploring the Foundations of Social Inquiry*, Cambridge University Press, p. 217.

[3] Mahoney, J. and Thelen, K. (2010) *Explaining Institutional Change: Ambiguity, Agency and Power*, Cambridge University Press, p. 31.

[4] Thelen, K. (2008) *How Institutions Evolve: The Political Economy of Skills in Germany, Britain, The United States and Japan*, Cambridge University Press, p. 293.

rooted in other elements of their employment whether they are – for example – part-timers, temporary workers, or members of a group subject to discrimination due to their gender or some other social characteristic.

The first chapter, by volume editor Julia López López, extends and develops the book's overarching approach. As this chapter underscores, increasing forms of employment that combine remote location and technologies with complex work status conditions have created a constellation of cases characterized by hybridization of forms, sources, and contents of regulation. From this hybridization emerges a complexity not only for remote workers but crucially and more broadly for the complete employment system. The chapter identifies the urgent necessity to frame the debate on vulnerability and on the regulation of remote workers through a methodology centered on institutional labor *interactions*. Relatedly, this contribution also emphasizes the implications of the interactive and holistic approach for policy-oriented analyses of the protection system, arguing that it is essential to take into account all elements of the definition of the employment relation of remote workers including working hours, the length of contracts, and the effects of such parameters on fundamental rights and labor conditions. The real complexity found in the combination of elements of location and technology has tended to mask other types of complexity in labor institutions present in employment and thus the overall pattern of interactions. These additional forms of complexity and their place in the holistic pattern of hybridization should, in the analysis of this chapter, be specified in order to fully appreciate the vulnerability of these workers in their fundamental rights and so as to fully develop debates on the future of labor law as a democratic institution. The "export" of labor institutions such as the right to digital disconnection from one regulatory terrain to others provides illuminating evidence of the transplanting of institutional provisions from remote work to other forms of employment, thereby offering an example of the interactions that characterize labor regulation today.

Building on its overall approach, this book focuses on ways in which all forms of employment are impacted by interactions between values and principles of labor regulatory systems: Sustainability, cooperation, collective action, and approaches to delimiting work teams in the case of remote work exert a broad impact on employment forms. In this vein, the chapter of Tonia Novitz on "The Sustainability of Remote Work: The Significance of International Institutions" analyzes the ways in which remote work can be regulated to address issues relating to the aspiration of sustainable development recognized by the international community in the United Nations (UN) 2030 Agenda. Different forms of remote work raise distinct issues, which are examined in her contribution with reference to the economic, environmental, and social dimensions of sustainability and the relationship between 'business and human rights'. Novitz argues that, while it is possible to reconcile various modes of remote work with sustainable development objectives, it should not be assumed that this will inevitably be the case. Rather, there are certain preconditions (or safeguards) which must be imposed on employers and obligations that will need to be placed on governments. Her chapter then proceeds to examine the ways in which international institutions could ensure that such preconditions are met, examining the potential contribution from UN human rights instruments, the International Labour Organization, and due diligence mechanisms to provision of such safeguards. Novitz suggests that the ways in which these institutions interact and enable access for worker voice and contestation will be vital for the longer-term sustainability of remote work.

The models of cooperation in the frame of remote work are analyzed in the chapter on "The Societal Value of Workplace Ties and the Challenge of Remote Work" by Cynthia Estlund. Estlund's chapter emphasizes how the rise of remote work and work-from-home, accelerated by the COVID-19 pandemic, is reshaping and disrupting the social dimension of work – that is, the incidence of cooperation, sociability, and solidarity (as well as conflict) among co-workers. Most of the research and discourse around the trend toward remote work centers naturally on its impact on firms (especially in terms of productivity) or workers (especially in terms of work–life balance). Her chapter focuses instead on how remote work and work-from-home may affect the social underpinnings of political life outside the workplace. In the analysis of Estlund, the quotidian experience of working together – traditionally, face-to-face, side-by-side, day after day, and often across salient lines of social division – generates weak and strong interpersonal bonds that can strengthen the foundations of a democratic society. The cumulative societal benefits of co-worker interactions are at risk insofar as a shift toward remote work tends to thin out and weaken workplace ties. That is especially likely because those societal benefits do not accrue to either workers or firms; she argues that they are "public goods" and spillover benefits of workplace interactions. Those social benefits may thus be neglected even while the preferences of firms and (some) workers regarding the social dimension of work will shape trends in remote work through labor markets and markets for workplace technology. Her chapter develops that thesis and then reflects briefly on whether and how the conventional institutional arsenal of labor and employment law might be deployed to increase the production of such public goods.

Fotis Vergis in his chapter on "Hybrid Action for a Hybrid World: Collective Freedoms and the Challenges of Digital Work Fragmentation" studies collective labor law institutions under the prism of remote workers and the impact on other forms of employment. This chapter notes that "remote work" and "telework," which used to be regarded as exceptional subcategories of labor engagement, became the norm for white-collar workers during the pandemic, and currently sit at the heart of modern work practices characterized by spatial fragmentation and supported by web-based technological tools. Recent years have seen the advent of *hybrid* labor arrangements, in which work is directly or indirectly provided through apps or similar pieces of software and other technological innovations ("information and communications technology"). In the holistic analysis of Vergis, the overarching work digitization phenomenon is, inter alia, defined by increasing delocalization and fragmentation of workplaces, and by the advent of algorithmic management which employs advanced software and AI-driven tools of worker control. "Platform work," for example, an emblematic instance of this perceived paradigm shift of hybridization, may itself become terminologically obsolete, as a variety of (broadly construed) digital "platforms" define the work experience of more "typical" non-gig workers, whether their services are provided at their employers' premises or not. The same, arguably, applies to our established understanding of "telework" as work performed outside the employer's premises. As this chapter points out, even work typically performed on-site includes nowadays elements of delocalization, from virtual meetings to the use of virtual workspaces, and from constant online communication as part of a worker's daily activities to work that is actually performed online in its entirety.

The chapter of Vergis revisits our understanding of "teleworking" and attempts to examine the appropriateness of existing collective labor law institutions to address the needs and particular conditions of workers engaged in digitized hybrid work, given that such processes and institutional structures had been developed with different work models in mind. It considers that a solution may lie with the extension of the scope and focus of the rights to collective organization and action, and with a reevaluation of their substantive content. With regard to work and workplace fragmentation that comes with work digitization, this chapter seeks solutions in worker empowerment through the redeployment of collective labor rights and institutions. Within that context, Vergis also briefly touches upon illustrative case studies that provide glimpses into possible avenues of traditional and alternative collective action tactics. Where appropriate, the relevant current EU framework is used to contextualize the discussion, particularly given the transnational characteristics that often define digitalized workplaces.

Takashi Araki, in his chapter on "Telework in Japan: A Game Changer for the Employment System and Labor Law Policy," points to the tendency to reinform teamwork in Japan and beyond. Until the COVID-19 pandemic, a working style in Japan that emphasized teamwork was predominant and telework was not widespread. However, due to the COVID-19 pandemic, a majority of companies had no choice but to introduce telework. Telework, where individual workers operate independently rather than collectively, was – in Araki's analysis – an entirely new way of working for many Japanese individuals. His chapter argues that to make telework function efficiently, a reevaluation of Japan's traditional employment system, where job descriptions are not specified in employment contracts and individuals agree only to become members of a company, became necessary. While it was previously considered an obligation for workers to comply with employers' transfer orders involving relocation, telework has introduced a new option of handling such orders without physically relocating. In this way, Araki suggests that telework has the potential to be a game changer in Japan's traditional employment system. However, there are diverse legal issues that need to be resolved when introducing telework.

The book also analyzes the debates and institutional interactions regarding several frontiers of labor law, namely subordination, territory, and responsibility. Several chapters examine institutional interactions and debates that lie on the borders of labor law and that are articulated around these themes. As such, these themes are intrinsically linked to labor law but also extend beyond it.

The concept of subordination, as a feature of labor law extending beyond the remote work systems, is analyzed by Adalberto Perulli in his chapter "Remote Working and Subordination." Remote working – which spread widely during the COVID-19 pandemic – is clearly today one of the main forms of innovation in the world of work. Perulli's chapter notes that in this case, as always, within innovation phenomena we have static elements, coming from the past, and dynamic elements, looking to the future and to overcoming the status quo. His chapter suggests that, consequently, the evaluation of remote work may be either conservative or innovative. In the first perspective, remote work can be considered as a simple re-proposition of the Fordist-Taylorist enterprise, with some space-time updates which, however, do not actually change the characteristics of employment as a not democratic relationship (involving the worker's submission to the employer's managerial, control and disciplinary power, lack of autonomy, personal dependence, etc.).

On the other hand, remote work can be recognized as the symptom of a broader cultural, organizational, and process change in the firm, allowing the worker to conquer new spaces of freedom and autonomy, which not only allows for a new balance in the relationship between work and life (as required, for example, by Directive 2019/1158/EU on work–life balance for parents and carers which refers to "flexible working arrangements" including "the use of remote working"), but also redefines both the factual and juridical connotations of subordination. His chapter analyzes this second perspective and, on the basis of legislation and collective bargaining, tries to define the elements of change in the concept and morphology of subordination within the employment relationship.

The implications of territory for labor law institutions are taken up in Alexandre de le Court's chapter on "Cross-Border Remote Workers and the Virtual Place of Work: New Pressure on the Territorial Application of Labour Law." De le Court's study suggests that the advancement of technology has significantly altered the characteristics of remote work in general, and cross-border remote work in particular. The varied categories of cross-border remote workers, including hybrid remote workers, permanent remote workers, digital nomads, platform workers, and crowd workers, present complex regulatory challenges. These workers, in De le Court's analysis, possess distinct characteristics and concerns, complicating both descriptive and normative analyses of remote work. Additionally, advances in technology and the growing possibilities for telework have altered the traditional remote work model, where the workers' physical locations were typically aligned with the countries or regions where their employers sold goods or services. An increasing number of remote workers are now able to provide services across borders, to markets and countries where they or their employers have no physical connection. The greater possibility of this new form of delocalization, alongside outsourcing or opening branches abroad, increases the weight of factors linked with workforce management when companies decide to have recourse to remote work, to the detriment of operational factors. The chapter argues that as there are more employment regulations to choose from, this increases the possibility for the employer to exploit lower labor standards in other countries and avoid responsibilities toward their workers. The greater access to cross-border remote workers also increases the supply of labor with a consequent increase in international competition between workers, which also extends to new types of jobs. Those new challenges to worker protection also intersect with the global debates on social dumping, wherein employers may seek to exploit lower labor standards in other countries while at the same time possibly raising employment prospects and prosperity in those same countries.

De le Court suggests that the new characteristics of cross-border remote work have called into question the existing frameworks for coordinating labor law and social security legislation. For instance, in the European Union, provisional extensions have been granted to rules implemented during the pandemic to accommodate telework without altering the previously applicable social security law. The current framework also causes some companies to deny cross-border remote work for their employees, limiting its function as a tool to increase freedom for employees. Also, several studies have begun to question the effectiveness of these rules in determining the applicable labor law for cross-border remote work situations, as they have not proven to adequately protect workers or prevent social dumping, particularly for some categories of remote workers. One of the main reasons is the traditional interpretation of the concept of the habitual place of work as the place where workers are physically performing their work and its central position as a connecting factor, rooted in the idea that it coincides with the socioeconomic environment in which the workers are embedded and thus where they will enjoy better protection. However, this interpretation, rooted in the principle of territoriality, does not fit well with the new realities of cross-border telework.

De le Court's analysis of the literature and jurisprudence in different cases shows that new interpretations of the place of work are brought forward with the view to better protect cross-border remote workers, both in Private International Law and in Labor Law, considering the increasingly virtual nature of the workplace. However, the principle of territoriality remains a strong argument in the hands of higher courts to limit evolution in that direction.

The chapter of Choi Sukhwan on "Remote Work and Redistribution of Responsibility: The Korean Case in Perspective" suggests that remote work in Korea, which rapidly accelerated mainly with digitalization and COVID-19, is posing challenging issues about traditional labor law in Korea. The practice of long working hours, the crisis of a low birth rate, and, consequently, an aging population demand fundamental changes of working style. In Choi's analysis, with the development of information and communication technology, traditional ways of direct command and supervision seem to be reduced, while the discretion of workers expanded. However, these very technologies also make possible more detailed direction by employers – even by the contractors of the employers. The character of the employment contract as a mutual contract presupposes fair distribution of obligation and responsibility. Changing situations surrounding working conditions such as remote work may propose re-distribution of responsibility. This chapter explores the impact of remote work in the perspective of employers' responsibility by taking into account the experience of Korean regulation and policies.

The interactions and new perspectives on fundamentals rights, technologies, and powers inside firms attract the attention of several contributors. Elias Felten takes up these concerns in his chapter on "Telework and Digital Surveillance: Legal Challenges on the Interface of Labour and Data Protection Law," a study on the implications of remote work and new technologies on privacy and dignity. Felten notes that the progressive digitalization of industries and services, which accelerated rapidly in the last decade, has direct effects on the organization of labor. Telework is first and foremost a consequence of the generally increased use of information technology in our professional and private lives. The organizational changes of labor due to digitalization, however, challenge the functionality and effectiveness of labor law. Felton argues that the employer's comprehensible concerns such as the idea that teleworkers might pursue private interests at home serve in practice as a justification for the implementation of significant monitoring measures. Hence, we face a significant paradox: Even though teleworkers enjoy a putative higher degree of autonomy because they are not present at the employers' premises and therefore not subject to the physical authority of the employer, they are at the same time exposed to a higher degree of dependency since the employers' authority is diffusing and condensing in digital control measures. Data protection gains therefore gain increasing importance in the labor context. Labor protection in many cases cannot be separated from data protection anymore and vice versa. However, Felten's chapter argues that this evolution is not sufficiently mirrored by the law. The chapter analyzes in its first part the existing shortcomings and loopholes exemplified by the problem of digital surveillance of telework. In its second part it seeks to identify possible legal mechanisms to create or even foster interaction between labor and data protection law.

The chapter of Miguel Rodrigez-Piñero Royo and Eusebi Colàs-Neila on "Remote Work and Artificial Intelligence: Threat or Chance for Worker's Rights?" focuses on the technological element – expressed in AI which is usually part of the definition of remote work. This chapter discusses how AI tools shape the organization and performance of remote work, how algorithms impact on remote workers' rights, and how trade unions and workers can harness these powerful instruments to improve working and living conditions.

Three hypotheses are considered. First, it is argued that AI systems and algorithmic management, the use and purpose of which is decided by the employer, induce a de facto deepening of the subordinate position of the worker. If we also consider the alteration of the classic locational element, and some effects of isolation eroding collective bonds with other workmates, a possible consequence may be making remote workers more vulnerable to the degradation of their labor and fundamental rights. Second, the chapter argues against technological determinism. The neutrality and objectivity that may seem intrinsic to digital technology are, in the perspective of Rodríguez-Piñero and Colàs-Neila, not genuine, and this is particularly predictable of AI: The parameters of digital technologies are given to them by human beings or institutions. In the analysis of this chapter, AI reproduces and amplifies hierarchies and situations of discrimination. However, a reversibility of their use, favoring workers and their representatives, is also possible. The invisibility and fragmentation of remote workers might be overcome with the use of digital mechanisms, which are also essential for the development of trade union organizing and protest activities. And finally, technological resources usually are more present in remote work than in traditional work provided at the workplace. There are, a priori, no particularities, beyond the fact that the alteration of the workspace entails a business decision to use AI systems or algorithms for its management or favors the use of applications specially designed for this type of performance.

This chapter is divided into four main sections. The first section contextualizes the use of AI in the employment relationship in a diachronic perspective, pointing out the convergences and divergences with previous technologies, to better understand the legal challenges posed by AI. The second section offers an approach to the concept of AI, pointing out some applications commonly used in remote work, to comprehend how it works and its consequences for workers' rights. This technical approach is needed to develop a proper risk assessment of AI in remote work, especially (but not only) regarding the right to equality and non-discrimination. The third section analyzes the complex multi-level regulatory framework applicable, which includes both heteronomous and autonomous labor standards, common to all workers and specific to remote working. This involves intersections with other fields of law in which digital technology is central such as data protection (i.e., GDPR), and emerging regulations of platform work (such as the European Commission's proposal of Directive) and AI (i.e., the EU's AI Act); and constitutional rules recognizing fundamental rights that can be exercised by workers in the employment relationship. In the light of this regulatory package, the following issues are reviewed by these authors: how the introduction and application of AI tools in remote work should take place; which tools can be used, and which cannot; who controls such use and how; what role workers' representatives may/should have; and which accountability mechanisms of the employer and/or the AI provider can be activated. The last section provides examples of how AI can improve the working conditions of remote workers and be used for their organization and representation by trade unions.

The final debates in the book are about rights as goals of labor law. This theme is prominent in the treatment of equality and non-discrimination in the chapter on "Telework and Work–Life Balance: Best Practices Addressing Gender Inequalities" where the author, Nuria Pumar, points out that telework presents two quite distinct faces as regards working time. In her perspective, in general the statistics associate remote work with the intensification of work and with longer, more irregular work schedules; yet, at the same time – and this particular characteristic is directly influenced by European regulations and the EU Framework Agreement on Telework – telework can constitute a working-time arrangement that facilitates a better reconciliation of work and family life, provided it is promoted in favor of workers' interests. Yet, when seeking to determine whether teleworking has a positive or negative impact on the work–life balance, the outcomes are clearly ambivalent, in Pumar's analysis. Indeed, the extant literature examining the implications of teleworking for gender equality provides a rather unsurprising conclusion, but one that should be kept very much in mind, and that is that teleworking in itself is no guarantee of co-responsibility or of the transformation of gender roles. On the contrary, due to the very nature of teleworking, but at the same time owing to business practices and prevailing social stereotypes, there is a risk that it may be perceived as the most "appropriate" working arrangement for women, in a way that perpetuates gender roles and, even, widens the labor gap. To address this danger, Pumar argues that socioeconomic and cultural alliances, policies, and regulations must all row in the same direction and, in their wake, take steps to eliminate all patriarchal structures and systemic discrimination.

Remote work is not a gender-neutral form of work because it brings paid work into the domestic sphere, a traditionally feminine domain where productive and reproductive spaces overlap. Developing that idea, Pumar's chapter analyzes the impact that labor legislation and business practices of so-called "indecent" working time have on women and explores the issues to which teleworking gives rise in relation to working time and the work–life balance. Additionally, and with the focus more firmly on business practices, the chapter addresses the opportunities afforded by telework as a working-time arrangement and the possible penalties that women teleworkers may have to face. In this sense, the negotiation of hybrid and reversible teleworking formulas facilitates, on the one hand, the visibility of teleworkers and, at the same time, their capacity to request to either work remotely or return to face-to-face work, considering their personal needs and their different life cycles.

However, Pumar suggests that, as with other measures of workplace conciliation, certain business practices and associated stereotypes can lead to teleworking becoming seen as the "mommy track," chosen above all by women, so that it becomes another manifestation of the so-called "flexibility stigma," linked to the exercise of motherhood and childcare.

In an effort at preventing or reversing such inequalities, the chapter undertakes an assessment of the guarantees and protections provided by the European regulatory framework and of best practices in European transnational collective bargaining, where the lynchpins of these guarantees are the principles of voluntariness and non-discrimination, as well as respect for fundamental rights. Pumar concludes that the implementation of teleworking, as a mode that is respectful of decent work and of a worker's fundamental rights, needs to be firmly anchored in regulatory and institutional frameworks and in collective bargaining, in ways that seek to promote equality and diversity in firms in a transversal and transparent fashion and in adherence with the principle of co-responsibility.

The last chapter on goals and challenges of remote work and other forms of employment is the study of José Luis Goñi Sein, Beatriz Rodríguez Sanz de Galdeano, Julen Llorens Espada, and & Uxue Del Río Ilincheta offering "An International Perspective on Occupational Health and Safety Challenges for Remote Workers." Their chapter examines the main challenges posed by remote working from the perspective of occupational health and safety protection. In their analysis, understanding the paradigm shift presented by this new way of rendering services requires a multilevel approach. This entails, first, an analysis of the applicable legislation on health and safety at work, and possible initiatives to ensure minimum standards of protection regardless of where the remote work is provided. In this regard, their chapter proposes a revision of the rules of conflict for the determination of the applicable law, as well as the need to work toward a specific homogenization of EU legislation on preventive obligations for remote work. Second, they argue that it is necessary to analyze how the fact that these workers can provide services anywhere and at any time affects health and safety at work and its regulations. To that end, the chapter analyzes the problem of applying the current concepts of effective working time and rest time to the new activity times that arise in remote work, reconsidering new interpretative tasks in accordance with the digital environment. These authors also examine the problems that arise in controlling working time and its recording in remote work, as well as the legal limits of the new forms of control used by companies to verify remote work activity. Their chapter argues for the need to articulate specific forms of digital disconnection in order to guarantee the correct protection of occupational health and co-responsibility at work, as well as the need to introduce online working time as a psychosocial risk factor in the workplace.

Finally, this study examines the implications of remote work for the management of occupational risk prevention, taking as a distorting element the fact that the worker no longer provides services in a workplace that is directly controlled and accessed by the company and externally administered prevention services. The authors focus on how occupational risk prevention planning is carried out, paying special attention to the new occupational risks that may appear in the digital sphere, such as cyber-bullying. They also take up the increase in more traditional psychosocial risks, and the difficulties that arise in achieving an effective assessment of these risks.

Through all these contributions and the volume's overarching framework, this book offers a new perspective on remote work systems and consequences, analyzing the interactions of labor law institutions holistically. Our work illuminates the transformations that this form of work has brought about and their implications for a complete understanding of increasingly complex employment systems. This contribution sheds light on numerous crucial debates including those that examine vulnerabilities, sustainability, cooperation, hybridization, subordination, territories, responsibility, new technologies, privacy, dignity, equality and non-discrimination and health and safety. Our holistic approach to remote work and its interactions serves to deepen our understanding of essentially the full range of themes addressed by scholars of work and labor both in law and in related disciplines.

# 1

# How Remote Work Redefines Labor Institutions

## *Applying an Interactive Approach*

*Julia López López*

## 1.1 REMOTE WORK AND HYBRIDIZATION OF EMPLOYMENT FORMS AS A CHALLENGE FOR LABOR REGULATION

This chapter applies the volume's interactive approach to the handling of remote work by labor institutions, underlining the complexity of labor contracts and their tendency to combine locational elements of work with other crucial dimensions of worker status such as the number of hours worked or the length of contract. The chapter devotes considerable attention to studying the construction of regulatory systems for remote work by highlighting the crucial role of the subsidiarity principle and the combinatory dynamics of levels, forms, objects, and rationales of regulation. Finally, this contribution also addresses policy-oriented questions, proposing the construction of a holistic frame of governance intended to reinforce labor rights for remote workers.

The combination of advancing technologies and transformations in our thinking about work has promoted increasingly diverse forms of *non-presence* at work. As the International Labor Organization (ILO) has underlined, the institutionally rooted statistical definition of this phenomenon is in itself a complex matter. Indeed, currently there is no fully agreed-upon international statistical definition of *remote work*. The challenges involved in the definition of such forms of employment are pointed out by the ILO:[1] As is elaborated in this ILO technical note, remote work can be described as situations where the work is fully or partly carried out in an alternative worksite.

In practice countries have used slightly different operational definitions of remote work, typically based on two different components (Eurofound 2021). One of those components specifies that the work is fully or partly carried out at an alternative

[1] ILO. COVID-19: Guidance for labor statics data collection. Defining and measuring remote work, telework, work at home-base work. ILO (2020), pp. 5–14; ILO (2023).

location other than the default place of work, whereas the second component involves the use of personal electronic devices such as a computer, tablet, or telephone to perform the work: The use of personal electronic devices is an essential part of the definition. Telework, as defined above, is a subcategory of the broader concept of remote work. It includes workers who use information and communications technology or landline telephones to carry out the work remotely. Similar to remote work, telework can be carried out in different locations outside the default place of work. What makes telework a unique category is that the work carried out remotely includes the use of personal electronic devices. Work at home refers to work that takes place fully or partly within the worker's own residence.

Work at home is part of the crosscutting variable "type of workplace" in the resolution concerning statistics on work relationships (ILO 2018), which provides information on the type of location where the work is usually performed. Based on the definition of the type of workplace provided in the resolution, work at home is any work taking place within a residential building or other type of dwelling in which the worker normally resides (ILO 2020, pp. 268–270). Thus, these concepts are interrelated and have some degree of overlap. Telework, for example, can be performed in the worker's home, and a home-based worker can also telework. One important point to underline in this constellation of forms of homework is the idea of hybrid forms that present important consequences not only for employers but also for employees (Countoris et al., 2023).

It is important to emphasize that the boom of home-based work includes very diverse combinations of the two elements of this genre's definition: the locational and the technological (Telework and ICT-based mobile work Publications Office of the European Union, 2020). These combinations vary by country and by sector of production. Thus, the locational element may refer to the worker's home or to another space of the worker's choice, and the technological factor is also significant, this being what differentiates it from remote work.

The diverse combination of location and technology in the current frame of labor regulation provides a challenge for the defense of fundamental rights for workers. This theme and its connection with political debates are taken up in *Labor Law and Democracy* (2022) by Mark Barenberg and other authors who focus on this challenge, by proposing a new labor law based on a deepening of democracy. From this perspective, the debate on the fundamental rights of remote workers stands as a component of the larger demand to intensify the democratic profile of labor regulation (López López, 2022). Harry Arthurs (2024)[2] has argued that strengthening the future of work-related law stands as part of a larger project of political and social transformation. All the institutions of labor law as a democratic institution should help in the implementation of principles and rights that lessen or reduce inequality. From this perspective the question that is raised here is whether or not new forms of

[2] Arthurs (2024), p. 31.

decentralized work and their management can help in that purpose. The historical context is a propitious one for posing this question: In 2021 the ETUC (European Trade Union Confederation) called for a year of more democracy.

The right to equality and nondiscrimination recognized for this type of employment should be interpreted as a key to democratic progress in the workplace, and thus to the goal of democratic deepening (Fishman, 2016, 2019; Roberts, 2022) – reflected, for example, in democracy at work and postindustrial justice.[3] A firm basis for pursuing that goal lies in the principle of the right to fair and decent work for all (Freedman et al., 2020). This constellation of interrelated themes identifies major issues at stake in the treatment of remote work.

Hybridization of employment status is reflected not only in the employment relation but also in the sources of regulation – including both hard and soft law and corporate social responsibility – and in forms of telework differentiated by their combinations of "presentiality" and remote work and their interrelationship with other contractual typologies such as part-time work and temporary work. An additional element of complexity involves the way in which telework challenges conventional understandings of national borders in the legal regulation of work.

## 1.2 INTERACTION OF ACTORS AND SOURCES OF REGULATION IN REMOTE WORK: ABOUT INVERTED SUBSIDIARITY

In a general sense the hybrid forms of combination between technological and locational innovations in work create challenging questions centered on principles of labor rights and the sources of regulation – and regulatory systems for remote workers. The pressure generated by this complex and fragmented reality of work-status has induced a hybridization of the regulatory model reflected both in the initiatives or practices of actors – supranational and national institutions, workers, entrepreneurs, unions and employers' associations – and in the sources of regulation – for example in law, collective bargaining, and agreements. This in turn puts in place consequences for the enforceability of regulations – as shaped by hard law, soft law, and intermediate categories – at multiple levels, including the international, supranational, regional, and local arenas. The resulting spillovers of such complex dynamics have to be understood in a holistic frame. More concretely, the spillover of regulatory consequences from the treatment of remote work to other arenas generates a complex and dynamic scenario involving the impact of home-work on the broader employment regulation system. One example is the role played by governance principles such as subsidiarity in the distribution of regulatory competences among actors. The interactions among levels, actors, and institutions involved in the governance of home workers create interesting spillovers that

[3] Cr Dukes, R. and Streeck, W. *Democracy Art Work: Contract, Status and Post-Industrial Justice* (2022) Wiley.

transform the complete employment regulation system. Crucially, given the multilevel interactions stressed here, it is necessary to introduce the principle of subsidiarity into debates on governance of new work arrangements.

The subsidiarity principle is, in practice, an important reference in handling the relations and interactions between different levels of policymaking and regulation whether the matters involved concern the updating of regulations initially formulated in the context of traditional forms of work, or other concrete issues. Subsidiarity implies the sharing of competences in governance across multiple "levels," through the principles of participation and proportionality. Supranational institutions under this principle only intervene in specifying regulations if, at the national level, it is not possible to achieve the goals stipulated in general terms at the supranational levels. International scholarship on this question has pointed to advantages of this principle centered on its respect for a variety of solutions to shared problems and in the specification of how to guarantee human rights (Carozza, 2003). An important contribution of Sciarra has elaborated the significance of this principle for the EU and for European labor law (Sciarra, 2023). The work of Bogg has identified connections between this principle and all coordinated human activity while specifying how it permits the promotion of decent work (Bogg, 2013).

The subsidiarity principle holds a great deal of concrete relevance for regulating remote work. In the construction of levels ruled by the subsidiarity principle the ILO Conventions serve as a floor of reference. A cornerstone is provided by the hard law regulation of domestic work in ILO Convention 177, Home work Convention (1996). This international norm defines homework, art COI 177, Article 1, as work carried out by a person, in his or her home or in other premises of his or her choice, other than the workplace of the employer for remuneration; which results in a product or service as specified by the employer, irrespective of who provides the equipment, materials, or other inputs used in the work. This Convention and Article also include the definition of the employer.

Article 5 of the Convention stipulates that national policy on homework shall be implemented by law, regulations, collective agreements, or arbitration. Consultation in the implementation of this stipulation at the national level is required in Article 3 of the Convention.

Using the lens of subsidiarity, this ILO Convention guarantees that its content serves as a minimal floor without undermining more favorable provisions applicable to some homeworkers under other international labor Conventions.

Thus, this Convention sets a minimal floor for national-level regulation. In Article 4, this minimal floor is developed as the promotion of equality of treatment for homeworkers when compared to the conditions applicable to the same or a similar type of work carried out within an enterprise. The Article includes under the principle of equality the homeworkers' right to establish or join organizations of their own choosing and to participate in the activities of such organizations; protection against discrimination in employment and occupation; protection in the field of occupational safety and health; remuneration; statutory social security protection; access to training; a minimum age for admission to employment or work; and maternity protection.

At the level of the European Union, the application of the subsidiarity principle is established in Article 5 of the Treaty; this principle raises very important questions about the role of the State and its limits (Carozza, 2003), and it holds broad implications for social actors (Bogg, 2013) and cooperation (Iglesias, 2017). The most crucial point in the case of remote work and its impact on employment regulation is the central role played by collective agreements at the European Union level to set the minimal floor of regulation and rights. In the governance of remote work, EU regulation has in effect implemented what we could call an "Inverted Subsidiarity" in which the ordering of instruments of regulation – either at the EU level or at the member state level – is quite different from the most common pattern. At the supranational level, EU regulation of remote work has been articulated around a Framework Agreement that is an EU-level collective bargaining accord that sets the principles of regulation, whereas the national-level implementation is pursued through both Agreements and statutory regulations. The bases of the Framework Agreement are, as in the international ILO Conventions, to protect equality and nondiscrimination and additionally the voluntary character of remote work, including its reversibility.

Until 2021 the Framework Agreement had only modest results. However, given prevailing circumstances during the pandemic, in 2021–2022 arrangements for the implementation of remote work expanded greatly in the member states. Different patterns of implementation by member states (involving hard law, soft law, and hybrid instruments) suggest that the regulation of homework has been characterized by a hybridization not only in the definition of the case but also in the sources of regulation and the results.

The historical basis for the key Framework Agreement extends back to the beginning of the twenty-first century: In 2001, the ETUC, the Union of Industrial and Employers' Confederations of Europe (UNICE)/the European Association of Craft, Small and Medium-Sized Enterprises (UEAPME), and the European Centre of Employers and Enterprises providing Public Services (CEEP) signed a framework agreement on teleworking. The purpose of the agreement was "to give more security to employed teleworkers in the EU." In order to fully understand this important accord, it is useful to analyze the regulatory period in which important Directives were approved and also to specify the interactions between those Directives, interactions which made them complementary to one another.

Key legislative provisions rooted in the Framework Agreement have been implemented in Austria, Belgium, Bulgaria, Croatia, Czechia, France, Germany, Greece, Hungary, Ireland, Italy, and Spain. One point which is very interesting is that the elaboration of national-level agreements on telework lacks an implementation of gender equality. The irradiation of the Framework on Telework in national-level collective bargaining is clear in the application of its voluntary status (in Belgium, France, Spain, Italy, and Luxembourg) but not in the defense of gender equality or equal pay. These latter objectives have to be guaranteed at the statutory level. The acquis communautaire guarantees these rights, and statutory regulation at the national level has to complement the deficits in social rights for remote workers. Directives on equality and nondiscrimination, on collective dismissal, health and safety, and information rights have to be applied to guarantee social rights for remote workers.

To understand the case of remote work regulation in a holistic way it is necessary to insert it within the normative cases of negotiated Directives. These Directives promoted many significant regulatory measures, including a greater protection of part-time work – Directive 97/81 – on fixed-term contracts and the prohibition of abuses – Directive 1999/70 – together with the Directives on equality – Directives 2010/41, 2006/54, and 2004/1113 – as well as later the Directive on reconciliation 2019/1158. This entire set of EU regulations was produced by both acting on the segmentation of workers' status and by building a regulatory common ground defending equality and nondiscrimination. The holistic frame of regulation, as is reflected, for example, in these Directives, is best understood as an instance of labor law institutions protecting vulnerability.

The flexicurity model promoted during that period was based on the combination of flexibility of entry and exit from employment with security rooted in steps designed to ensure the employability of workers through vocational training and unemployment coverage. This model was based on a series of balances between flexibility and security measures. Within this scheme, the remote work model did not take off in a generalized manner until the global outbreak of the pandemic.

From 2001 to 2020 the implementation or impact of the 2001 Telework Agreement was modest. This was not the case with the Part-Time Agreement (1997), which, as a negotiated Directive, had an impact on the organization of the member countries in this area and which took voluntary work and the principle of equality and nondiscrimination as the basis for the regulation of that form of work. Thus, the first important developments in forms of regulation of part-time work and telework date from two decades ago, encompassing several common principles – voluntariness and reversibility – and fundamental rights – equality and nondiscrimination. However, the impact of these regulatory principles on the management and the prevalence of telework was not significant until the pandemic. These modest results of the Telework Agreement might initially have appeared to reflect the fact that the regulatory document was an agreement between negotiating partners rather than a Directive as was the case with the 1997 regulation of part-time work. However, during the pandemic, the application and use of the 2001 Agreement grew very substantially, thus suggesting that the earlier limitation in its application was based on factors other than its formal character. Crucially, in a comparison of these two management instruments – on part-time work and teleworkers – in terms of content, the Telework Agreement presents a thoroughness in the recognition of fundamental rights that does not appear in the Directive on part-time work, nor in that of temporary employment.

In my analysis, the economic context and the policies chosen to overcome the COVID crisis were decisive. The pandemic-based economic crisis was marked by the end of austerity-oriented economic adjustment policies and the implementation instead of interventionist policies of another paradigm. In this sense, the COVID pandemic has meant not only an economic, social, and humanitarian crisis worldwide but also a change in the economic paradigm shaping how the crisis was faced. In the previous crisis, the dominant response paradigm in Europe emphasized austerity, an approach that was questioned by a very significant sector of economists (Akerlof and Shiller, 2009; Piketty, 2014). The response to the COVID crisis instead promoted economic expansion. Economic practice in this context facilitated remote work and telework not only to address the public health situation that the pandemic brought about but also as an approach to the organization of work in the future. In this sense the analysis of remote work and workers should be contextualized by placing these phenomena within a time of paradigm shift intended to address the economic crisis not through austerity and cutbacks but instead through a model of intervention with public policies of social spending and through flexible approaches to the organization of work.

The definition provided by the Telework Agreement in Article 2 tries to cover the various manifestations of this type of contract, thereby reflecting its underlying complexity. Telework is defined as a form of organization and/or performance of work using information technology, within the framework of an employment contract or employment relationship, in which work that could also have been performed on the employer's premises is usually performed away from those premises.

This Agreement has been incorporated – in its distinctive form of implementation – in the different national models and is reflected in the norms, conventions, and instruments of corporate social responsibility which, in cases such as Spain, Portugal, Italy, or Austria, have transplanted it into the national legislation of the member countries. There is a dynamic of implementation in a process that is inverse to the cases of part-time and temporary contracts in which the hard law norm (namely in a negotiated Directive) is located initially at the community level and then radiates to the member countries, whereas in the case of teleworking the Agreement (itself an example of soft law) radiates to the member countries, where it ultimately becomes hard law (manifested in legislation or collective bargaining agreements) and in all cases the central underlying principles embodied in the regulatory approach – namely voluntariness and reversibility – and the linkage to fundamental rights are preserved.

This application of the subsidiarity principle presents several important features. A main one is that collective bargaining is, in this instance, the instrument providing the initial minimal floor at the EU level. This holds consequences in the interaction of levels of regulation and degrees of enforceability of the regulatory systems, because the initial EU floor is not a hard law instrument. However, in some member states the rules agreed upon in the Agreement have been transformed into hard law regulation at the national level. Crucially, the Charter of Fundamental Rights stipulates in its Article 51 that rights guaranteed by the Charter must be applied when the member states are implementing other elements of EU law. This means that a holistic reading of the acquis communautaire and its implications for applying negotiated framework agreements – in our case for home workers – leads to the promotion of the principles and rights elaborated in the Charter under the principles of subsidiarity and proportionality. In this instance the subsidiarity principle ultimately leads to a strengthening of enforceability in many member states.

In 2001, the Telework Agreement included a series of rights for teleworkers, putting in place hallmarks of this type of work that do not exist to the same extent in the negotiated part-time and temporary contracting Directives. In this sense, this Agreement has an intensity in the content of labor rights that presents a noteworthy potential for development. Together with the fundamental rights that are recognized, there are two principles that I view as significant, that of voluntariness and that of reversibility, both of which incorporate labor rights into the management of remote work. The process of being able to influence the choice between forms of work implies a right of worker participation that is also guaranteed in the implementation of reversibility. This voluntariness in the case of part-time teleworkers is reinforced by the interaction of the different regulations (Prassel, 2016; Novitz, 2022).

The principle of voluntariness reinforces the consensual nature that the implementation of these forms of work organization has in the legal framework established by the Agreement, an approach that repeats the legal framework for part-time work in the 1997 Directive and the Agreement that gave rise to it. It is a form of implementation of the negotiation process that has provided the basis, for example, in the Spanish case, for the Courts to require employers to justify refusals to make changes requested by the worker in an application of the reversibility principle.

Another crucial point is that the elaboration of national-level agreements on telework lacks an implementation of the commitment to gender equality. The irradiation of the Framework on Telework in national-level collective bargaining is clear in the application of this type of work's voluntary status (Belgium, France, Spain, Italy, Luxembourg) but not in the defense of gender equality or equal pay or training (Eurofound dates, Telework in the EU: regulatory frameworks and recent updates, 2020).

The analysis of the principles and fundamental rights of teleworkers in the regulatory order and of that order's interaction with other forms of labor relations is of fundamental importance in assessing how to deepen democracy in labor relations. The axes underpinning and articulating social rights have to be interconnected to the right of equality and nondiscrimination, understanding the meaning of equality as dignity (Barnard and Hepple, 2000; Hepple, 2001), a principle that has one of its most important inscriptions in the broadly understood right of participation. Thus, the starting point, in my assessment, is to articulate the rights of teleworkers around fundamental rights that are key to structuring progress in democracy. This involves, above all, the rights of equality and nondiscrimination as manifestations of dignity, an approach that promotes not only the elimination of discrimination but also the correction of differential gaps in outcomes.

As I have argued, the Telework Agreement, with its long history of management of labor relations, is the key reference for embedding the regulation of this form of work in an affirmation of fundamental principles and rights of labor relations not only at the EU level but also at the national level. At the level of the member countries, regulation instruments vary according to national models; in addition to the domestic legal norms there are national collective agreements and other soft law instruments resulting from corporate social responsibility.

Concerning the rights that are included in the different instruments at the level of the member countries, and that could be grouped around equality and nondiscrimination, it is useful to view them as vectors of progress in the improvement of democratic structures (Roberts, 2022). The rights of equality and nondiscrimination – in their provision for conciliation, training and participation, and including the management of the rights to health according to the Directive 89/391CEE, and to the specific Directives, national legislation, and the relevant collective agreements – offer an itinerary of progress in elaborating democratic structures in the workplace. The right to equality and nondiscrimination is further nourished by another set of fundamental rights, namely, the rights to dignity and privacy, the contents of which are defined in the Agreement, in national regulations, in collective agreements and in corporate social responsibility.

The telework legal framework guarantees that the employer should respect the private life of the teleworker. In the Spanish case, this is elaborated in interaction with EU rules related to the right to privacy and the use of digital devices in the workplace, as is provided for in Spain's Organic Law 3/2018, of December 5, on the Protection of Personal Data and guarantee of digital rights and at the EU level in Regulation (EU) 2016/679 of the European Parliament and of the Council of April 27, 2016, on the protection of natural persons.

The interactions between the right to equality and the principle of inclusive solidarity have a main reference in the Charter of Fundamental Rights. Underpinning those interactions, understanding equality as inclusive solidarity (López López, 2022), are initiatives to address the conciliation of family and work life, technological training, and to elaborate collective rights in all levels of participation such as social dialogue, collective bargaining, and the freedom to protest and to obtain information. For example, Directive 91/533/EEC establishes that the employer facilitates pertinent written information to the teleworker. If the employer undertakes online supervision of telework, the means used must be proportionate to the objective and introduced in accordance with Directive 90/270 EEC, relating to display screens. Digital disconnection, as a recognized right, is linked to work and rest times, and to the principle of reconciliation of work and family life, as well as occupational health and can therefore be inserted within the right to equality and nondiscrimination that has been presented here as a major point of reference. Collective bargaining agreements as well as corporate responsibility instruments also play a crucial role entering into the regulation of this form of work. This interest by labor relations negotiating partners in telework and its regulation does not occur in the same way for part-time work and temporary work, although it should be said that there are differences in the intensity of this coverage according to sectors of activity.

A useful example in the Spanish case is the sector collective agreement for the financial sector[4], which in its Article 14 integrates the principle of voluntary work for telework by employees is to be reflected not only in the implementation of telework arrangements but also in their reversibility. The collective agreement also provides mechanisms to guarantee some working time in the workplace.

In its Article 14, this agreement specifies the rules or principles of telework as voluntary and reversible, either by the will of the company or by the worker. It also includes, in Article 15, the digital rights of the workforce, which, among other points, include the right to digital and labor disconnection, training, and participation. In the collective agreement, digital disconnection is understood to be rooted within the limits set between work and rest time and with an impact on life planning.

Digital disconnection is linked to the right to health and with the reduction of technological fatigue or stress. Finally, the right to worker training is defined in this collective agreement by integrating the right to digital education. Companies commit to training their personnel in the digital competences and skills necessary to face the digital transformation and thus facilitate their digital reconversion and adaptation to new jobs, as well as their participation rights in the implementation of algorithms within the right to artificial intelligence.

On the other hand, collective bargaining agreements are making advances in the definition of forms of discrimination that occur in the technological environment. For example, the second bargaining agreement of Telefonica[5] defines cyberbullying through the principle of prevention. This content of collective bargaining agreements on existing categories of protection against discrimination and harassment in technological fields is important. A framework collective agreement was signed

[4] Official Journal of the European Union June 6, 2024.

[5] Resolución de 17 de marzo de 2022, Official Journal of the European Union 29 march 2022, II Convenio colectivo de Telefónica de España, SAU, Telefónica Móviles España, SAU, y Telefónica Soluciones de Informática y Comunicaciones de España, SAU.

between employers and employees (ANEC 2023)[6], which includes the commitment to promote telework as a flexible and negotiated form of work. The agreement includes the right to digital disconnection and promotes policies of human control of IA.

Levels of regulation, sources of regulation, and regulatory contents all interconnect labor institutions in a broad governance scenario that holds important consequences. These consequences are to be found in both principles and rights – including voluntariness and equality and nondiscrimination, privacy and dignity – and in substantive results – for example limiting the employers' power to extend working time and in the right to digital disconnection – and creating a common floor of fundamental rights for all workers.

## 1.3 A FRAGMENTED REGULATORY FRAMEWORK TO PROTECT VULNERABILITY: RECONSTRUCTING THE HOLISTIC APPROACH FOR REMOTE WORK

Key values for labor law and labor institutions are freedom, autonomy, dignity, equal respect, democracy, and social justice (Collins et al., 2018). In the goal of achieving decent work for all, including home-based workers, the argument presented here underscores the advantages offered by a holistic approach not only for promoting scholarly understanding but also in practical terms for addressing the human needs of workers. The interactions among actors, institutions, and rules reinforce the agency of actors (as is reflected in the voluntary character of work status and in negotiation) and the fulfillment of the guarantee of equality and nondiscrimination by leveraging interconnections between specific treatments of that principle. Home-based work has changed the rules of more traditional forms of employment, for example, in the entrepreneurial power to design the workplace. The hybridization of forms of regulation and governance and the complexity of the spectrum of forms of work in the labor market have established a complex new scenario that can only be fully understood through a holistic perspective. Moreover, the interactive application of rules generated by multilevel regulatory systems is crucial to maintain the visibility of workers and the enforceability of labor rights. Decent work for all in the Agenda of the ILO is understood to require respect for international labor standards shaped through social dialogue and promoting the rule of law at the national and international levels through nondiscriminatory laws and policies for sustainability. In a scenario of fragmented labor law protections that address specific types of vulnerability one by one, it is crucial to construct and apply a complete system of protection for remote workers that ties together different components of

6 Resolución de 19 de mayo de 2023, V Acuerdo para el Empleo y la Negociación Colectiva, Official Journal of the European Union May 31, 2023.

vulnerability. This interactive approach holds the promise of strengthening fundamental rights for remote workers by drawing on their multiple forms of vulnerability.

I have argued that the evolution of legal regulation of remote work can contribute to such ends not only because of how it is handled as a specific matter but instead because of how it interacts with other types of work and their regulation. The overall legal structure of labor regulation provides strong grounds for fortifying the defense of worker rights through such interactions.

## REFERENCES


Akerlof, G. A., & Shiller, R. J. (2009). *Animal spirits: How human psychology drives the economy, and why it matters for global capitalism*. Princeton University Press.

Arthurs, H. (2024). A rose by any other name: WORK law as law power. In G. Davidov, B. Langille, & Gillian Lester (eds.), *The Oxford handbook of the law of work* (p. 31). Oxford University Press.

Barenberg, M. (2022). A new labor law for deep democracy: From social democracy to democratic socialism. In A. Cornell & M. Barenberg (eds.), *The Cambridge handbook of labor and democracy* (pp. 13–36). Cambridge University Press.

Barnard, C., & Hepple, B. (2000). Substantive equality. *Cambridge Law Journal*, 59(3), 562–585.

Bogg, A. (2013). Subsidiarity or freedom of association? A perspective from labour law. *American Journal of Jurisprudence*, 58(1), 123–153.

Carozza, P. G. (2003). Subsidiarity as a structural principle of international human rights law. *American Journal of International Law*, 97(1), 38–79.

Collins, H., Lester, G., & Mantouvalou, V. (eds.). (2018). *Philosophical foundations of labour law*. Oxford University Press.

Cornell, A. & M. Barenberg (eds.) (2022). *Labor law and democracy*. Oxford University Press.

Countouris, N., De Stefano, V., Piasna, A., & Rainone, S. (2023). *The future of remote work*. European Trade Union Institute (ETUI).

Eurofound. (2020). *Telework in the EU: Regulatory frameworks and recent updates*. Publications Office of the European Union.

(2021). https://www.eurofound.europa.eu/en/european-industrial-relations-dictionary/telework.

Fishman, R. M. (2016). Rethinking dimensions of democracy for empirical analysis: Authenticity, quality, depth, and consolidation. *Annual Review of Political Science*, 19, 289–309.

(2019). *Democratic practice: Origins of the Iberian divide in political inclusion*. Oxford University Press.

Freedman, S., du Toit, D., Graham, M., Howson, K., Heeks, R., van Belle, J. P., Mungai, P., & Osiki, A. (2020). Thinking out of the box: Fair work for platform workers. In A. Bogg, M. Ford, & T. Novitz (eds.). *King's Law Journal*, 31(2), 236–253.

Hepple, B. (2001). Equality and empowerment for decent work. *International Labour Review*, 140(1), 5–18.

Iglesias, M. (2017). Subsidiarity and international human rights tribunals: Deference to states or cooperative division of labor? *Derecho PUCP: Revista de la Facultad de Derecho*, 79, 192–222.

ILO (5 June 2020). Covid-19: Guidance for labour statistics data collection, pp. 5–14.

(2023). Remote work, telework, work at home based work. *International Conference of Labour Statistics*.

López López, J. (2022). Pursuing democratic depth in the age of multinational powers and soft law regulation: The case of platform workers' protests. In A. Cornell & M. Barenberg (eds.), *The Cambridge handbook of labor and democracy* (pp. 307–316). Cambridge University Press.

Novitz, T. (2022). Sustainability as solidarity unbound: Labour rights and collective voice in the United Nations sustainable development goals and the European Union. In J. López López (ed.), *Inscriptions of solidarity: Labour law and beyond* (pp. 150–170). Cambridge University Press.

Piketty, T. (2014). *Capital in the twenty-first century*. Belknap Press of Harvard University Press.

Prassl, J. (2016). The interaction of EU law and national law: Between myth and reality. In A. Bogg, C. Costello, & A. C. L. Davies (eds.), *Research handbook on EU labour law* (pp. 42–64). Edward Elgar Publishing.

Publications Office of the European Union (2020). Telework and ICT-based mobile work: Flexible working in the digital age, new forms of employment series. Luxembourg.

Resolución de 19 de mayo de (31 May 2023). V Acuerdo para el Empleo y la Negociación Colectiva. Ufficial Bolletin.

Roberts, K. M. (2022). Labor and democracy: Constructing, deepening, and defending citizenship rights. In A. Cornell & M. Barenberg (eds.), *The Cambridge handbook of labor and democracy* (pp. 36–59). Cambridge University Press.

Sciarra, S. S. H. (2023). *"Recourse" to and "Discourse" Convention: an asset for democracy*. European Court of Human Rights.

2

# The Sustainability of Remote Work

## *The Significance of International Institutions*

*Tonia Novitz*

### 2.1 INTRODUCTION

This chapter analyses the ways in which remote work can be regulated to address issues relating to sustainability. This is done by identifying different forms of remote work, and considering what issues they raise with reference to the three economic, environmental and social pillars reflected in the United Nations (UN) 2030 Agenda, which set out the Sustainable Development Goals (SDGs) in 2015[1]. It is argued that, while it is possible to reconcile remote work with sustainability objectives, it should not be assumed that this will inevitably be the case. Much more needs to be done in regulation of the world of work to achieve this.

Accordingly, the chapter goes on to consider which international institutions have the capacity and mandate to exercise regulatory influence over remote work from a sustainability perspective. This examination bears in mind the procedural as well as substantive facets of a sustainable development agenda. In this context, the chapter analyses the diverse (but arguably interconnected) roles currently played by United Nations (UN) mechanisms and its agencies, including the International Labour Organization (ILO). These are compared and contrasted with the infusion of sustainability into corporate codes of conduct as an aspiration for decent work. It is suggested that the lack of collective worker voice within current corporate social responsibility (CSR) mechanisms and the importance of acknowledging the role of the state could obstruct the participatory approach to "just transitions" advocated by the ILO.

[1] UN General Assembly Resolution Transforming our world: the 2030 Agenda for Sustainable Development, 25 September 2015 A/Res/70/1. https://sustainabledevelopment.un.org/post2015/transformingourworld/publication.

## 2.2 WHAT IS "REMOTE WORK" FOR THE PURPOSES OF OUR ANALYSIS?

For statistical purposes, the International Labour Office (the administrative organ of the ILO) has defined "remote work" broadly as "situations where the work is fully or partly carried out on an alternative worksite other than the default place of work" (ILO 2020: 1). In a subsequent joint "technical brief" issued by the ILO and the World Health Organization (WHO), "telework" has been further defined as "the use of information and communications technology (ICT) – such as desktop computers, laptops, tablets and smartphones – for work that is performed outside the employer's premises" (ILO/WHO 2021: 1). The brief observes that this can also be termed "e-work" and "remote work"; and that it can take diverse forms. For example: at home, at a secondary workplace designated by an employer, or at "another location", which could presumably include a library, a coffee shop or even on transport such as a train (ILO/WHO 2021).

"Crowd work" (as a facet of platform work) is another variant of "remote work", which had become common prior to the pandemic, because of reduced transaction costs for employers and consumers (De Stefano 2024: 813). "Crowd work" entails the creation of a system whereby those seeking to supply their services bid for a task on an internet platform and then perform this job online for a set fee in the time they have been allotted (Prassl 2018: 1–12; and De Stefano 2016). Moreover, the payment made for "on demand" services need not amount to a living wage (De Stefano 2024: 813). This kind of work can involve "the offshoring and outsourcing of business services from developed to developing countries using information and communications technologies" (ILO 2010: 1).

There is also increasing demand for "hybrid" work, referring to a combination of remote telework and work "in-person" on the employer's premises (see also ILO 2020a). Employers often want to ensure that workers are sighted in-person at least one or two days a week to maintain exercise of managerial control and enhance productivity (Ionescu 2022).

It is evident that some jobs have to be performed personally, such as physical care and cooking, but remote work is becoming ubiquitous in labour markets across the globe. One key question is how this practice should be regulated in accordance with the fundamental precepts of sustainable development.

## 2.3 APPLICATION OF THE SUSTAINABLE DEVELOPMENT GOALS (SDGS) TO THE ISSUE OF REMOTE WORK

Initially, telework as a form of remote work was lauded for its contribution to sustainable development, due to reduction of the pollutants associated with travel (White et al. 2010). However, this will be the case only if other aspects of our lifestyles are changed (as outlined by Moos et al. 2006), and even then, seems an unduly limited assessment. Instead, it would make more sense to engage in more detailed interrogation of a range of the SDGs set out in the 2030 Agenda, which requires thinking about the economic, environmental and social objectives that they represent and how they interact, such that "no one is left behind" whether in current or future generations (cf. World Commission on Environment and Development 1987: 51; Novitz 2024: ch 1).

It is worth emphasising that the aims of the 2030 Agenda are numerous, encompassing economic growth and "decent work" in SDG 8, but also protection of the planet, in relation to: agriculture (SDG 2); water (SDG 6); energy (SDG 7); climate change (SDG 13); oceans and seas (SDG 14); as well as ecosystems and biodiversity on land (SDG 15). Further, there are social objectives which have implications for decent work, such as: preventing poverty (SDG 1); promoting health (SDG 3); education (SDG 4); gender equality (SDG 5); industry, innovation and infrastructure (SDG 9); reducing inequalities (SDG 10); aspiring to sustainable cities and communities (SDG 11); and responsible consumption and production (SDG 12). Moreover, important supplementary measures for achievement of the SDGs are set out in SDG 16 (concerned with peace, justice and strong institutions) and SDG 17 (which stresses the importance of global partnerships).

In the context of the COVID pandemic, one of the key objectives for remote work was the preservation of health for those at work (and their families), which can be defended in terms of SDG 3 (Belzunegui-Eraso and Erro-Garcés 2020), while also having environmental benefits regarding travel (Riggs 2020). Governments, employers and workers (and their representatives), as well as international institutions, now have more extensive policy choices to make regarding why they might enable remote work, the preconditions for doing so, and the ways in which its usage should be regulated.

### 2.3.1 *The Focus on the Employer's Economic Objectives*

Remote work can be presented as an *economically* sustainable way forward for business, corresponding to ambitions for "economic growth" that foreground SDG 8 and associated goals. See, for example, SDG target 8.1, which seeks to "Sustain per capita economic growth in accordance with national circumstances ..." Remote work could even be regarded as a means to achieve target 8.2, which aims to achieve "higher levels of economic productivity through diversification, technological upgrading and innovation, including through a focus on high-value added and labour-intensive sectors". Arguably, the prevalence of business interests in design of the SDGs is notable here (Pingeot 2014; Scheyvens et al. 2016). However, the desirability of economic growth which involves the ever-increasing expansion of business interests and profits has increasingly been questioned (see for example Zekić 2024).

The reasons that employers have chosen to continue forms of remote work seem to be primarily economic. Some time prior to the pandemic, it was observed (by Van Horn and Storen 2000) that:

> Telework programs can ... lower overhead expenses for companies... For some firms, telework programs have reduced office space needs. ... IBM reported savings of $1 billion on real estate costs from 1992 to 1997... most companies will use telework to save on future real estate costs.

Indeed, the traditional boundaries of the workplace have long been eroding (Tomassetti 2018: 63). It is evidently cheaper for an employer to outsource to the worker the onus of finding a place to do their work (Lord 2020). The cost of past requirements to provide heating, water coolers, photocopiers and printers are reduced for the employer, but not necessarily for the worker. For example, hikes in expenditure on domestic energy consumption have seldom been addressed, nor have the inefficiencies that they entail (Akgüç et al. 2023: 45–46, 51–53; Shi et al. 2023).

Pursuit of the economic benefits of remote work by employers has been supplemented by the hybrid work strategies identified above, which seek to enhance worker productivity by expecting part time telework to be combined with some selective physical engagement with the workplace (Licite-Kurbe and Leonovica 2021). Hot desking means that office spaces can be smaller (and cheaper), while attendance in the workplace can be rotated. Indications are that such practices can unduly limit worker flexibility and autonomy, but also may have some welcome social effects for workers when they make contact with their colleagues (Dale et al. 2024), arguably in line with psychological health under SDG 3.

The expansion of cf enables employers to subcontract services from one country to be performed in another. This practice can involve payment on an ad hoc piece-rate basis reflecting lower wages in the third country, rather than guaranteeing longer term or higher incomes (Graham and Anwar 2019: 21–22; ILO 2021: 44, 51). Crowdwork across borders also raises issues relating to time differences in terms of night working, as well as lengthy and often unregulated working time (Novitz 2020a).

In all these ways remote work can be utilised to reduce employers' costs and the profitability of business, but at the expense of those who perform that work. This does not bode well for sustainable economic growth, which would be expected to aid equality with and between states (SDG 10). There are also other environmental and social sustainability objectives that need to be addressed.

### 2.3.2 *Environmental Sustainability and Remote Work*

As regards the *environmental* effects of remote work, the employer's carbon footprint might seem to reduce with their costs. For example, in the absence of any demand to attend a workplace, workers' travel and thereby associated pollutants could diminish. After all, during the pandemic pollution was dramatically reduced if only temporarily (Moglia et al. 2022). SDG 7 (energy) and SDG 13 (climate change) may be relevant here. The problem is, as observed above, that there may also be environmental inefficiencies in the heating, electricity supply and lighting of numerous homes as opposed to one entire workplace. This could be overcome as a problem if the employer permits remote working in other shared public spaces, such as libraries, but that would also depend on their provision by the state (i.e. local or national government).

If remote work is envisaged which is not solely home-based, then reduction of pollution associated with transport needs to be considered more strategically through co-ordinated government strategies, whether national, regional or transnational. It will matter whether the place where work is conducted is walkable, cyclable or reachable through public (or private) transport which entails minimal emissions (cf. Akgüç et al. 2023). The environmental impact of hybrid work could also be reduced (as it is for full time in-office work) through public provision of non-polluting transport. For example, trams, trains and electric buses could be helpful, as could cycle and pedestrian lanes. But that transport system would also need to be inclusive of people with various needs, so that no one is left behind[2]. This role for the state (as opposed to private enterprise) requires participatory engagement with the population, respecting the "responsive, inclusive, participatory and representative decision-making at all levels" contemplated in target SDG 16.7 (cf. Novitz 2020b).

There is arguably a problematic confusion between digital and green "tech", which are not necessarily compatible. Assumptions that the digital is "clean" in terms of energy need to be interrogated. There is emerging research on the effects of cobalt mining as a source of digital hardware[3]; but also with problems associated with recycling that equipment. These are indicative of the off shoring of exploitative labour provision, but also have consequences for environmental pollution[4]. More computer usage in the context of remote work may not, therefore, necessarily avoid environmental harms, such as climate change (SDG 13). Indeed, it is becoming apparent that "[d]igitalization is not only an *instrument* to resolve sustainability challenges", that is, to achieve green transitions. Rather, it is "also fundamental as

[2] Cf. SDG target 11.2: "By 2030, provide access to safe, affordable, accessible and sustainable transport systems for all, improving road safety, notably by expanding public transport, with special attention to the needs of those in vulnerable situations, women, children, persons with disabilities and older persons."

[3] Raised in a question before the European parliament in 202www.europarl.europa.eu/doceo/document/E-9-2022-002207_EN.html. See also www.amnesty.org/en/latest/campaigns/2016/06/drc-cobalt-child-labour/; and www.beroeinc.com/article/child-labor-and-cobalt-mining/. For recent academic evidence, see Krummel and Siegfried 2021.

[4] See EU proposals for recycling through a "circular economy" at: https://ec.europa.eu/info/law/better-regulation/have-your-say/initiatives/12797-Designing-mobile-phones-and-tablets-to-be-sus tainable-ecodesign_en. See Ahirwar and Tripathi 2021.

a driver of disruptive change", such that sustainable policies have to address "the threats, opportunities, and dynamics of the digital revolution" (De Felice and Petrillo 2020).

These tensions when making structural change and reorganising forms of work and protection can be viewed through the prism of "the imperatives of a just transition of the workforce and the creation of decent work and quality jobs in accordance with nationally defined development priorities", referred to in the preamble to the Paris Agreement[5]. In these ways environmental sustainability can be linked also to social sustainability.

### 2.3.3 *Social Sustainability*

Remote work can pursue *socially* sustainable objectives by promoting inclusion in the labour market of those otherwise excluded by reason of prejudice, such as women (who still tend to take on the main societal role as care givers as is recognised by SDG 5) and access for those with disabilities (Jesus et al. 2020; Schur et al. 2020). This could entail job creation in line with SDG target 8.3 and "full and productive employment" under target 8.5. Remote work that is genuinely social redistributive of jobs and income could further serve the purposes of SDG 10, especially targets 10.1 ("income growth"), 10.2 ("empower and promote the social, economic and political inclusion of all, irrespective of age, sex, disability, race, ethnicity, origin, religion or economic or other status") and 10.3 ("ensure equal opportunity and reduce inequalities of outcome…").

However, we know that remote work may include those who are most systematically disadvantaged but, perhaps for that very reason, provide minimal income and social well-being for those kinds of workers. Certainly, we know that remote work did not necessarily promote equality during the COVID-19 pandemic (Adams-Prassl et al. 2020; de Laat 2020).

For sustainability purposes, remote work should be (at a minimum) "decent work" (for which see the very title of SDG 8), not performed in precarity and certainly not enabled by "unacceptable forms of work" (McCann and Fudge 2017). Otherwise, there would seem to be a failure to adhere to SDG target 8.8 which seeks to "protect labour rights… for all workers", including those who are "in precarious employment". Failure to ensure "employment status" and coverage under national labour laws can cause problems for this class of often "invisible" workers (Crain et al. 2016). They may end up only being scrutinised by their employers' algorithmic management and digital surveillance (Aloisi and De Stefano 2022), while being unseen and unprotected by the state regulatory bodies, such as labour inspectorates.

[5] See the Paris Agreement, 12 December 2015. Available at: https://unfccc.int/sites/default/files/english_paris_agreement.pdf.

There should also be a determination to address SDG target 8.7: "immediate and effective measures to eradicate forced labour, end modern slavery and human trafficking and secure the prohibition and elimination of the worst forms of child labour". As the case of cobalt mining demonstrates (e.g. Krummel and Siegfried 2021), digital hardware has been revealed to come at the cost of informal, forced and child labour in countries of the Global South. De Stefano (2024: 807) has also observed that the invisibility of remote work could lead to enticement of child labour into crowd work, with all the systemic deprivations that entails.

In terms of freedom of association and the effective right to collective bargaining, SDG 8 and the associated targets are silent, but SDG indicator 8.8.2 confirms the relevance of "national compliance with labour rights (freedom of association and collective bargaining)" and ILO standards relating to these. This is consistent with the insistence of the UN Special Rapporteur in 2018 that "freedom of association" as well as protection of trade unions and the right to strike are to be understood as included in the "fundamental freedoms" referred to in SDG target 16.10[6]. However, realisation of these rights in the context of remote work can be obstructed by the lack of regular face-to-face contact in the workplace, alongside the forms of surveillance which can stifle collective organisation (Dukes and Streeck 2023: 121; Rogers 2023: ch 4).

Issues also arise regarding other SDGs. One example is SDG 3 since, as the ILO/WHO Brief (2021) makes clear, health and safety issues can arise within the home (or any other location) as a workplace. Home working has the capacity to promote health in accordance with SDG 3, but not if living conditions are crowded, unsanitary, the systems of supervision create work-related stress or the hours become unduly long.

Also relevant is SDG 4 regarding education, which would seem to require that an employer should enable some training for those who are engaged in remote work in terms of lifelong learning (Moglia et al. 2022: 11). Moreover, there will need to be forms of social protection, including protection from poverty under SDGs 1 and 8. Also notable here is target 10.4, which demands "policies, especially fiscal, wage and social protection policies" that "progressively achieve greater equality".

There is again a role for government in supporting and sharing the costs of remote work by establishing sustainable cities (SDG 11), which may need to be fostered by, for example, wider email/Wi-Fi access from people's houses and other potential work-related spaces such as public libraries, parks and private coffee and other shops. This could also bring autonomy of movement (and hours) to those who work

[6] *Report of the Special Rapporteur on the rights to freedom of peaceful assembly and of association*. Item 74(b) of the provisional agenda, General Assembly, 73rd Session, A/73/279. 7 August 2018, paras 6, 58 and 87–89.

remotely, facilitating their connections with others, enabling freedom of association (SDGs 8 and 16) even for precarious workers. However, the degree of freedom of speech, assembly and association engendered in this way will also depend on the protection of civil liberties in public spheres by the state and in private spaces by employers. There also remain live issues as to the extent to which digital spaces are public or private and how they can and should be regulated by government (Beverungen et al. 2022).

If social sustainability safeguards are absent (as they would seem to be in many, if not most, countries across the globe in the context of platform work, for which see ILO 2021), then the question is how they can be created. In crafting appropriate regulatory responses, there will need to be engagement with SDG 16, which seeks to "Promote peaceful and inclusive societies for sustainable development, provide access to justice for all and build effective, accountable and inclusive institutions at all levels". This involves giving effect to fundamental rights recognised under SDG target 16.10, such as freedom of speech, assembly and freedom of association, as well as making them operative in accordance with target 16.7 as a means to achieve just transitions[7].

Moreover, the 2030 Agenda recognises that economic, environmental and social facets of sustainable development, not only influence each other but also have no respect for geographical borders, operating across the supply chains that shape labour markets today. This means that achieving the SDGs should involve the deliberations and actions of not just a single state or civil society actor, but a "global partnership" under SDG 17. In other words, sustainable policymaking does not only have a substantive dimension, but requires multilevel inclusive and collaborative processes, involving governments as well as business and also, representatives of those who perform remote work. This SDG again evokes the aspirations of social participation in a "just transition".

## 2.4 INTERNATIONAL INSTITUTIONAL PROMOTION OF SUSTAINABILITY IN REMOTE WORK

This part of the chapter examines how international institutions can shape compliance with sustainability. The question is whether, in compliance with SDG target 17.14, there is any likelihood of "policy coherence for sustainable development". The potential for gravitation towards a unified stance and strategy is probed here with reference to international soft law promoting sustainability at the UN and the ILO. The utilisation of the term "sustainability" by business in corporate codes of conduct is analysed in terms of compliance with the precepts of decent remote work.

[7] Ibid.

### 2.4.1 *UN Supervisory Mechanisms Devoted to the SDGs*

The UN High Level Political Forum on Sustainable Development (HLPF) was established in 2013 (before the adoption of the 2030 Agenda) as the supervisory body responsible for the planned SDGs and more generally to "promote the review and stocktaking of progress in the implementation of all sustainable development commitments"[8]. The HLPF was to "provide political leadership, guidance and recommendations for sustainable development"[9], but effective "orchestration" (cf. Abbott and Bernstein 2015) has proved elusive. This may be attributed to the time-restrictions imposed on a partial and annual voluntary national review (VNR) process together with the lack of any binding force of supervisory findings. While organisations such as the ILO have engaged enthusiastically in HLPF procedures, their voices can be lost due to problems of scale and resources, despite recent attempts at reform (Beisheim and Fritzsche 2019). In short, the limited resources of the HLPF have also limited its influence.

Different SDGs receive different levels of scrutiny in the VNR, depending on the frequency of their discussion at the HLPF. For example, so far, SDG 8 (which encompasses "decent work") was only considered for the first time through the VNR in 2019 and again in 2021 in the wake of the COVID-19 pandemic. Despite the extensive use of remote work at that time, subsequently, there has been remarkably little said about its use in the VNR before the HLPF, although digital services have received attention. The Political Declaration adopted at the SDG Summit in 2023 made minimal reference to work (remote or otherwise), merely stating that "We also remain resolved to create conditions for sustainable, inclusive and sustained economic growth, shared prosperity and decent work for all, and equal pay for work of equal value, taking into account different levels of national development and capacities."[10]

More interesting comment can however be found in two further SDG reports from the UN Secretary-General in 2024. The first was a report on "eradicating poverty" that stressed the importance of establishing adequate social security protection for those reliant on digital and platform work, arguably in line with arguments relating to SDG 10 above[11]. A second report on "long-term impacts of

[8] UNGA Resolution The Future We Want, 27 July 2012, UNGA A/RES/66/288, para 76. See also Novitz and Pieraccini 2020.

[9] UNGA Resolution Format and organizational aspects of the high-level political forum on sustainable development, 9 July 2013 A/RES.67/290, para. 2.

[10] Political declaration of the high-level political forum on sustainable development convened under the auspices of the General Assembly A/HLPF/2023/L.1, 15 September 2023, para. 14.

[11] Report of the UN Secretary-General, Reinforcing the 2030 Agenda for Sustainable Development and eradicating poverty in times of multiple crises: the effective delivery of sustainable, resilient and innovative solutions E/2024/52, 1 May 2024, para. 45.

current trends" considered in more detail the trend towards digitalisation of work[12]. One problem identified was that technological change can now "allow workers to serve multiple clients remotely from their homes, vehicles or co-working spaces instead of working full-time for a single employer"[13]; another being that "many of these new forms of work fall outside the scope and coverage of labour laws and regulations, since an employer may be in one place while a worker is on the other side of the world"[14]. The Secretary-General observed that the result had been a rise in "informal and precarious employment"[15] and thereby a global increase in "working poverty"[16]. The report advocates action by governments, as well as workers and employers relating to access to social security, training and labour law protections[17]. The report also expressly notes "recognition of the need for international action"[18]. It is not, however, immediately obvious where such action will be taken and how.

### 2.4.2 *Sustainable Development and "Decent" Remote Work at the ILO*

International action has arguably begun at the ILO, which began to grapple with regulatory issues arising from remote work in the context of the COVID-19 pandemic. An example was the guidance issued by the employers' bureau (ACT/EMP) at the ILO regarding management of home working (ILO 2020b; analysed in Beebeejaun and Gunputh 2022), but which did not refer to sustainable development.

If we are to consider ILO promotion of sustainable development, in line with SDG 8, we may wish to return to consider the basic requirements of "decent work" elaborated at the ILO. These are understood to include (i) promoting employment; (ii) enhancing social protection; (iii) promoting social dialogue and tripartism; and (iv) respecting, promoting and realising the fundamental principles and rights at work[19]. The latter consists of (a) freedom of association and the effective recognition of the right to collective bargaining; (b) the elimination of all forms of forced or compulsory labour; (c) the effective abolition of child labour; (d) the elimination of discrimination in respect of employment and occupation; and (since 2022) (e) a safe and healthy working environment[20]. The relevance of these has been considered

[12] Report of the Secretary-General, Long-term impacts of current trends on the realization of the Sustainable Development Goals E/2024/55, 3 May 2024, paras 22–38.

[13] Ibid., para. 24.

[14] Ibid., para. 25.

[15] Ibid., para. 32.

[16] Ibid., para. 34.

[17] Ibid., recommendations listed at para. 86.

[18] Ibid., para. 26.

[19] See ILO Declaration on Social Justice for a Fair Globalization 2008, Art. I(A).

[20] Article 2 of the ILO Declaration on Fundamental Principles and Rights at Work 1998, adopted at the 86th Session of the International Labour Conference (1998) and amended at the 110th Session (2022).

above, in relation to the SDGs in which these facets of "decent work" and labour rights are manifested. From that discussion it is also apparent that there is also a strong argument that the tendency to label those engaged in many forms of remote work as independent contractors needs to be addressed to overcome the threshold for access to protections in these many regards under national employment and labour laws. In this respect, it is evident that revision of and elaboration on ILO Employment Relationship Recommendation No. 198 (2006)[21] is not only timely, but long overdue (cf. Creighton and McCrystal 2016; De Stefano 2021).

In terms of the intersection of remote work with the environmental and social pillars of sustainability, in 2015 an ILO Tripartite Meeting of Experts agreed ILO Guidelines on Just Transitions[22]. One of the important facets of this document was its focus on the process governing "how we get there" (Galgóczi 2020: 369). The ILO Guidelines made express reference to the 2030 Agenda[23], contemplating that key economic, social and environmental policies should be pursued through tripartite social dialogue and via collective agreements "at all levels"[24].

The 2019 Centenary Declaration on the Future of Work stated in Article II(A) that the ILO should be "(i) ensuring a just transition to a future of work that contributes to sustainable development in its economic, social and environmental dimensions". This would seem to require "(ii) harnessing the fullest potential of technological progress and productivity growth", but notably doing so "through social dialogue, to achieve decent work and sustainable development". Again, tripartite participatory engagement was contemplated to ensure "a just sharing of the benefits for all..." Even more pertinent is the insistence by the International Labour Office, in its 2019 report *Time to Act for SDG* 8, that trade unions and collective bargaining are vital to securing the SDGs, especially for female, migrant and other marginalised groups of workers (ILO 2019: 69–75). This endorsement of collective representative engagement is also to be found in the ILO WESO Report on platform work in 2021 (ILO 2021; Novitz 2021: 654–655).

There is no apparent forthcoming standard-setting on "remote work" per se, but the ILO Governing Body has placed "platform work" on the International Labour Conference agenda in 2025[25]. This decision may yet have implications for how remote work is performed and could address questions of employment status and statutory protections for those engaged in crowdwork. We have yet to see whether any Convention or Recommendation will be phrased in sustainability terms, but the

[21] Text available at: www.ilo.org/dyn/normlex/en/f?p=NORMLEXPUB:12100:0::NO::P12100_INSTRUMENT_ID:312535.

[22] ILO Guidelines for a just transition towards environmentally sustainable economies and societies (ILO 2015) available at: www.ilo.org/wcmsp5/groups/public/—ed_emp/—emp_ent/documents/publication/wcms_432859.pdf.

[23] ILO Guidelines n.22, para. 15(c).

[24] Ibid., paras 17–18.

[25] ILO Governing Body, *Minutes of the Policy Development Section* GB.347/POL/PV, 347th Session, Geneva, 13–23 March 2023 (ILO 2023), 3–16.

ILO Director-General's current mission to lead a "global coalition for social justice" has been linked by him explicitly to sustainable development, as well as the fostering of global partnerships[26].

### 2.4.3 *Reference to Sustainability in Global Corporate Governance and Its Limitations*

Historically, corporate codes of conduct have been less likely to promote freedom of association and collective bargaining; focussing rather on other issues, such as child or forced labour which business sees as setting a minimal level playing field (Hepple 1999: 358; Anner 2012). A recent study conducted in 2021 cast doubt on whether this has changed since adoption of ostensible sustainability objectives (Kuruvilla 2021: 151–155).

Indeed, corporate enthusiasm for engagement with a sustainability discourse has been contrasted with the reluctance of commercial interests to endorse harder binding human rights norms (Bellace 2015). The suspicion has been that what makes the discourse of sustainability attractive to business is precisely the soft law, non-binding nature of the international legal regime on this topic. There has also been a trend whereby sustainability-oriented codes place more emphasis on environmental as opposed to social objectives, which has meant that their relevance to labour conditions has often been negligible (Kuruvilla 2021: 11; Lashitew 2021).

However, that corporate approach may be changing, judging from the content of recently revised documents, such as H&M's "Sustainability Commitment"[27] and Santander's "Sustainability Strategy", which govern their engagement with third party contractors[28]. These are interesting initiatives, because they self-consciously reference both environmental and social facets of sustainable development together, alongside the language of "responsible business conduct" (RBC) and "economic, social and governance" (ESG) norms. Both documents seek to be "inclusive" in terms of their treatment of work. Santander does so by listing "human rights" to be respected which accord with core ILO labour standards, while H&M recognises the extension of these entitlements to "all" forms of work, referring for example expressly to "platform work". They both acknowledge the legal right to organise and join trade unions. In this respect, H&M goes further in terms of provision for a parallel track where lawful access to trade union representation is prevented in the country

[26] Update on the Global Coalition for Social Justice GB.347/INS/4, 20 February 2023, 4–7; and Report of the Director-General: Advancing Social Justice (ILO 2023), 25, 29–30.

[27] Updated most recently in 2022 and available at: https://hmgroup.com/sustainability/standards-and-policies/sustainability-commitment/. See for a historical perspective Menashe 2020.

[28] Available at: www.santander.co.uk/sustainability; and www.santander.co.uk/content/dam/sites/santander-uk-sustainability/resources/documents/Code%20of%20Supplier%20Responsibility_vfinal.pdf. See for earlier comment Bajo and Curbelo (2021).

concerned. Neither mentions "remote work" or "telework" directly as a specific issue to be interrogated, which is interesting given that this could be an increasingly pertinent issue in relation to global suppliers, but one might expect these types of work to be covered by the general obligations stated. To that extent these promises of policy commitments to sustainability seem indicative of continuing change and improvement in the content and implementation of these corporate codes.

Both H&M and Santander documents also make reference to the processes of risk assessment associated with "due diligence". In this way, they reflect the evolving international instruments concerning multinational corporate governance that have emerged on the global regulatory stage. These include: the Organisation for Economic Co-operation and Development (OECD) Guidelines for Multinational Enterprises (1976 and revised most recently in 2023)[29], the ILO Tripartite Declaration concerning Multinational Enterprises and Social Policy (1977 and revised most recently in 2022)[30], the UN Global Compact created in 2000 (revised in response to the 2015 UN SDGs)[31] and the UN Guiding Principles on Business and Human Rights (adopted 2011 regarding which there is also ongoing revision and adaptation)[32]. Their evolution and elaboration over decades, responding specifically to ILO norms, have led to normative interaction and some cohesion between the norms they espouse, but they have their limitations (Novitz 2024: ch6). None of these instruments refer explicitly to remote work either, but they have been promoting due diligence.

The problem is that, while the due diligence approach to a respect, protect and remedy human rights framework might have initially been perceived by business as threatening (Bellace 2015); its current manifestation has had less influence than was initially thought. The reason may be that due diligence tends to be more reactive to breaches of human and labour rights, rather than being proactive for their prevention (Landau 2023: 185). This may also be due to the failure to adequately engage in this process representatives of the workers most affected by a corporation's conduct, especially when they work casually through platforms or remotely (see Brudney 2023; Marshall et al. 2023). The participatory dimension of just transitions in the green and digital sphere has therefore yet to be successfully realised. But more than this, corporate governance measures on sustainability can only take us so far since, as

[29] OECD Guidelines for Multinational Enterprises on Responsible Business Conduct 2023 available at: www.oecd.org/en/publications/oecd-guidelines-for-multinational-enterprises-on-responsible-business-conduct_81f92357-en.html; see also the OECD Due Diligence Guidelines for Responsible Business Conduct: www.oecd.org/en/publications/oecd-due-diligence-guidance-for-responsible-business-conduct_15f5f4b3-en.html.

[30] The 2022 edition of the ILO Tripartite Declaration is available at: www.ilo.org/empent/Publications/WCMS_094386/lang–en/index.html.

[31] Based online at: www.unglobalcompact.org/.

[32] John Ruggie, Guiding Principles on Business and Human Rights: Implementing the United Nations 'Protect, Respect and Remedy' Framework, 17th sess, Agenda Item 3, UN Doc A/HRC/17/31, 21 March 2011 annex ('UNGPs').

identified above, achievement of sustainability for remote work requires coordinated engagement from government (at all levels) together with corporations and worker representatives. This suggests that a tripartite model for regulation, as advocated by the ILO, could be helpful for inclusive global partnerships which set more detailed parameters for sustainable remote work.

## 2.5 CONCLUSION

This chapter has explored the arguments for regulating remote work from a sustainable development perspective, with reference to economic, environmental and social objectives. It has also established that the SDGs in the 2030 Agenda do not only set substantive objectives but also contain procedural norms, which are also essential for just transitions which concern the transformation of the labour market to encompass digital remote work.

The chapter has highlighted the growing interest of UN institutions, including the ILO, in regulation of remote work, and the ways in which this has been connected to aspirations for sustainability. In particular, it does seem that ILO standards concerning decent work have not only shaped facets of the content of SDG 8, but also the text of recent corporate sustainability commitments. The difficulty is that while the texts of these corporate codes respect substantive aspects of fundamental labour standards espoused by the ILO, they have yet to operationalise due diligence commitments in a way likely to respect ILO Guidelines for a Just Transition.

There has to be greater appreciation that trade unions (and other representatives of those who provide services in the contemporary labour market) alongside governments can and should make a meaningful contribution to due diligence risk assessment. More than this, there needs to be commitment from business to proactive engagement in tripartite social dialogue and policy design on issues such as remote work. Finally, corporate self-regulation cannot replace much-needed government engagement with the preconditions for sustainable remote work, such as transport, public spaces and other smart city infrastructure, but also the effective enforcement of labour laws designed to address the more exploitative possibilities of remote work. The dynamics of the interactions between the tripartite policy actors in this sphere now require greater attention from the ILO, being the next step towards genuine global partnership for sustainability.

## REFERENCES

Abbott, K.W. and Bernstein, S. (2015) The High-Level Political Forum on sustainable development: Orchestration by default and design. *Global Policy* 6, 3: 222–233.

Adams-Prassl, A., Boneva, T., Golin, M. and Rauh, C. (2020) Inequality in the impact of the coronavirus shock: Evidence from real time surveys. *Journal of Public Economics* 189: 104245

Ahirwar, R. and Tripathi, A.K. (2021) E-waste management: A review of recycling process, environmental and occupational health hazards, and potential solutions. *Environmental Nanotechnology, Monitoring & Management* 15: 100409.

Akgüç, M., Galgóczi, B. and Meil, P. (2023) Remote work and the green transition. In Countouris, N., De Stefano, V., Piasna, A. and Rainone, S. (eds), *The Future of Remote Work*. Brussels: European Trade Union Institute, 45–59.

Aloisi, A. and De Stefano, V. (2022) Essential jobs, remote work and digital surveillance: Addressing the COVID-19 pandemic panopticon. *International Labour Review* 161, 2: 289–314.

Anner, M. (2012) Corporate social responsibility and freedom of association rights: The precarious quest for legitimacy and control in global supply chains. *Politics & Society* 40, 4: 609–644.

Bajo, A. and Curbelo, D. (2021), Sustainable Marketing in banking sector. The case of Santander in Spain. *Proceedings of the European Marketing Academy*, 50: 94756.

Beebeejaun, A. and R P Gunputh, R.P. (2022) A Critical Analysis of the Mauritius Workers' Rights (Working from Home) Regulations 2020 in the Wake of COVID-19. *Industrial Law Journal* 51, 1: 174–193.

Beisheim, M. and Fritzsche, F. (2019) The UN High-Level Political Forum on Sustainable Development: An orchestrator, more or less?' *Global Policy* 13, 5: 683–693.

Bellace, J.R. (2015) Pushback on the right to strike: Resisting the thickening of soft law. In Blackett, A. and Trebilcock, A. (eds), *Research Handbook on Transnational Labour Law*. Cheltenham: Edward Elgar, 181–193.

Belzunegui-Eraso, A. and Erro-Garcés, A. (2020) Teleworking in the context of the Covid-19 crisis. *Sustainability* 12, 9: 3662.

Beverungen, D., Hess, T., Köster, A. and Lehrer, C. (2022) From private digital platforms to public data spaces: Implications for the digital transformation. *Electronic Markets* 32, 2: 493–501.

Brudney, J.J. (2023) Hiding in plain sight: An ILO Convention on labor standards in global supply chains. *Chicago Journal of International Law* 23, 2: 272–341.

Crain, M., Poster, W. and Cherry, M. (eds) (2016) *Invisible Labor: Hidden Work in the Contemporary World*. Oakland: University of California Press.

Creighton, B. and McCrystal, S. (2016) Who is a worker in international law. *Comparative Labor Law and Policy Journal* 37, 3: 691–725.

Dale, G., Wilson, H. and Tucker, M. (2024) What is healthy hybrid work? Exploring employee perceptions on well-being and hybrid work arrangements. *International Journal of Workplace Health Management*. Advance access available at: https://doi.org/10.1108/IJWHM-03-2024-0041.

De Felice, F. and Petrillo, A. (2020) An interdisciplinary framework to define strategies for digitalization and sustainability: Proposal of a "digicircular" model. *IET Collaborative Intelligent Manufacturing* https://doi.org/10.1049/cim2.12013.

de Laat, K. (2020). *Remote Work and Gender Inequality Throughout and Beyond the COVID-19 Pandemic*. Toronto: Institute for Gender and the Economy. Available at: https://tspace.library.utoronto.ca/bitstream/1807/131739/1/de%20Laat_2020_Remote%20Work.pdf.

De Stefano, V. (2016) *The Rise of the "Just-in-Time Workforce": On-Demand Work, Crowdwork and Labour Protection in the "Gig-Economy"*. Geneva: ILO Conditions of Work and Employment Series Working Paper No. 71.

(2021) Not as simple as it seems: The ILO and the personal scope of international labour standards. *International Labour Review* 160, 3: 387–406.

(2024) Online work. In Davidov, G., Langille, B. and Lester, G. (eds), *The Oxford Handbook of the Law at Work*. Oxford: Oxford University Press, 805–818.

Dukes, R. and Streeck, W. (2023) *Democracy at Work: Contract, Status and Post-Industrial Justice*. Cambridge: Polity Press.

Galgóczi, B. (2020) Just transition on the ground: Challenges and opportunities for social dialogue. *European Journal of Industrial Relations*, 26, 4: 367–382.

Graham, M. and Anwar, M. (2019) The global gig economy: Towards a planetary labour market? *First Monday* 24: 4.

Hepple, B. (1999) A race to the top – International investment guidelines and corporate codes of conduct. *Comparative Labour Law and Policy Journal*, 20: 347–363.

ILO. (2010) *Offshoring and Working Conditions in Remote Work*. Geneva: ILO.

(2015) *Guidelines for a Just Transition towards Environmentally Sustainable Economies and Societies*. Geneva: ILO. Available at: www.ilo.org/wcmsp5/groups/public/—ed_emp/—emp_ent/documents/publication/wcms_432859.pdf.

(2019) *Time to Act for SDG 8: Integrating Decent Work, Sustained Growth and Environmental Integrity*. Geneva: International Labour Office, ILO.

(2020a) *Defining and Measuring Remote Work, Telework, Work at Home and Home-Based Work*. Geneva: ILO. Available at: www.ilo.org/wcmsp5/groups/public/—dgreports/—stat/documents/publication/wcms_747075.pdf.

(2020b) *An Employers' Guide on Working from Home in Response to the Outbreak of COVID-19*. Geneva: ILO. Available at: www.ilo.org/wcmsp5/groups/public/—ed_dialogue/—act_emp/documents/publication/wcms_745024.pdf.

ILO/WHO. (2021) *Healthy and Safe Telework Technical Brief* – Geneva: ILO/WHO. Available at: www.ilo.org/wcmsp5/groups/public/—ed_dialogue/—lab_admin/documents/publication/wcms_836250.pdf.

ILO. (2021) *The Role of Digital Labour Platforms in Transforming the World of Work*. Geneva: ILO World Employment and Social Outlook (WESO) Report.

(2023) *Sustainable Development, Decent Work and Social Justice: An Update on Progress towards SDG 8*. Geneva: ILO Policy Brief.

Ionescu, C.A., Fülöp, M.T., Topor, D.I., Duică, M.C., Stanescu, S.G., Florea, N.V., Zamfir, M. and Coman, M.D. (2022) Sustainability analysis, implications, and effects of the teleworking system in Romania. *Sustainability* 14, 9: 5273.

Jesus, T.S., Landry, M.D. and Jacobs, K. (2020) A "new normal" following COVID-19 and the economic crisis: Using systems thinking to identify challenges and opportunities in disability, telework, and rehabilitation. *Work* 67, 1: 637–46.

Krummel, D. and Siegfried, P. (2021) The dark side of Samsung's value chain: The human costs of cobalt mining: Blood, sweat and cobalt. *Journal of Geoscience and Environment Protection* 9, 2: 182–203.

Kuruvilla, S. (2021) *Private Regulation of Labor Standards in Global Supply Chains*. Ithaca: Cornell University Press.

Landau, I. (2023) *Human Rights Due Diligence and Labour Governance*. Oxford: Oxford University Press.

Lashitew, A.A. (2021) Corporate uptake of the Sustainable Development Goals: Mere greenwashing or an advent of institutional change? *Journal of International Business Policy* 4, 1: 184.

Licite-Kurbe, L. and Leonovica, R. (2021) Economic benefits of remote work from the employer perspective. *Economic Science for Rural Development Conference Proceedings* 55. Available at: https://llufb.llu.lv/conference/economic_science_rural/2021/Latvia_ESRD_55_2021-345-354.pdf.

Lord, P. (2020) The social perils and promise of remote work. *Journal of Behavioral Economics for Policy* 4, COVID-19 Special Issue: 63–67.

Marshall, S., Landau, I., Shamir, H., Barkay, T., Fudge, J. and van Heerden, A. (2023) *Mandatory Human Rights Due Diligence: Risks and Opportunities for Workers and Unions* Melbourne: RMIT/TraffLab/Monash.

McCann, D. and Fudge, J. (2017) Unacceptable forms of work: A multidimensional model. *International Labour Review* 156, 2: 147–184.

Menashe, M. (2020) Private actors as transnational regulators: The case of freedom of association. *Industrial Law Journal* 49, 1: 1–34.

Moglia, M., Hopkins, J. and Bardoel, A. (2022) Telework, hybrid work and the United Nation's Sustainable Development Goals: Towards policy coherence. *Sustainability* 13, 6: 9222.

Moos, M., Andrey, J. and Johnson L.C. (2006) The sustainability of telework: An ecological-footprinting approach. *Sustainability: Science, practice and policy* 2, 1: 3–14.

Novitz, T. (2020a) The potential for international regulation of gig economy issues. *King's Law Journal* 31, 2: 275–286.

(2020b) Engagement with sustainability at the International Labour Organization and wider implications for collective worker voice. *International Labour Review* 159, 4: 463–482.

(2021) Gig work as a manifestation of short termism – the sustainability problem? *Industrial Law Journal* 50, 4: 636–661.

(2024) *Trade, Labour and Sustainable Development: Leaving No One in the World of Work Behind*. Cheltenham: Edward Elgar.

Novitz, T. and Pieraccini, M. (2020). Agenda 2030 and the Sustainable Development Goals: "Responsive, inclusive, participatory and representative decision-making"? In: Pieraccini, M. and Novitz, T. (eds), *Legal Perspectives on Sustainability*. Bristol: Bristol University Press, 39–66.

Pingeot, L. (2014) Corporate influence in the post-2015 process. Working Paper available at: www.cid.org.nz/assets/Key-issues/Beyond-2015/Corporate-influence-in-the-Post-2015-process.pdf.

Prassl, P. (2018) *Humans as a Service: The Promise and Perils of Work in the Gig Economy*. Oxford: Oxford University Press.

Riggs, W. (2020) Telework and sustainable travel during the COVID-19 era. Working Paper available at: https://papers.ssrn.com/sol3/papers.cfm?abstract_id = 3638885.

Rogers, B. (2023) *Data and Democracy at Work: Advanced Information. Technologies, Labor Law and the New Working Class*. Boston: MIT Press.

Scheyvens, R., Banks, G., and Hughes, E. (2016) The private sector and the SDGs: The need to move beyond 'business as usual. *Sustainable Development* 24, 6: 371–382.

Schur, L.A., Ameri, M. and Kruse, D. (2020) Telework after COVID: A "silver lining" for workers with disabilities? *Journal of Occupational Rehabilitation*, 30: 521–536.

Shi, Y., Sorrell, S. and Foxon, T. (2023) The impact of teleworking on domestic energy use and carbon emissions: An assessment for England. *Energy and Buildings* 287: 112996.

Tomassetti, P. (2018) Labor law and environmental sustainability. *Comparative Labor Law and Policy Journal*, 40, 1: 61–88.

Van Horn, C.E. and Storen, D. (2000) Telework: Coming of age? Evaluating the potential benefits of telework. Working Paper available at: http://zdalniej.pl/wp-content/uploads/2011/09/Telework_Coming_of_Age_Evaluating_the_Potential_Benefits_of_Telework.pdf.

White, P., Christodoulou, G., Mackett, R., Titheridge, H., Thoreau, R. and Polak, J. (2010) The impacts of teleworking on sustainability and travel. In Manzi, T., Lucas, K., Lloyd Jones, T. and Allen, J. (eds), *Social Sustainability in Urban Areas*. London: Routledge, 159–178.

World Commission on Environment and Development (WCED) (1987) *Our Common Future*. Oxford: Oxford University Press.

Zekić, N. (2024) Labour law for degrowth and meaningful work. In Bueno, N., ter Haar, B. and Zekic, N. (eds), *Labour Law Utopias: Post-Growth & Post-Productive Work Approaches*. Oxford: Oxford University Press, 51–70.

# 3

# The Societal Value of Workplace Ties and the Challenge of Remote Work

*Cynthia Estlund*

## 3.1 INTRODUCTION

Paid work generates pay and work. And much more. Workers also gain intangible "goods" at work – status, sociability, skill development, and feelings of belonging, fulfillment, and accomplishment – and suffer "bads" – risks to physical and psychological health and safety, stress, harassment, conflict, and the sheer diversion of time from the rest of life – leisure, nonwork relationships and activities, or sleep. Much of what workers seek and get from a job – both the goods and the bads – hinge on their relationships with co-workers, including those above or below them in the workplace pecking order as well as their peers. And much of what paid work generates for employers – the labor that enables firms to bring goods and services to market – also depends on how well workers get along and collaborate with their co-workers. Both firms and workers derive value from good or at least functional working relationships and suffer when those relationships are fraught or dysfunctional. We can call that the social dimension of work.

The rise of remote work and "work from home," accelerated by the COVID pandemic but apparently here to stay, has disrupted the social dimension of work and our understanding of it. Most of the discourse around that trend centers naturally on its impact on firms or workers in various sectors and layers of the labor market. Firms obviously worry about how workers' productivity is affected by remote work. Firms' interests in employee recruitment, morale, and retention also compel them to care about what at least some workers want out of, and outside of, work. Workers and those concerned for their welfare, for their part, focus on the impact of remote work on workers' ability to thrive and advance at work and to achieve a decent work–life balance, and on how equitably those abilities are distributed, as well as on workers' ability to organize and bargain collectively.

I want to focus here instead on how remote work and work-from-home might affect our social and political infrastructure outside of the workplace. My argument here builds on a proposition I develop at length elsewhere: The daily experience of more-or-less diverse co-workers working together, and the resulting connections and connectedness – especially those that cross salient lines of social division – can strengthen the foundations of a sustainable democratic society (Estlund 2003, 2022). The growth of remote work and work-from-home has implications for the cultivation of that diffuse but crucial societal resource.

Importantly, the cumulative societal benefits of co-worker interactions – traditionally, face-to-face, side-by-side, day after day – are not internalized by either workers or their employers. Those are positive externalities of relationships and interactions within firms; and they are "public goods" in the sense that we all benefit from them whether or not we contribute to them[1]. Both labor market dynamics and the market for workplace technologies will reflect interests and preferences of employers and of at least some workers regarding the social dimension of work, including the impact of remote work arrangements; but they will not reflect the crucial societal spillover benefits of remote work. This chapter will develop that thesis and then reflect briefly on whether and how the conventional institutional arsenal of labor and employment law could be deployed to increase the production of those public goods.

## 3.2 HOW WORKING TOGETHER CAN GENERATE "BRIDGING BONDS" AND STRENGTHEN DEMOCRACY[2]

Most democratic theorists agree that a sustainably democratic society requires at least a thin sense of shared identity and shared membership in the polity. That in turn rests on a substrate of social ties – not only intimate ties among close family and friends but also weaker ties among strangers or once-strangers who may serve as a social bridge to the society as a whole. Recalling Tocqueville's famous reflections on Americans' penchant for associations, social scientists and theorists have argued that those diffuse, cross-cutting social ties arise from associating with others and cooperating toward shared ends (Putnam 2000). Civil society at its best cultivates overlapping networks of purposeful cooperative activity and diffuse feelings of trust and reciprocity – forms of "social capital" that enable people to cooperate in shared undertakings and that help to hold a society and a polity together (Fung 2003; Putnam 2000).

Most contemporary accounts of civil society center on voluntary associations formed around charitable, religious, political, cultural, or even recreational aims; workplace associations are seen as peripheral at best, tainted as they are by economic necessity, hierarchy, and subordination (Cohen and Arato 1992: ix;

[1] For economists, "public goods" are goods that are both non-rivalrous (one person's enjoyment of the good does not limit another's) and non-excludable (enjoyment of the good cannot be limited, e.g., to those who pay for it or contribute their share). E.g., Varian 1992: 414.

[2] This section draws heavily on Estlund (2003, 2022).

Ehrenberg 1999: 235; Habermas 1996: 366–367; Post 1991: 289). Other accounts, including those of Tocqueville and especially Durkheim, included cooperation in the productive sphere among the associations that fostered social integration. I contend that work-based ties are of distinctive value in a diverse democratic society – in part because of their very involuntariness (Estlund 2003). How can that be?

To begin with, the need to make a living leads most adults to spend much of their lives at work and interacting with co-workers – much more time than they spend in "voluntary associations."[3] That social interaction happens in the course of the work itself, before and after work, during breaks, around the proverbial (and increasingly metaphorical) water cooler, and in the digital sphere. And it includes a lot of talking. Co-workers talk about the work itself, about shared working conditions – a speed-up of production, a rumor of layoffs, a disagreeable supervisor – and about family, politics, popular culture, sports, and other stuff of daily life. Over weeks, months, or even years of working together, co-workers often develop ties of affection, empathy, loyalty, solidarity, and friendship. Obviously, workplace ties can also be infected by conflict, resentment, abuse, or humiliation. But given all that is at stake in a job, people often find ways to work through or around conflicts and to get along well enough to get the job done. The *involuntariness* of bonds among co-workers may give them a resilience that is hard to replicate in voluntary associations.

The history of organized labor offers especially powerful evidence of the strong bonds that can form through common work (Estlund 2022). Shared workplace grievances have long provided a rich medium for the growth of solidarity, a willingness to take risks and make sacrifices for the group, and a platform for organizing and collective action. But it is not only shared grievances that can unite co-workers. Working together creates a base of common experiences and interests, and can generate social ties grounded in shared pride and purpose, shared frustration, or both.

The relative resilience and density of workplace ties is especially important because those ties connect people who neither grew up together nor chose each other as associates. Co-workers are *comparatively* likely to come from different cultural, religious, racial, and ethnic backgrounds – compared, that is, to families, neighborhoods, religious congregations, or most voluntary associations (Estlund 2003: 7–10, 61–69. See also Briggs 2007; Darling-Hammond et al. 2019; Tomaskovic-Deney et al. 2006). And given the relative intensity and duration of workplace relationships, ties among co-workers of different racial and ethnic identities often have a chance to deepen and even grow into friendships (Estlund 2003: 9–12; see also 33–35). But from a societal standpoint, those strong ties of interracial

[3] On average, American adults spend 4.35 hours per day engaged in "work and work-related activities," and just over 15 minutes per day in "organizational, civic, and religious activities." Bureau of Labor Statistics 2019.

friendship are less important in themselves than is the larger reservoir of weaker positive interracial ties among co-workers, out of which friendships can sometimes grow.

The point is not that intergroup relations at work are wholly positive. Clearly out-group biases and in-group affinities persist, and harm groups that are still under-represented in good jobs and especially in management (Estlund 2003: 77–83). At the same time, piles of social scientific evidence accumulated over many decades back up the so-called "contact hypothesis" first advanced in the 1950s (Allport 1954) – that is, the proposition that ongoing contact and cooperation among individuals from diverse groups can counter stereotypes and biases and contribute to more positive and egalitarian intergroup relations and attitudes (Estlund 2003: 74–76; see also Darling-Hammond et al. 2019; Tropp and Pettigrew 2006; Paluck et al. 2019)[4]. Personal connections across group lines – what Putnam calls "bridging ties" (Putnam 2000) – not only can counter stereotypes and biases; they also can provide a medium for the exchange of experiences and opinions and the cultivation of empathy and broad-mindedness that may shape political preferences, enable compromise, and enrich public discourse.

The workplace is a uniquely prolific source of those bridging ties because it fosters interpersonal cooperation, informal sociability, solidarity, and shared experiences and interests across often-divisive group lines. The daily experience of working together across differences, multiplied over legions of working adults, thus strengthens the social foundations for democratic governance in a heterogeneous society, albeit in diffuse and incalculable ways.

Before turning to the impact of remote work, more must be said about the compulsory nature of workplace ties – both the economic hold of the workplace on individuals and the power managers exercise there. The economic compulsion to sell one's labor and the managerial compulsion to cooperate in production are at the heart of enduring critiques of capitalism[5]. Those elements of compulsion, on some accounts, disqualify workplace associations from the vaunted domain of civil society. But the semi-compulsory nature of workplace associations also gives workers powerful motives to overcome conflict and friction, and to carry on cooperating with co-workers with whom they might not have chosen to associate, rather than simply walking away. Workers answer to managers who have powerful means and motives to induce workers to overcome their differences and cooperate productively. Those managerial imperatives have generated a cottage industry of corporate diversity initiatives and consultants, with mixed results for intergroup relations[6]. But as long

[4] One study found that white individuals who had at least one black co-worker displayed significantly less racial bias than those who did not, and found clues that the link is causal. Darling-Hammond et al. (2019).

[5] Anderson (2017) has recently elaborated these critiques.

[6] Scholarly assessments of those programs are mixed. Compare Hawkins (2017) (a largely positive account) with Leong (2013: 2165) and Kim et al. (2012) (more skeptical).

as employers have a modicum of diversity within their workforces – a state of affairs that the legal prohibition of employment discrimination helps to ensure – they have solid bottom-line incentives to figure out how to promote intergroup cooperation at work. A crucial byproduct of that cooperation is the profusion of "bridging ties" across group lines, with their spillover benefits for society.

State regulatory compulsion also plays a role in workplace associations. As noted, managers manage and workers work under the shadow of antidiscrimination laws, which make workforces more diverse than they might otherwise be. Those laws also help to counter the interpersonal conflict or harassment that might otherwise follow from workforce diversity by making employers accountable for harassment and discrimination, direct and indirect. Those legal pressures reinforce managers' operational reasons for promoting at least a modicum of civility among co-workers[7]. In turn, relatively civil and cooperative relations among diverse co-workers help to enrich the roots of public discourse and social solidarity in individuals' daily lives.

Again, I do not mean to overstate either the demographic diversity of existing workplaces or the law's efficacy in combatting discrimination, stratification, and intergroup conflict at work. Workplaces are not nearly as diverse or integrated as they could or should be after all these years. But we should ask: compared to what? Compared to the voluntary associations at the core of conventional conceptions of civil society? Unfortunately, many people choose – when their choices are unconstrained – to live and associate with others from similar backgrounds and racial and ethnic identities. But diverse societies must find ways and places to cultivate connectedness, empathy, and reciprocity across group lines. And that may require the convergence of legal, economic, and organizational constraints that can be found in the workplace but rarely elsewhere.

## 3.3 THE IMPACT OF REMOTE WORK ON THE SOCIETAL RESERVOIR OF BRIDGING TIES

That brings us to the question of how the rise of remote work might affect workplaces' capacity and tendency to cultivate this societal resource of intergroup connectedness, empathy, and reciprocity. It is too soon, if not simply impossible, to measure this particular effect of remote work empirically. But anyone who is persuaded of the societal value of working together should be seriously concerned about the sheer reduction in face-to-face contact, side-by-side cooperation, and interstitial sociability entailed by the rise of remote work.

We should start by recognizing that the production of civically virtuous workplace ties is and has always been entirely *incidental* to the pursuit of positive social ties by

7 Up to a point, that is. Managers operating under the shadow of liability can go too far in suffocating sociability among co-workers, for example, through overbroad and censorious "zero-tolerance" harassment policies: Estlund (2003: 157–159, 163–164).

workers and firms for their own reasons. Social ties form at work mainly because, since the Industrial Revolution and the advent of capitalism, the production of marketable goods and services has required firms to convene workers in common spaces – in factories, loading docks, offices, hospitals, retail outlets, and so on – and to coordinate their work and induce their cooperation with each other and with supervisors. (To be sure, as workers began to organize themselves against capital, they and their leaders had other reasons to convene and form bonds – reasons grounded in solidarity and collective power. We'll return to that distinctive dimension of workplace connectedness below.)

Most social ties within the workplace arise because those ties benefit firms, workers, or both in tangible or intangible ways. Firms depend to varying degrees on cooperation, teamwork, and camaraderie among workers (and they lose out from most forms of conflict, which may undercut morale or generate turnover)[8]. Stated differently, firms have an interest in cultivating "intrafirm social capital," or useful social ties, for the sake of productivity, retention, and recruitment (Ben Hador 2016: 1121–1122; Sözbilir 2018: 94; Westlund and Adam 2010: 904). Workers for their part are social beings; once convened and compelled to cooperate, they will often form friendly ties, friendships, and some sense of community with co-workers, even apart from the cooperation their bosses demand from them. Some might also engage in or suffer from degrading treatment, exclusion, and bullying; things clearly can go badly among co-workers. But both workers and firms have powerful reasons to cultivate friendly or at least functional ties that enable them to get things done together.

I have argued that those ties also have value to the whole society through their contribution to the social and political cohesion that diverse and pluralist democracies require. But those societal benefits have never motivated the production of those social ties. The societal value of working together is a positive societal externality of the organization of work within firms, and a public good, that we have largely failed to appreciate and that might be very hard to cultivate deliberately and directly. So we should attend to what motivates firms and workers to produce this incidental public good, and what forces might push in the other direction, including the rise of technologies of remote work.

Let's first look at this landscape from the standpoint of firms and managers. Whenever interpersonal cooperation or "teamwork" is required to produce what they bring to market, firms will try to organize and manage work so as to cultivate productive worker relationships and reduce counterproductive conflict (Brown et al. 2021: 681). Social relationships at work can motivate workers (Borghouts et al. 2022: 10–12), increase job satisfaction (Charalampous et al. 2019: 56), and ease emotional demands that affect work performance (Parker et al. 2022: 1623–1624). Cultivating those relationships might require face-to-face, in-person interaction, both planned

[8] Familiarity and trust within teams, even if "highly virtual," may reduce team conflict (Alves et al. 2022: 854).

and unplanned. Or it might not – depending partly on the evolving state of the art of virtual and remote work technologies.

Managers, along with the consultants and researchers who advise them, have to assess the effectiveness of remote technologies versus in-person interaction in promoting cooperation and productivity (Meluso et al. 2022: 16–17). And managers in turn will demand from the tech sector innovations in remote co-working technologies that improve the productivity of remote work (Bloom et al. 2021: 4–5; Zhu et al. 2021: 4–5). Managers will have to figure out, as those innovations are developed and brought to market in response to firms' demands, how to best use technology and how much face-time – with co-workers and with supervisors, managers, and team leaders – is still needed for workers to carry out their jobs well, to trust each other, and to resolve conflicts. Considerations like these appear to be motivating a push to get workers back on site for at least a few days per week or even full-time (Microsoft WTI 2022). They might continue to lead managers going forward to require some of in-person working-togetherness that incidentally generates virtuous social spillover.

Then again, some managers might find that virtual meetings and remote team production work well enough – especially as technology improves and workers and managers get used to it – to get what their firms need out of workers. Some might find that remote work reduces the risk of harassment or other forms of potentially disruptive conflict among workers (Alves et al. 2022: 854). Part of the unique societal value of workplace interaction comes from individuals' feeling compelled to work through or around conflict, especially across lines of social division; but managers would probably prefer simply to minimize those conflicts, and remote work might seem to allow them to do that. Some managers (like my brother-in-law) might find that moving their entire business online through remote technologies improves the bottom line if only by avoiding the significant real estate expenses entailed by traditional office work (Barrero et al. 2023: 13). Those cost savings might more than offset the incremental productivity losses, if any, of remote versus in-person synchronous production (JLL 2016). Different firms and managers will settle on different mixtures of in-person and remote work that gets the job done. But let us be clear: Whatever mix of remote, in-person, and hybrid work is good enough and productive enough for firms might not be good enough to forge the resilient workplace ties – especially those across group lines – that society needs.

To some degree, the decisions of firms and managers will have to take into account how *workers* view the respective virtues of in-person and remote work. Some workers have institutional channels within firms for pressing their own interests; we will return to those below. But labor markets also afford channels for workers, including those without collective representation, to assert their interests. In particular, workers who are "in demand" – who have skills that employers need and cannot easily replace – are in a position to make some demands of their own or to be choosy. In tight labor markets – as in the United States in recent years – even some less-skilled workers might be sufficiently "in demand" to make some implicit demands on employers or to shop around for preferred working conditions as well as higher wages. To be sure, these dynamics affect only jobs that can feasibly be done remotely; that proviso disproportionately knocks out many low-wage workers[9]. But in a large swath of the labor market, it matters what in-demand workers demand in terms of in-person versus remote or hybrid co-working arrangements (for jobs in which the latter are feasible). Let's examine their perspectives on remote work.

Some in-demand workers might prefer a more sociable work environment, with supportive supervisors and co-workers and positive social dynamics. In one survey, 61% of employee respondents identified less socializing as a top concern of working even partly remote (Glint 2021). So, too, some ambitious workers believe that more face-time with bosses will help them to advance within the organization (Glint 2021). (And there is some evidence to support that belief; Bloom et al. 2015: 170.) So far, however, studies suggest that many workers – especially but not only women with children – place a higher priority on better work–life balance[10]. Those workers are gravitating to employers and jobs that offer flexibility in work time and location and less or no commuting time[11]. Some workers might even prefer to avoid face-time with co-workers who are annoying, or biased, or simply different from themselves; those co-workers were not, after all, the people with whom they'd have chosen to spend thirty, forty, or more hours per week. Involuntary association is not an unmitigated benefit to workers even if it serves societal interests.

For various reasons, many workers are now seeking out remote work and work-from-home options, partly because of its greater flexibility and compatibility with family demands and home life. Some workers – perhaps especially women – appear willing to give up, in exchange for that flexibility, some compensation or whatever edge more in-person face-time might give them in climbing the organizational ladder (with unsettling implications for gender equality that are beyond the scope of this chapter)[12]. Managers seeking to recruit or retain those in-demand workers might feel obliged to supply a good deal of what those workers want, and to offer more remote work opportunities than managers might otherwise prefer[13]. Employers have to balance workers' demands – or those of in-demand workers! – against their

[9] Barrero et al. (2023: 2) identify fully in-person employees as the lowest paid on average. On the other hand, technological developments might gradually expand the scope of "remote-capable" work.

[10] Henley Business School (2022: 14–15). One study found 53% of employee respondents (and 56% of women with children) said they were more likely to prioritize their health and well-being than before the pandemic. Microsoft WTI 2022.

[11] Barrero et al. (2022: slide 8) and Mas and Pallais (2017: 3726). Microsoft WTI (2022) found that lack of flexible hours and location is one of the top five reasons respondents quit their jobs; that appears especially true for women. Anders (2022). Henley Business School (2022: 15) finds that some workers are willing to accept lower compensation to work from home.

[12] Hering (2024) finds that 29% of female survey respondents would take a 10% or 20% pay cut in return for more flexibility at work.

[13] Aksoy et al. (2022: 2) describe a steady increase in employer willingness to allow more work from home from January 2021 to June 2022.

own need to maintain productivity and whatever level of worker interaction and cooperation that requires.

Employers catering to workers who want more flexibility and less mandatory face time, as well as those seeking to reduce real estate costs, are driving up business demand for digital tools that make remote work more seamless and productive (Bloom et al. 2021: 4–5). Some employers in some sectors are striving to make remote workplace interactions, including those between remote and in-office workers in hybrid settings, more like face-to-face interactions, and more socially rich and inclusive[14]. Some employers, and therefore some developers and vendors of workplace technologies, attempt to replicate the informal, unplanned "water cooler" interactions that characterize in-person workplaces[15]. That's a good thing from the societal working-together perspective; more "life-like" forms of remote engagement should incidentally generate more of the societally valuable connections and feelings of connectedness. On the other hand, the more employers can get what *they* want out of workplace interactions through remote technologies, the more they might be inclined to substitute remote for in-person work.

In short, some employers and some workers, for their own reasons, value the social dimension of work, including the informal, incidental worker-driven interactions that have traditionally occurred at work, and that generate spillover value to society. But both workers and employers are pulled in both directions – toward and away from remote work; and in the meantime, both innovations in remote work technologies and workers' and bosses' growing familiarity and comfort with them are enabling a shift toward more remote work in much of the economy. It would be surprising if the various arrangements that firms and workers arrive at in different sectors and organizations – even if they continue to include some in-person work – end up generating as much of the workplace connectedness and especially the bridging ties that society has derived in the past from workplace interaction, and that it needs now more than ever.

## 3.4 THE CONFOUNDING ROLE OF WORKER SOLIDARITY, SELF-ORGANIZATION, AND UNIONS

A confounding factor is worker solidarity. It is confounding in part because this is a form of workplace connectedness that employers generally do not value and often seek to avoid. That is especially true in industrial relations systems like that in the

[14] For examples, see Zhang et al. (2022: 1–2) and Margariti et al. (2022: 7).

[15] Reed and Allen (2021: 114–115) recommend reserving time in meetings for social interactions. Sendra and Grensing-Pophal (2023) provide several case studies of how executives foster casual encounters, including teambuilding sessions, icebreakers, virtual social events, and online games. Burton (2023) even discusses the use of artificial intelligence tools to monitor employees' mood and encourage the formation of informal connections outside of their normal professional network. See also Bleakley et al. (2021: 410–412, 413–414, 424–425).

US, in which unionization is an all-or-nothing proposition that plays out at the enterprise and facility level based on majority rule, and in which employers have powerful means and motives to resist unionization.

In the United States, unionization requires an intensive campaign by unions and pro-union workers for majority support; and the campaign is largely conducted under the noses of hostile employers who invest heavily in both crude and sophisticated forms of "union avoidance." Brishen Rogers, in his recent book *Data and Democracy at Work*, shows how US employers deploy workplace technologies – especially surveillance and monitoring technologies – not, or not only, to enhance productivity but to frustrate workers' ability to organize themselves and exercise countervailing power (Rogers 2023). Employers may do that in part by organizing production so as to minimize workers' occasions to congregate in person (without surveillance), and to minimize their opportunities to share grievances informally, and to develop the kind of mutual trust that is usually a prerequisite for union organizing. Unionization is not impossible but is much more challenging where workers do not have extensive daily contact at work – where they do not work together physically.

US employers are most anxious to squelch the solidarity that might lead to unionization among workers who need it most – those with little or no individual bargaining power and little ability to make demands on or shop around among employers. In many of those jobs, whether in the dwindling non-unionized manufacturing sector or in the large and growing service sector, workers' physical presence is a necessity and remote work is not feasible. But where remote work is feasible and unionization is perceived as a "risk" to be managed and minimized, employers have an additional powerful incentive to shift away from in-person, face-to-face workplace interaction and to frustrate informal social interaction among workers by design. And even if employers conclude that they need to cultivate informal interactions among remote workers to elicit their cooperation and collective creativity, employers may be able to impede oppositional solidarity-building, for example, by monitoring workers' interactions.

Other confounding aspects of this dimension of workplace connectedness – solidarity and self-organization among workers in latent or overt opposition to employers – lie in the role of workers' organizations. Workers' organizations plainly benefit from the social dimension of work; they might therefore have reasons, and potentially some power, to push back against the rise of remote work. Or they might not.

Workers collectively benefit from solidarity that strengthens their collective institutions and their collective bargaining power. That solidaristic connectedness is a public good among workers – a public good, again, in the sense that all may gain from that solidaristic connectedness whether or not they contribute to it. The production of public goods suffers from an inherent collective action problem: Because individuals cannot capture for themselves the gains from building solidaristic ties, they may be unwilling or at least undermotivated to shoulder the risks and burdens of producing those ties. But unions can help to overcome this collective action problem by serving as collective and institutional vehicles for promoting solidaristic ties and self-organizational activities among workers for the good of all.

Solidaristic connectedness and self-organization among workers can also benefit the society at large, as argued above, by bridging intergroup differences among workers and promoting cross-racial connectedness that builds on workplace ties. As I have written elsewhere: "Unions at their best can promote intergroup connectedness at the workplace and within unions, and can make mutually reinforcing moral and material arguments for intergroup solidarity. That can make [unions] especially credible proponents of racial inclusion and progressive class-based policies and politics beyond the workplace" (Estlund 2022). Effective unions with diverse worker constituencies have to find ways to counter the kind of racially divisive appeals that are corroding democracies across the developed world. That is just one of many ways in which a strong labor movement can fortify democratic norms and institutions (Roberts 2022).

Unfortunately, the rise of remote work potentially weakens organized labor at its roots in daily interaction among workers under shared working conditions. Remote and at-home work seems like an especially poor medium for the kind of intense organizing that is required in the United States, given its decentralized enterprise-based system of union organizing and bargaining. Remote work thus seems likely to exacerbate the long-term trend of union decline, most dramatic in the United States, and to pose one of many challenges to unions' revival.

These might be reasons why unions might deploy some of whatever power they do have to push back against remote work, at least in some settings and some forms. To do that, however, they would presumably have to convince their worker-constituents to resist remote work rather than welcoming it. Stated differently, empowering workers to pursue their own interests and make demands on employers through unionization is unlikely to put the brakes on the rise of remote work unless that is what workers want. Workers might prefer to use their collective bargaining power to expand their ability to work from home; the benefits in work–life balance are bound to weigh more heavily in workers' own calculus than the societal value of informal, spontaneous, non-instrumental co-worker interactions, and their diffuse benefits to worker solidarity, collective power, and social integration. So there are lots of good reasons for society to improve the legal infrastructure for union organizing and a stronger collective voice for workers. But those reforms might not do much to fend off whatever threat remote work poses to the future societal reservoir of connections and connectedness that flows from working together.

The same dilemma puts in question the usefulness of other traditional labor law mechanisms in responding to the rise of remote work. We could probably devise regulatory interventions that would put a societal thumb on the scale in favor of in-person shared work (though that's not an easy task, and limitations of space and imagination prevent my undertaking it here!). The societal value of working together – if my argument above is persuasive – *might* help to justify those interventions despite the preferences of individual workers and their families for more remote work and a better work–life balance. But even if it were normatively justified for society to weigh in on the side of in-person working together, where is the political constituency for regulatory interventions of this sort if they are not aligned with workers' preferences?

## 3.5 CONCLUSION

Part of the value of working together is captured by employers, and part of it is captured by workers. But both workers and employers have interests and aims that, all things considered, might point them toward greater substitution of remote work for in-person co-working. In the meantime, technology is increasingly enabling both workers and especially employers to get what they need out of the social dimension of work without in-person interaction. That is a problem – again, if my argument above is persuasive. The societal spillover benefits of working together are not captured by either employers or individual workers; they are "externalities" that are likely to be undersupplied if left to the parties to pursue their own interests through market mechanisms. That means that the demands and interests of workers and employers – even if successfully channeled into collective bargaining – may lead them to converge on various mixtures of in-person and remote work that fail to serve society's interests in the spillover benefits of working together, and especially of working together across lines of social division.

There are still plenty of good reasons to pursue institutional reforms that empower workers collectively and strengthen their collective institutions. But those face strong headwinds, and will have to be reimagined, in a remote-work environment. For example, legal interventions might be designed to facilitate workers' remote engagement with each other and with workers' organizations free from employer surveillance. (Clearly more needs to be thought and said about this, but not here.) If a mix of traditional and innovative labor law reforms can help workers to build stronger collective institutions, those reforms and those stronger institutions could help to cultivate workers' solidaristic ties, and perhaps offset the thinning out of workplace ties themselves.

A profound challenge to that traditional labor law project – reimagined or not – lies in the mutual dependency of working together and solidarity: Growing and strengthening workers' organizations will help to fortify workers' feelings and experiences of solidarity; yet that project also *depends on* those feelings and experiences, which might be impoverished in a world of remote work. Still, if worker organizations can gain greater power to shape working conditions and workplace technologies, then their institutional interest in cultivating solidarity may lead them to find new ways of fostering bonds among workers even with the rise of remote and hybrid work. Or so we must hope for the sake of democracy's future.

## REFERENCES


Aksoy C. G. et al. (2022) Working from home around the world. Becker Friedman Institute Working Paper No. 2022-124, University of Chicago. Available at https://bfi.uchicago.edu/wp-content/uploads/2022/09/BFI_WP_2022-124.pdf.

Allport, G. (1954) *The Nature of Prejudice*. Reading, MA: Addison-Wesley.

Alves, M. P. et al. (2022) Can virtuality be protective of team trust? Conflict and effectiveness in hybrid teams. *Behaviour & Information Technology* 42, 7: 851–868. Available at https://doi.org/10.1080/0144929X.2022.2046163.

Anders, G. (2022) What job hunters really want: 43% of women seek to cut workplace stress. *LinkedIn Blog*. Microsoft Study. Available at https://www.linkedin.com/pulse/what-job-hunters-really-want-43-women-seek-cut-workplace-anders/.

Anderson, E. (2017) *Private Government: How Employers Rule Our Lives*. Princeton: Princeton University Press.

Barrero, J. M., Bloom, N., and Davis, S. J. (2022) Survey of working arrangements and attitudes April 2022 updates. *WFH Research*. Available at https://wfhresearch.com/wp-content/uploads/2022/04/WFHResearch_updates-April-2022.pdf.

(2023) The evolution of working from home. Stanford Institute for Economic Policy Research Working Paper No. 23-19, Stanford University. Available at https://siepr.stanford.edu/publications/working-paper/evolution-working-home.

Ben Hador, B. (2016) How intra-organizational social capital influences employee performance. *Journal of Management Development* 35, 9: 1119–1133. Available at https://doi.org/10.1108/JMD-12-2015-0172.

Bleakley, A. et al. (2021) Bridging social distance during social distancing: Exploring social talk and remote collegiality in video conferencing. *Human–Computer Interaction* 37, 5: 404–432. Available at https://doi.org/10.1080/07370024.2021.1994859.

Bloom, N., Davis, S. J., and Zhestkova, Y. (2021) COVID-19 shifted patent applications toward technologies that support working from home. *American Economic Association Papers and Proceedings* 111: 263–266. Available at www.aeaweb.org/articles?id=10.1257/pandp.20211057.

Bloom, N. et al. (2015) Does working from home work? Evidence from a Chinese experiment. *The Quarterly Journal of Economics* 130, 1: 165–218. Available at www.jstor.org/stable/26372598.

Borghouts, J. et al. (2022) Motivated to work or working to stay motivated: A diary and interview study on working from home. *Proceedings of the ACM on Human-Computer Interaction* 6, CSCW2: 1–26. Available at https://dl.acm.org/doi/pdf/10.1145/3555121.

Briggs, X. de S. (2007) "Some of my best friends are . . .": Interracial friendships, class, and segregation in America. *City & Community* 6, 4: 263–290. Available at https://doi.org/10.1111/j.1540-6040.2007.00228.x.

Brown, S. G., Hill, N. S., and Lorinkova, N. M. (2021) Leadership and virtual team performance: A meta-analytic investigation. *European Journal of Work and Organizational Psychology* 30, 5: 672–685. Available at https://doi.org/10.1080/1359432X.2021.1914719.

Bureau of Labor Statistics (2019) *American time use survey – 2018 results*. Table 8a. Available at www.bls.gov/news.release/archives/atus_06192019.pdf.

Burton, A. (2023) Genpact is using A.I. to flag employee dissatisfaction and tying leaders' bonuses to the results. *Yahoo! Finance*. Available at https://finance.yahoo.com/news/genpact-using-flag-employee-dissatisfaction-110000748.html.

Charalampous, M. et al. (2019) Systematically reviewing remote e-workers' well-being at work: A multidimensional approach. *European Journal of Work and Organizational Psychology* 28, 1: 51–73. Available at https://doi.org/10.1080/1359432X.2018.1541886.

Cohen, J. L. and Arato, A. (1992) *Civil Society and Political Theory*. Cambridge, MA: MIT Press.

Darling-Hammond, S., Lee, R. T., and Mendoza-Denton, R. (2019) Interracial contact at work: Does workplace diversity reduce bias? *Group Processes & Intergroup Relations* 24, 7: 1114–1131. Available at https://doi.org/10.1177/1368430220932636.

Ehrenberg, J. (1999) *Civil Society: The Critical History of an Idea*. New York: New York University Press.

Estlund, C. (2022) Coming apart: How union decline and workplace disintegration imperil democracy. In Cornell, A. and Barenberg, M. (eds.), *The Cambridge handbook of labor and democracy*. Cambridge: Cambridge University Press, 163–179.

(2003) *Working Together: How Workplace Bonds Strengthen a Diverse Democracy*. New York: Oxford University Press.

Fung, A. (2003) Associations and democracy: Between theories, hopes, and realities. *Annual Review of Sociology* 29: 515–539. Available at www.jstor.org/stable/30036978.

Glint (2021) Concerns on virtual work in a hybrid world. Microsoft Study.

Habermas, J. (1996) *Between Facts and Norms*. Cambridge, MA: MIT Press.

Henley Business School (2022) The four-day week: The pandemic and the evolution of flexible working. *Henley Business School*. White Paper. Available at www.henley.ac.uk/the-four-day-week.

Hering, B. B. (2024) Women want flexibility at work, FlexJobs survey finds. *FlexJobs*. Available at www.flexjobs.com/employer-blog/women-want-flexibility-at-work-flexjobs-survey/.

JLL (2016) A surprising way to cut real estate costs. Available at www.jll.ca/en/trends-and-insights/workplace/a-surprising-way-to-cut-real-estate-costs.

Margariti, E. et al. (2022) Automated mapping of competitive and collaborative overlapping talk in video meetings. *ACM CHI EA'22*, Article 311: 1–8. Microsoft Study. Available at https://doi.org/10.1145/3491101.3519612.

Mas, A. and Pallais, A. (2017) Valuing alternative work arrangements. *American Economic Review* 107, 12: 3722–3759. Available at https://doi.org/10.1257/aer.20161500.

Meluso, J., Johnson, S., and Bagrow, J. (2022) Flexible environments for hybrid Collaboration: Redesigning virtual work through the four orders of design. *Design Issues* 38, 1: 55–69. Available at https://doi.org/10.1162/desi_a_00670.

Microsoft WTI (2022) Great expectations: Making hybrid work work. *Microsoft WorkLab: Work Trend Index* 2022. Available at www.microsoft.com/en-us/worklab/work-trend-index/great-expectations-making-hybrid-work-work.

Paluck, E. L., Green, S. A., and Green, D. P. (2019) The contact hypothesis reevaluated. *Behavioural Public Policy* 3, 2: 129–158. Available at https://doi.org/10.1017/bpp.2018.25.

Parker, A., Waldstrøm, C., and Shah, N. P. (2022) The coevolution of emotional job demands and work-based social ties and their effect on performance. *Journal of Management* 49, 5: 1601–1632. Available at https://doi.org/10.1177/01492063221087636.

Post, R. (1991) Racist speech, democracy, and the first amendment. *William & Mary Law Review* 32: 267.

Putnam, R. (2000) *Bowling Alone: The Collapse and Revival of American Community*. New York: Simon & Schuster.

Reed, K. M. and Allen, J. A. (2021) *Suddenly Virtual: Making Remote Meetings Work*. Hoboken, NJ: John Wiley & Sons.

Roberts, K. (2022) Labor and democracy: Constructing, deepening, and defending citizenship rights. In Cornell, A. and Barenberg, M. (eds.), *The Cambridge Handbook of Labor and Democracy*. Cambridge: Cambridge University Press, 36–48.

Rogers, B. (2023) *Data and Democracy at Work: Advanced Information Technologies, Labor Law, and the New Working Class*. Cambridge, MA: MIT Press.

Sendra, C. and Grensing-Pophal, L. (2023) Replacing "water cooler moments." *SAP Best Practice Guide*. Available at www.sap.com/resources/replacing-water-cooler-moments.

Sözbilir, F. (2018) The interaction between social capital, creativity and efficiency in organizations. *Thinking Skills and Creativity* 27: 92–100. Available at https://doi.org/10.1016/j.tsc.2017.12.006.

Tomaskovic-Deney, D. et al. (2006) Documenting desegregation: Segregation in American workplaces by race, ethnicity, and sex, 1966–2003. *American Sociological Review* 71, 4: 565–588. Available at https://doi.org/10.1177/000312240607100403.

Tropp, T. F. and Pettigrew, L. R. (2006) A meta-analytic test of intergroup contact theory. *Journal of Personality and Social Psychology* 90, 5: 751–783. Available at https://doi.org/10.1037/0022-3514.90.5.751.

Westlund, H. and Adam, F. (2010) Social capital and economic performance: A meta-analysis of 65 Studies. *European Planning Studies* 18, 6: 893–919. Available at https://doi.org/10.1080/09654311003701431.

Varian, H. R. (1992) *Microeconomic Analysis*, 3d ed., New York, NY: Norton.

Zhang, Y. et al. (2022) VirtualCube: An immersive 3D video communication system. *IEEE Transactions on Visualization and Computer Graphics*. 28, 5: 2146–2156. Microsoft Study. Available at https://arxiv.org/pdf/2112.06730.pdf.

Zhu, C. et al. (2021) MediaSum: A large-scale media interview dataset for dialogue summarization. *arXiv preprint*: arXiv.2103.06410. Microsoft Study. Available at https://arxiv.org/pdf/2103.06410.pdf.

# 4

# Hybrid Action for a Hybrid World

## *Collective Freedoms and the Challenges of Digital Work Fragmentation*

*Fotis Vergis*

### 4.1 INTRODUCTION

'Remote work' and 'telework', which used to be regarded as exceptional subcategories of labour engagement, became the norm for white-collar workers during the pandemic, and currently sit at the heart of modern work practices characterised by spatial fragmentation and supported by web-based technological tools. The experience of recent years, in other words, has been the increasing advent of *hybrid* labour arrangements, where work is directly or indirectly provided through apps or similar pieces of software and other technological innovations ('information and communications technology' or ICT)[1]. The overarching work digitisation phenomenon is, inter alia, defined by increasing delocalisation and fragmentation of workplaces, and by the advent of algorithmic management that employs advanced software and AI driven tools of worker control. 'Platform work', for example, an emblematic example of this perceived paradigm shift of hybridisation, may itself become terminologically obsolete, as a variety of (broadly construed) digital 'platforms' define the work experience of more 'typical' non-gig workers, whether their services are provided at their employer's premises or not. The same, arguably, applies to our established understanding of 'telework' (cf. Anderson et al., 2007) as work performed outside the employer's premises (Messenger 2022: 2;[2] Eurofound and ILO 2017: 5–6). Even work

[1] For relevant ILO projects see, ILO, The Future of Work in Information and Communication Technology, GLO/17/20/JPN, www.ilo.org/projects-and-partnerships/projects/future-work-information-and-communication-technology (last accessed 25 September 2024).; European Foundation for the Improvement of Living and Working Conditions and the International Labour Organization (Eurofound and ILO 2017), Working Anytime, Anywhere: The Effects on the World of Work, Luxembourg: Publications Office of the European Union and Geneva: ILO, eurofound.link/ef1658 (accessed 25 September 2024). Indicatively, on ICT, see also Anderson et al. 2007.

[2] Who also notes the difficulty of literature to encapsulate the concept, leading not just to a diversity of definitions, but, ultimately, to confusion (Messenger 2022: 9).

typically performed on-site includes nowadays elements of delocalisation, from virtual meetings to the use of virtual workspaces, and from constant online communication as part of a worker's daily activities to work that is actually performed online in its entirety.[3]

This chapter attempts to examine the appropriateness of existing collective labour law institutions to address the needs and particular conditions of workers engaged in digitised hybrid work, given that such processes and institutional structures had been developed with different work models in mind. It considers that a solution may lie with the extension of the scope and focus of the rights to collective organisation and action, and with a re-evaluation of their substantive content. With regard to work and workplace fragmentation that come with work digitisation, it seeks solutions in worker empowerment through the redeployment of those collective labour rights and institutions. Within that context, the chapter will also briefly touch upon illustrative case studies that provide glimpses into possible avenues of traditional and alternative collective action tactics. Where appropriate, the relevant current EU framework will be used to contextualise the discussion, particularly given the transnational characteristics that often define digitalised workplaces.

### 4.1.1 *From Telework to Digitised Hybrid Work*

It is notable that, at European level, it was the social partners who had the foresight to more closely engage with the regulation of telework at a time when the expansion of internet-based work was in its relatively early stages. The Framework Agreement concluded on 16 July 2006[4] defined telework as 'a form of organising and/or performing work, using information technology, in the context of an employment contract/relationship, where work, which could also be performed at the employer's premises, is carried out away from those premises on a regular basis'. That definition encapsulates the traditional understanding of telework as a model identified with remote work, that is, work that is undertaken away from the employer's premises (Niles 1975, 1988; Eurofound and ILO 2017: 5–6).

The more recent 2022 Framework Agreement on social security arrangements[5] for habitual cross-border telework[6] offers a more nuanced take. Telework is now approached as any activity 'which can be pursued from any location', including

3 Interestingly, as early as 2002 Bailey and Kurland had described telework as an early form of virtual work (Bailey and Kurland 2002: 384).

4 The 2006 Framework Agreement was concluded between the social partners (European Trade Union Confederation, ETUC; Business Europe; the European Centre of Employers and Enterprises providing Public Services, CEEP; and the European of Craft, Small and Medium-Sized Enterprises, UEAPME). cf. Prosser 2011.

5 Specifically, aiming to introduce exceptions to Regulation (EC) No 883/2004 of the European Parliament and of the Council of 29 April 2004 on the coordination of social security systems.

6 Framework Agreement on the application of Article 16 (1) of Regulation (EC) No. 883/2004 in cases of habitual cross-border telework. This multilateral agreement, which, as of

such performed 'at the employer's premises or place of business' (Art.1(c)), is not carried out at the employer's premises or place of business (Art.1(c)(1)) and 'is based on information technology to remain connected to the employer's or business's working environment as well as stakeholders/clients in order to fulfil the employee's tasks assigned by the employer or clients, in case of self-employed persons' (Art.1(c)(2)). It is this second element that can be crucial in an expanded reconceptualisation of the concept that would include work performed at the premises of the employer but primarily through technological tools that either require the worker to be constantly connected to the employer's virtual workplace or environment or constitute the means by which her service is offered.

The Explanatory Memorandum attached to the 2022 Framework Agreement supports that reconceptualisation. It notes the 'explosive accrual' of (traditional) telework because of the COVID-19 pandemic[7] (cf. Sostero et al. 2023; Bruurs 2023; Nyberg et al. 2021), but also that, even after that exceptional period, telework has carried on as 'a permanent new way of work'. In defining telework as a concept, the Explanatory Memorandum highlights that genuine telework is 'completely location-independent'[8] and emphasises its reliance on a constant 'digital connection to the company's infrastructure' and its working environment. This digital connection, through which work is performed, is treated as an integral part of the model[9]. However, the Explanatory Memorandum adds that connection to the employer's environment, though necessary and 'normally and habitually present', does not necessarily need to be required 100 per cent of the working time.[10] Hence, it appears to exclude manual activities undertaken beyond the employer's premises from the concept of telework. At the same time, though, it also opens the door for a conceptual transition from telework to hybrid digital work (cf. Vartiainen and Vanharanta 2024).

In other words, in circumstances of work digitisation, under which digital work and virtual/online working environments have been regularised and become the norm, it might be useful to reshape our concept of telework so that it does not *necessarily* equal remote work (regular or not; synchronous or asynchronous).

September 2024, has been countersigned by 22 states (including Switzerland, Norway and Liechtenstein), was the result of discussions within an ad hoc working group of the Administrative Commission for the Coordination of Social Security Systems, which began as an emergency reaction to the force majeure that was the COVID-19 pandemic. See also Administrative Commission for the Coordination of Social Security Systems, Guidance Note of 21 June 2023 (AC 137/23), available at European Commission, Employment, Social Affairs and Inclusion, Official Documents, https://ec.europa.eu/social/main.jsp?catId=868 (last accessed 25 September 2024).

7 Explanatory Memorandum to the Framework Agreement on the application of Article 16 (1) of Regulation (EC) No. 883/2004 in cases of habitual cross-border telework, pg.1, https://socialsecurity.belgium.be/sites/default/files/content/docs/en/international/explanatory_memorandum_to_the_framework_agreement.pdf (last accessed 25/09/2024).

8 Ibid., p. 2 (on Art.1: definition).

9 Ibid.

10 Ibid.

Rather, the model of digitised work, clerical or other, performed in the physical world (e.g. delivery gig work) or wholly online, inherently entails elements of tele-performance or tele-control that fragment spatiality and shape workers' commitment and experience. The constantly 'logged on' worker ('logging on' itself having become a form of digitally punching in to enter the virtual workspace) essentially operates beyond the physical confines of her cubicle, workstation, or office. She is connected with colleagues with whom she does not necessarily share the same premises – and they can all be subject to rigorous digital monitoring and management by their employer (see Iannuzzi and Campolongo 2023; Eurofound and ILO 2017: 26–27)). The issues that had been identified by the 2006 Framework Agreement as particularly pertinent to teleworkers, with regard to data protection (Art.5), privacy (Art.6), the required equipment (Art.7), health and safety (particularly as regards 'visual display units', i.e. screens of any kind) (Art.8), training (Art.10), but also the risk of isolation (Art.9) and disconnection from their colleagues (Art.11), today apply to any worker operating within a wholly digital or hybrid environment. Therefore, it might be more useful to identify *elements* or *levels* of teleworking in each individual case lying within the spectrum that is digital and hybrid work[11], and adjust our established norms, rights, and institutions accordingly to address the various relevant challenges, rather than treat telework as a mode of work that is not only exceptional, but also supposedly wholly separate (Di Martino and Wirth 1990; Golden and Fromen 2011; Golden et al. 2008; Hill et al. 2001, 2003, 2010; Kurland and Bailey 1999; cf. Anderson et al., 2007) to a now almost obsolete 'norm'.

The proposition that telework has changed over the years is not new. Messenger (Messenger 2022) documents the three-stage evolution from the stationary 'home office' to the 'mobile office' (i.e. working not just from home, but from virtually anywhere), to, finally, the 'virtual office' (Messenger 2022: 13–15; Messenger and Gschwind 2016; cf. Hill et al. 2003), with communication and information technology having merged to allow assets, data, and, ultimately work itself to exist primarily in a virtual space rather than the physical office. Messenger has rightly suggested that the emphasis should be placed on noting the evolution of ICT that led to this paradigmatic change, rather than on working from afar ('tele') in relation to the employer's premises, or on the concept of flexibility[12] in organising work. His identification of 'intermediate spaces'[13] where work is performed (e.g. the elevator at or the sidewalk around the typical business workplace) that are still defined with reference to the employer's premises stricto sensu (Messenger 2022: 14) is important to help understand what the new digital working model entails.

[11] Messenger's concept of 'instantaneous telework' (Messenger 2022: 10) would fit nicely within such a reconceptualisation.

[12] On the suggested advantages and concerns of work flexibility for both employers and workers, see, inter alia, Kelliher and de Menezes 2019.

[13] That is, separate to the employer's premises, any location outside those that would define mobile work, and the worker's home.

However, it is suggested that what technological development and increased instantaneous connectivity demand reconsidered is our very concept of what lies afar ('tele') in telework as an element of hybrid digital work. Instead of focusing on where the worker is physically present in relation to the business premises, we ought to note what actually lies beyond that physical space: data and assets crucial to the performance of the work (which exist in the cloud and remote servers rather than cabinets or hard drives); clients and, often, colleagues (with emails and virtual meetings substituting for physical even within the employer's premises); and, ultimately, work itself, which primarily consists of activities performed in the virtual space, on or through ICT devices and tools. Employers, particularly after the end of the heights of the COVID-19 pandemic, are eager to have their workers return to business premises, seeking to exert greater control[14] over them (cf. Gschwind and Vargas 2022: 40, 59) than what the already intrusive management and monitoring software would allow. That, however, does not change the hybrid nature of work to be performed under this new evolving paradigm.

### 4.1.2 *Genuine Telework and Digitised Hybrid Work*

The challenges, practicalities, and substance of collective labour engagement of hybrid digital workers have not been the subject of much attention; even under the more traditional understanding of telework, they have gone largely been unnoticed by literature and legislators. The 2002 Framework Agreement, under Art 11 ('Collective Rights Issues'), did recognise the importance of teleworkers' full inclusion in collective processes, stipulating that they have the same collective rights as workers at the employer's premises, but offering little as to how that is to be achieved. The one notable exception is its demand that communication of teleworkers with worker representatives is unimpeded and relevant obstacles prohibited. This could be read, inter alia, as the social partners acknowledging perhaps the greatest hurdles full or partial teleworkers face in building a consciousness of shared experience and interest, and funnelling that into mechanisms of solidarity: isolation (Beauregard et al. 2013: 4, 28–34; Gschwind and Vargas 2022: 54–56; Eurofound and ILO 2017: 37) and detachment ('being cut-off')[15] (Beauregard et al. 2013:4; 28–34) from their colleagues and peers, which weakens the interpersonal bonds between them (Beauregard et al. 2013: 25–28)[16].

It is suggested that these hurdles apply to all engaged in digital work, regardless of the level of remoteness that characterises their duties, from fully remote teleworkers (be it 'home office' or 'mobile office' as such) to those that might be physically

[14] Control related concerns and mistrust of workers have long informed employers' practices (see Bailey and Kurland 2002: 388–389).

[15] Beauregard et al. 2013: 30.

[16] Expectedly, that appears to be less of a problem for part-time teleworkers: Beauregard et al. 2013: 28.

stationed at the employer's premises but offer their services in its 'virtual office', engaged in work that does not actually allow physical proximity and interaction with their coworkers. Moreover, the technological advancements and ICT tools that define the digital work model fragment work spatially and substantially (furthering micro-specialisation, and artificial work fragmentation, including into what Graeber would have regarded as 'bullshit jobs') (Graeber 2018). De-spatialisation is crucial. Making the common physical workspace redundant in favour of the 'mobile office' or the virtual working environment that requires minimal (if any) physical face-to-face interaction deprives workers of the spatiality of workplace community as the place they meet and interact[17] to forge the commonality of their experience, their labour consciousness and, ultimately, to organise and act. Communication and interaction between coworkers is the minimum prerequisite for building the interpersonal bonds, the shared experience, and the sense of shared interests and problems that are required for substantive and formal solidarity to emerge, that is, for sentiments of solidarity and formal mechanisms through which common understanding, action and mutual aid can be funnelled.

The digital work model, which includes the established concept of telework and its proposed reconceptualisation, has been argued to be characterised by multifaceted fragmentation: legal; technological; organisational; spatial; social (Della Porta et al. 2022: 222–224). Although platform work encapsulates all, as perhaps the most emblematic example of this modern paradigm, teleworking does not escape these varieties of fragmentation. Delocalisation of work, to the detriment of commonality (cf. Moriset 2004), but also to the detriment of developing full bourgeois citizen consciousness, is, as we have remarked, the most common feature of teleworking. Further, though, attempting to contain telework into a separate category that only encompasses fully remote work (with the caveat of the 2006 Framework Agreement, as discussed above) reveals the risk of splitting digital work into separate categories, if not legal statuses and contractual modalities. The variety of ICTs and digital services upon which teleworking is based fuels technological fragmentation, creating respective varieties of working experience, automated management and surveillance, work standardisation and individualisation. Finally, the virtual workspace promotes organisational fragmentation, that is, compartmentalisation, but also integration, interaction and intra-employee competition beyond physical borders. It is useful, therefore, to keep in mind the digital paradigm context in which our contemporary understanding of teleworking is situated.

In that regard, we also need to recall that work digitisation, as applied in the modern work and workplaces, constitutes part of the most recent evolutionary stage of the variety of free market capitalism that has been dominant globally since the late 1980s (Srnicek 2017: 11; 13–25) and its preference for 'liberal' (i.e., unregulated) labour markets. It ushers in a new emblematic paradigm of economic, market and

[17] cf. Wells et al. 2021: 322–324, making a similar point with regard to platform work.

business organisation (Srnicek 2017: 27 ff.), promoting ever-increasing dematerialisation of capital production, financialisation and intangible 'services products' that often, in turn, define the new workplace paradigm (examples range from cloud computing and data processing, communication and work management platforms, to crowdwork and digital micro-work supplementing more 'regular' in-house digital work). Such services and platforms used by employers are not under their direct control but developed and offered by companies and providers increasingly conglomerated under the control of just a few corporate entities. In other words, zooming out from the microlevel of digital work as such, the systemic context reveals a movement away from the liberal free market ideal towards a stage of capitalist neofeudalism (Dean 2020; Kuttner and Stone 2020; Supiot 2013: 129–145, 2017: 214–225; cf. Morozov 2022) facilitated by, and clad in, technological advancement (Kobrin 1998; Mazzucato 2019; Varoufakis 2023, 2021).

It is within this broader contemporary paradigm that we must situate any analysis of digital work, including a reconceptualisation of telework. And it is within this context that more comprehensive re-evaluation of the concepts of work and the workplace, and a respective reconsideration of traditional legal institutions might be due. Instead of piecemeal intervention through regulating supposedly distinct forms of work, taxonomised into convenient conceptual boxes (telework; platform work), we should perhaps start by considering whether the scope and substance of established (in this case, collective) labour rights, processes and mechanisms should be reshaped to fit the needs of the digital work paradigm.

## 4.2 COLLECTIVE LABOUR RIGHTS AND DIGITAL WORK

Within this new digital market paradigm, and if established labour law concepts and norms are to be reconsidered accordingly, someone may wonder why any attention at all should be given to rethinking collective labour rights, beyond just ensuring that digital workers are covered by established regulations (cf. Eurofound and ILO 2017: 44–45, 48–49, 60). However, the mere tokenistic expansion of the scope of existing collective labour institutions to cover (full or hybrid teleworker) might be missing the importance digital collective autonomy might have in combating the multifragmented nature of digital work.

Collective labour law rights and processes do not simply aim to rebalance the inherently unequal employment relationship (indicatively, Vergis 2019). The functions they perform promote both individualistic (e.g. economic freedom) and collective (e.g. solidaristic; class-related; systemic) objectives, as they serve all three uncommodifiable (Polanyi 2001: 72–79) aspects of a worker's identity: that of a person, that is, an autonomous individual whose personal freedom ought to be respected; that of a bourgeois citizen (i.e. member of a particular societal arrangement); and that of a political citizen, a member of a particular polity (Schmidt am Busch 2012: 71). Workers' associations, such as trade unions, embody and promote communal values, like cooperation, solidarity (Zimmer 2022) and mutual aid (Van Den Abbeele 2022), and, ultimately, the sense of human interdependence and commonality of interests, as opposed to the individualistic, selfish ethos, the 'atomism ascendant' (Kohler 1995: 291–296), of neoclassical economic perceptions (Levine 2001: 559–560). They have the potential to re-embed the (never neutral) market in its specific social, societal, institutional and political context (see Polanyi 2001; Veitch 2013; Wood et al. 2019).

Digital work and teleworking, defined by fragmentation, dehumanisation, depersonalisation and de-spacialisation of labour, epitomise work commodification and can decouple labour from its personal, and, hence, social, nature. Such commodification of labour amounts to perhaps the most grievous disembedding of the economy from its social context, a separation that inevitably leads to social reaction (Polanyi 2001: 136–140, 156–157; Wood et al. 2019: 935–936). That paradigmatic shift, therefore, is what makes renewed emphasis on collective labour law imperative. Ensuring effective access to collective rights, institutions and processes in the digital workplace constitutes a democratic (and market-democratising)[18], re-embedding safety valve.

Further, in a digital market where technological resources and ownership of data and the ICT to access them exacerbate the power imbalance between capital and labour, collective autonomy remains the prime means of forcing access to the relevant information and redressing power inequality. It also holds the key to addressing the isolation inherent in digital teleworking and facilitate labour and social solidarity (Lester 2011; Zimmer 2022) building and processes of mutual aid (cf. Van Den Abbeele 2022).

### 4.2.1 *Collective Bargaining: Legal Avenues and Transnational Potential*

In the European context, as discussed, the 2006 Framework Agreement on Telework did recognise the need for teleworkers to have equal and full access to collective labour rights, but did not offer anything on how that could actually be achieved. Further, advancements in digital work made it easier, and more common, for such working arrangements and virtual working environments to transcend national borders. This transnational element of teleworking (see Bruurs 2023) saw an explosion during the COVID-19 pandemic (cf. Nyberg et al. 2021 on the relevant challenges), to the point of making imperative the adoption of the 2022 Framework Agreement to regulate the social security related challenges that arose. This cross-border character could necessitate the re-evaluation of transnational collective labour processes within the context of the EU common market. It is a question, however, whether that would be even possible, and, if so, what

[18] See Dukes 2008: 343, 346, 2014: 18–19; Kahn-Freund 1983: 23; cf. Derber 1970; Nelson and Howell 1993; Webb and Webb 1902 (2nd ed), (1st ed. 1898).

particular form regulatory intervention to facilitate collective labour engagement, transnational or not, could take.

#### 4.2.1.1 Taking Inspiration from the Platform Work Directive

Even at the level of the narrowest of interventions, whereby the EU would introduce certain minimum requirements related to the substantive exercise of collective labour rights for teleworkers, the EU Platform Work Directive[19] (PWD) could serve as inspiration, even in its eventual, diluted version.

It is important that the Preamble to the finally proposed Directive, as eventually approved by employment and social affairs ministers at the Council meeting on 11 March 2024, explicitly acknowledges the risks inherent in increased work digitisation and the introduction of new technologies. The dangers it recognises, of furthering the inherent power imbalance between employers and workers, increased surveillance (and its effect on privacy), and lack of transparency of employer decision making, associated with digital work, and the potential adverse effects on working conditions, equal treatment, and health and safety at work (Point 4, PWD Preamble), are present regardless of the form digital work takes and are not specific to platform work. The same applies regarding algorithmic management and its depersonalised nature and opacity (Point 8, PWD Preamble), as well as the de facto cross-border nature of (online) digital work (Point 9, PWD Preamble). It should be noted that the PWD Preamble explicitly recognises the need for the exercise of collective bargaining rights to be protected against these dangers, and, particularly, those arising from automated management and the transnational nature of digital tools and platforms (Point 14, PWD Preamble).

The Directive is silent on collective labour rights per se. However, importantly, it introduces subject specific information and consultation rights (Articles 9 and 17 upd.PWD), requires the engagement of workers' representatives on certain issues (Article 9(1) and (4) upd.PWD) and emphasises the need of transparency as regards the algorithms and, more generally, the digital tools employed by platforms. Those elements could form the basis of a comprehensive piece of legislative intervention that would cover digital work as a genus field. Transparency as regards the capabilities of ICT tools and other pieces of software and digital resources that define and affect teleworking, for example, is crucial for the effective protection of digital workers. The same applies as regards interventions that would counter their isolation and ensure the effective, unmediated, and unmonitored communication between them while logged into their virtual workspace and/or workplace.

[19] See Proposal for the Directive of the European Parliament and of the Council on improving working conditions in platform work – Analysis of the final compromise text with a view to agreement, 7212/24 ADD1 (with reference to 2021/0414(COD)), 8 March 2024. Cf. previous version: Proposal for a Directive of the European Parliament and of the Council on improving working conditions in platform work, 2021/0414 (COD) in COM (2021) 762 final.

The final version of the Platform Work Directive addresses general information rights of worker representatives as regards automated monitoring and decision-making systems under Article 9(1) upd.PWD. Further, though, it stipulates that such comprehensive and detailed information is always due *prior* to 'the use of those systems or to the introduction of changes affecting working conditions, the organisation of work or monitoring work performance'. It is clear that this right to information is not self-standing but is to be considered as a necessary condition for effective consultation (Article 13 upd.PWD) and dialogue, including in the form of collective bargaining, as corroborated by the Directive's Preamble (point 22, PWD Preamble). Guaranteeing effective access to information is crucial, given the opaque nature of technical algorithmic processes and the imbalance of resources (including technical expertise)[20] between the employer and digital workers.

It should be noted that the PWD does not limit information and consultation rights to trade unions. Its broad understanding of the concept of worker representatives, as members of an organised entity, but also its reference to representatives that do not fall within that organisational context (Art.15 upd.PWD), acknowledges impliedly the possibility of proto-unions or other grassroots structures or initiatives emerging (Aloisi and Potocks-Sionek 2022: 41), including through the borderless channels of the digital, online working environment.

It is also important to note that Article 20 of the final version of the Directive introduces a right to private communication between workers and between them and their representatives. Such a right would be crucial to all digital workers, including teleworkers as currently conceived or under the broader concept proposed in this chapter. Under Article 20 upd.PWD, Member States are placed under the duty to ensure that digital labour platforms create and offer their workers the ability, through the platform's own infrastructure or similarly effective means, 'to contact and communicate privately and securely with each other, and to contact or be contacted by representatives of persons performing platform work' (i.e. both unions and ad hoc representatives, as above).

The Directive's Preamble explicitly acknowledges that the creation of secure digital communication channels is imperative to offset the spatial fragmentation of work, lacking a common workplace[21] where workers can have the opportunity to 'get to know' and communicate with each other. Importantly, the Preamble adds that this opportunity should be guaranteed not simply to ensure social interaction, but also with a 'view *of (workers) defending their interests*'. In that, the PWD effectively

20 The updated PWD attempts to bridge expertise gap by granting the representatives of platform workers with the right to be assisted by an expert of their choice assessing the technical information (Article 13(3) upd.PWD). In cases of digital platforms that employ more than 250 workers, the relevant cost is to be covered by the platform, insofar it is 'proportionate'.

21 An earlier version of the Preamble had used broader wording ('common place of work') that might be more appropriate to emphasise the physical character the digital/virtual workplace is lacking.

appears to recognise the need for collective labour organisation and action in digital work, since that is how workers' interests can actually be defended. Any other interpretation would make the introduction of the communication and contact provision meaningless. In that, the communication right under Article 20 upd. PWD might prove crucial in the sharing of information and experiences, and the forging of familiarity and commonality that have been seen (Hertwig et al. 2024; Maffie 2020; cf. Sorian and Cabanes 2020) to be prerequisites of the development of a collective participation ethos among digital communities.

As EU competence formally does not extend to regulating labour associations, collective bargaining, and strikes (Article 153(5) TFEU), the PWD does not prescribe anything beyond information and consultation rights.

#### 4.2.1.2 Exercise of Transnational Association Rights under EU Law?

Freedom of association is enshrined in Article 12(1) CFREU, which almost verbatim replicates Article 11 ECHR. The Community Charter[22] (CC) and the European Social Charter (ESC) are useful when attempting its interpretation, with the latter, in Article 5 ESC, establishing the potential for 'international' organisation and, hence, transnational collective labour processes. According to the European Committee of Social Rights, Article 5 ESC introduces a positive obligation (cf. Waldron 1993: 8 on the nature of collective labour rights) for states to legislate to protect the right to organise and its effective exercise, a duty that cannot compensated by reference to custom (Harris and Darcy 2001: 89). In that regard, a level of internal autonomy of worker organisations is to be safeguarded against legislative intervention or employers' interference (Harris and Darcy 2001: 96, 98). The European Court of Human Rights concurs, reading into Article 11 ECHR a positive obligation of the state to establish and maintain legal mechanisms and institutions (particularly trade unions[23]) that will accommodate the effective enjoyment of the relevant freedom[24], with an eye to collective bargaining[25]. Any restrictions should be construed narrowly, with states enjoying only a slim margin of appreciation[26]; collective organisation as such cannot be prohibited[27].

22 Inter alia, see Bercusson (1990).

23 ECtHR *Wilson, NUJ et al v. The UK* (Application Nos 30668/96, 30671/96, and 30678/96), judgment of 2nd July 2002, para. 48; K. Ewing, The implications of Wilson and Palmer, ILJ, 2003, p. 6.

24 ECtHR *Demir and Baykara v. Turkey* (Application No 34503/97), judgment of 12 November 2008. Cf. *Council of Civil Service Unions et al v. UK* ("GCHQ"), Decision of 20th January 1987, Application No 11603/85, 50 DR, 228. For extensive analysis of the relevant case-law, see Dorssemont (2010).

25 ECtHR *Wilson, NUJ et als v. The UK* (Application Nos 30668/96, 30671/96, and 30678/96), judgment of 2nd July 2002, para. 48. See also Ewing 2003: 6.

26 *Wilson, NUJ et al*, para. 119.

27 Cf. *Demir and Baykara v. Turkey*, op. cit., para. 127.

Similarly, a systematic reading of Article 12(1) CFREU, taking into account the ECHR and the ESC under the light of the fundamental normative values and objectives of the EU (particularly, Articles 2 TEU and 3(3) paras 1–3 TEU), and given the transnational potential of digital work, should lead to a positive obligation on the EU, when not precluded by territoriality and local elements, that would trigger the exclusive competence of Member States, to create the framework that facilitates and realises (transnational) worker organisation and engagement. Despite the apparent finality of its wording, therefore, it could be (perhaps controversially) suggested that Article 153(5) TFEU only prevents EU intervention where the relevant exclusive competence of Member States can indeed be exercised, that is, at the *national* level. Digital work wholly or partially provided online, in the virtual space, can escape national boundaries. The same applies for the ICTs, platforms, pieces of software and data that make digital work possible. Under the virtual workplace and market paradigm, territoriality and, hence, jurisdiction triggering the exclusive national competence should not necessarily be judged merely on the basis of where a worker happens to stand when engaging in digital work. The code that underpins algorithmic management and shapes the virtual working environment and the data that define and embody the service provided exist beyond national borders, as does the virtual space that shapes the experience of communicating and engaging with clients, coworkers, and assigned tasks. It might be, therefore, that what requires regulation is the transborder digital market itself. That leaves EU law as the only regulatory level that can ensure the enjoyment of relevant rights, in line with the fundamental principles and objectives of the Union, including as regards its pursuit of a social market economy (Article 3(3) TEU).

#### 4.2.1.3 Transnational Collective Bargaining in the EU: Legal Bases?

Article 28 CFREU[28] on collective bargaining and collective action explicitly covers the European level[29] exercise of both rights, and, as such, in principle also guarantees *transnational* collective bargaining and collective action. As such, it could be the springboard to elevate the Social Dialogue mechanism under Articles 152 and 154–155 TFEU to more than just a supplementary legislative process (see also Riesenhuber (2012): 71–87, 152–160) and into a vehicle for a transnational collective bargaining mechanism.

Interpretation of the Charter on collective bargaining should draw for inspiration from the Community Charter, the European Social Charter (ESC), the European Convention on Human Rights (ECHR), and relevant ILO Conventions (particularly, Conventions 87 and 98 (Dorssemont and Rocca 2019: 471–476). The imperative of ensuring effective communication between digital workers, for example,

[28] For a thorough discussion, see Dorssemont and Rocca 2019.

[29] See Explanations, Article 28 CFREU.

should be read under the light of the duty of the ESC signatory parties to 'promote', without unnecessarily interfering (Dorssemont and Rocca 2019: 473–474), 'joint consultation' (6(1) ESC) and 'machinery for voluntary negotiations' (6(2) ESC) between workers and employers. However, joint consultation and voluntary negotiations are impossible without the ability of workers to exchange information and coordinate before attempting communication and dialogue with the employer, processes which States are to promote refraining from any unnecessary intervention (Świątkowski 2007: §7.2.2, 213–214)[30].

The Social Dialogue[31] provisions of Article 152 and Articles 154–155 TFEU can provide the legal vehicle for an EU transnational collective organisation and bargaining process. According to Article 154(1) TFEU, the fundamental objective of Social Dialogue is the promotion of the autonomous process of balanced dialogue between management and labour. A key aspect of Social Dialogue is its capacity to function as an autonomous regulatory mechanism through the option for the Social Partners to conclude an agreement under Article 155 TFEU. When such an agreement refers to matters under Article 153 TFEU and the social partners so request, it can also take the form of legislation on the decision of the Council, following the relevant proposal by the Commission[32].

Criticisms as to a representativity[33] and legitimacy deficit (Barnard 2012: 79–85; Betten 1998: 30–36; Riesenhuber 2012: 155) of Social Dialogue as a legislative mechanism[34] subside if we consider Social Dialogue to be an instrument of collective autonomy (Bercusson 1999; cf. Fredman 1998: 408–409). In that sense, the process is to be approached as an extension of the relevant autonomous regulatory mechanism of private law and industrial relations (Bercusson 1999). Within this context, Bercusson (1999) has suggested that the term 'representation' refers to the interests represented, rather than the individuals who are members of the interacting worker and employer parties. However, even under the view that Social Dialogue is a vehicle for transnational collective bargaining, there are structural deficits of the current framework that could have that collective process producing uneven results. Most notably, in the absence of a complementary transnational framework for collective action to rebalance the inherent inequality of negotiating power between workers and employers, employers and their interests could dominate the process (Fredman 1998: 409–410).

30 With reference to European Committee of Social Rights Addendum to Conclusions XI-2, 22–23 (Ireland).

31 For thorough discussion, see Franssen 2002; Welz 2008; cf. Hepple 1993.

32 But cf. C-928/19 P, *EPSU v. Commission*, ECLI:EU:C:2021:656.

33 CFI T-135/96, *UEAPME/Council*, 17.06.1998, ECLI:EU:T:1998:128, paras. 88–90. For the criteria of representativity, see COM (93) 600, para. 24. See, also, Betten, 1998; Franssen 2002: 192–199.

34 See CFI T-135/96, *UEAPME/Council*, op. cit., paras 66–67.

That deficit notwithstanding, though, the procedure under Article 155(2) TFEU is to be understood as a form of erga omnes extension of collective agreements, a regulatory choice of giving effect to collective autonomy (Bercusson 2009: 582; Ryan 2003: 88–89) and a transnational collective labour law enforcement mechanism. The substantive recognition of collective autonomy at EU level by Article 152 TFEU supports this view. A combined reading of Article 152 TFEU and Articles 154 and 155 TFEU, under the light of the express recognition of an EU fundamental right to collective bargaining (Article 28 CFREU), confirms that Social Dialogue is to be now primarily acknowledged as a sui generis manifestation of collective autonomy[35] at transnational level (Bercusson 2009: 578; cf. Lo Faro 2000: 74–83).

Even at a bare minimum, though, the wording of Article 152 TFEU implies an obligation of the Union vis-à-vis collective labour institutions that is not necessarily related to the formal process of Social Dialogue as a sui generis mechanism and is not confined to it. Article 152 TFEU clearly stipulates that the Union ought to both 'recognise', but, perhaps more importantly, 'promote' the role of social partners 'at its level'. That is not to be approached as an empty declaration. It forces the EU to recognise the role, function, and legal identity of worker and employer organisations and associations of national or transnational nature and actively support and accommodate them in the pursuit of their systemic function. Arguably, that encompasses accommodating the work and evolution of collectivities (e.g. virtual such; groupings that transcend national borders) that might not necessarily fit the formal, established understanding of social partners or workers' representatives, but do perform a similar function for digital workers involved and pursue similar objectives (see above on Art.15 upd.PWD). At a minimum, it cements the duty to introduce norms guaranteeing effective communication between digital workers that would allow their self-organisation.

### 4.2.2 *Collective Action: Case Studies and Potential*

As regards collective action, given the limitations of the Charter (Article 51(2) CFREU) and the competences of the EU (Article 153(5) TFEU), the established reading of Article 28 CFREU suggests that it cannot be interpreted as giving rise to a (new) transnational right to strike that can exist separately and in addition to relevant national rights (Bercusson 2009: 209–210, 243–244). Regardless, national-level cases of collective action undertaken by digital workers are useful in examining the relevant challenges and drawing lessons from potentially innovative practices that might illustrate what (even transnational) digital industrial action might evolve to encompass, within or beyond the confines of the law.

Examples of platform workers' mobilisation are indicative of how, similarly to their out-of-the-box self-organisation strategies, collective action tactics of gig

[35] CJEU C-271/08, *Commission/Germany*, 15.07.2010, ECLI:EU:C:2010:426, para. 39.

workers employed also fell outside the conventional toolbox of established trade unions (see Della Porta et al. 2022: 224–238; Tassinari and Maccarrone 2017: 354–355, 2020: 45–46). It is interesting that in some cases, the lack of experience in labour organising per se and the absence of support by 'traditional' trade unions proved to be a strength and a source of experimentation and tactical innovation. Workers turned to their non-labour mobilisation experiences, forged through prior participation in other social, political, and grassroots movements (such as the student movement; housing and urban collectives) (Della Porta et al. 2022: 225), aiming to engage consumers and the general public and disrupt the employer's market image (e.g. calling for review bombing and boycotts). Cross-pollination of experiences and tactics (Forsyth 2022: 116–131, 146–164) was vital in adopting unconventional modes of collective action not against production processes, as is typically the case, but aimed at marketing and the point of consumption.

Digital workers engaged in full or hybrid teleworking, on the other hand, seem to have adopted relatively more conventional forms of collective organisation, coordination, and action, as illustrated by the examples of Gizmodo and Onion (G/O Media) workers in the United States and Teleperformance workers in Greece.

The G/O Media group, formed in 2019 as a result of the merger of the two original employer companies, owns and operates a number of news websites and blogs (including specialised outlets that focus, inter alia, on social and political issues, technology, entertainment, sports, gaming, automotive news)[36]. The peculiarity is that these are strictly digital media, operating under conditions of enhanced digitisation of work, with telework as the main model, particularly post-COVID. The trade union (GMG Union)[37], representing the Group's workforce of writers and copywriters, journalists, artists, podcast and video producers, editors and social media managers of the various media, was the first in the United States to be set up in the digital media sector and the first to call for ('digital', as it called it) strike action of indefinite duration in June 2022. As the G/O workers had revealed, for two years during the pandemic (2020–2022) the company had applied a remote work model for the entirety of the workforce, with telework becoming the default, allocating work and shifts so as to cover the full extent of US time zones and continuous 24-hour operation of its outlets. Part of the dispute that arose with the employer company was its demand that workers 'return to the office', located in New York; for many, that would now involve having to relocate to the city, with all the cost and personal stress and difficulty that might come with. Interestingly, therefore, in this case, in addition to other demands (such as those related to wage, leave and working time, compensation in the event of termination of employment, various health benefits, and anti-discrimination issues), worker mobilisation and, ultimately,

[36] The outlets in question are Gizmodo, Jezebel, The Root, Lifehacker, Kotaku, io9, Jalopnik.

[37] https://gmgunion.com/who-is-gmg-union (accessed March 2024; down as of 25 September 2024).

industrial action sought to preserve, rather than avoid, work digitisation. Specifically, it aimed to safeguard the (initially urgently) established conditions of teleworking and to prevent the imposition of a return to a more 'traditional' physical work regime.

In the case of 'Teleperformance Greece' workers, the employer, a national subsidiary of a French multinational, offers its services to companies or entities that are in need of customer communication and support, telemarketing, content moderation and debt collection, with Teleperformance workers being allocated to the relevant tasks. Its workers are engaged either at Teleperformance's premises, whereby, however, work is provided wholly through ICTs (internet; phone), or outside of those as traditional fully remote teleworkers. Privatisation and liberalisation policies have triggered a boom in outsourcing of tasks and departments covered by Teleperformance, with a respective pressure upon its workers to engage in an increasingly diverse array of tasks, clients, and subjects, and increasing pressures as to wage, working hours, and working conditions, but, also, job security, all issues which workers soon brought to the fore.

In the dispute that arose, Teleperformance Greece workers, beyond demands on the above, also raised health and safety concerns (requesting, inter alia, regular breaks and a compensatory bonus for the mandatory constant use of earpiece/headphones) and noted the need for timely notification before reassignment to new tasks and clients and for relevant information about those. Moreover, though, and importantly as regards digital (tele)work, they alluded to the increasing legal, organisational, and social fragmentation that was brought about by the company's model and subcontracting practices, explicitly noting the problem of isolation and dissociation this working model caused. In fact, in its inaugural announcement, SETEP, the company-level trade union teleworkers established[38], declared: 'No employee of Teleperformance, will ever feel alone again, no one will ever feel easily replaceable and fear in the isolation of teleworking'[39]. Lastly, Teleperformance workers demanded that the employer fully cover the cost of wholly remote telework (i.e. equipment, internet connection, energy and heating costs), and asked to be guaranteed full disconnection from all systems at the end of the daily working hours.

It is worth noting that neither Teleperformance nor G/O Media digital workers fully embraced radical tactics, with minor exceptions (particularly in the case of G/O). Teleperformance workers were the more 'traditional' of the two groups, manoeuvring within the confines of established trade union structures and institutions under Greek law. Their initial action was sanctioned, and thus legally 'covered', by a sectoral trade union, before they eventually formed a company level

[38] https://setep.gr/ (accessed 5 September 2024).

[39] Joint statement by SETIP & SETEP, Piraeus, Tuesday 13 February, 2024, https://setep.gr/joint-statement-by-setip-setep/ (accessed 25 September 2024).

such in February 2024. Their strategy consisted of typical trade union organisation and a number of non-consecutive single day strikes, in the form of typical removal of labour. G/O workers, despite framing their action as 'digital', also largely employed conventional tactics and negotiation avenues. Through their company group-level trade union, they called for indefinite strike action, which was complemented by holding small picket lines at the employer's offices.

However, it is worth noting two elements that do not necessarily appear in 'common', non-digital, action which were critical in the eventual success of the G/O action in particular. First, G/O workers set up robust digital networks of communication, which effectively, for a good deal of the mobilisation, nullified the delocalisation of their work. Second, they made good use of social media to engage the company's target audience and call for a boycott of the Group's websites and blogs. The layout of those webpages, which typically includes a comments section, allowed readers, that is, G/O's audience, to flood them with comments and images that expressed support and solidarity towards the striking workforce, intensifying the visibility of the mobilisation and putting pressure on the company. Further, digital workers employed at other similar media showed their support by intensifying the online coverage and visibility of the G/O workers' mobilisation. The result of digital Sustainable Development Goals and the careful mix of simple digital and conventional action was that an agreement with the employer was reached within only four days from the beginning of the strike.

It appears, therefore, that there is an understandable tendency to gravitate towards established vehicles and forms of action, in a form of 'institutional replication', since these are the only means guaranteed to fall within the protective scope of the current labour laws. However, cracks of innovation do appear, as digital workers attempt to adapt those traditional forms of struggle into the digital and de-spatialised circumstances of their work and working environments. It is interesting, in particular, how outreach, synergies with not just the employer's customer base but the broader public and consequent forms of digital action that would harm the employer's market reputation, rather than disrupt production as such (e.g. calls to boycott; digital campaigns; review bombing), appear to be more prominent in the digitally integrated market.

## 4.3 CONCLUSION

The ascending dominance of digitisation in most white-collar jobs, which involves multiple elements of (full or partial) remoteness, questions the established, narrower understanding of telework as defined by the worker's location and construed as a supposedly separate category of work that poses equally distinct challenges. Digital work, including teleworking in all its forms, promotes isolation, fractures the commonality of the workplace and the working experience, and, ultimately, tests the limits of concepts and processes of collective organisation, solidarity, and action that developed out of radically different production paradigms. The elements of power imbalance and resource and information asymmetry that typically characterise the employment relationship as unequal and justify rebalancing mechanisms such as collective autonomy are certainly present, if not enhanced, in the modern digital workplace and the opacity of its underlying processes. Work, regardless of whether it is offered at the premises of the employer or beyond, depends upon a piece of technology possibly developed, but certainly owned by the employer, under the sole command of whom it is, serving that party's business interests. That alone should be reason enough to warrant not just relevant information and consultation rights, but a full-fledged framework for collective organisation and action, as a counterbalancing mechanism. Further, though, collective labour rights are systemically necessary to prevent the complete commodification and de-humanisation of labour that risks disembedding work from its social context and stripping it of its interpersonal character.

Guaranteeing that teleworkers are caught by established collective rights and norms is necessary, but not sufficient. Regulators should carefully consider the intricacies of digital work and the opacity of the technological means through which it is organised and performed, and adjust the relevant rights accordingly. It might be that some unconventional thinking is required of legislators and judges alike to tackle the challenges of a working model that can escape physical and national boundaries, including as regards utilising the hidden options EU law and its purposive and systematic interpretation might provide.

In that respect, it might be that digital workers are ahead of the game. Through their mobilisation, they have highlighted the needs and demands that have arisen specifically with reference to digital work. Alternative tactics and novel synergies have already been developed, indicating routes of solidarity, mutual aid, organisation, and active promotion of worker interests that do not necessarily fall within pre-prescribed norms and institutional models. These forms of action take advantage of the features and strengths of the digital environment from which they sprung, attempting to traverse established legal options and gaps. However, ultimately, their success depends on the level of commitment and resilience of workers. In turn, that resilience will rely on the robustness of support and mutual aid networks, and the synergies that might be facilitated by digital means but, ultimately, will have to manifest in the physical realm that is the streets, where labour struggle always returns, and the fragments of solidarity are put back together.

## REFERENCES

Administrative Commission for the Coordination of Social Security Systems, Guidance Note of 21 June 2023 (AC 137/23), available at European Commission, Employment, Social Affairs and Inclusion, Official Documents, https://ec.europa.eu/social/main.jsp?catId=868 (last accessed 25 September 2024)

Aloisi, A. and Potocks-Sionek, N. (2022), De-gigging the labour market? An analysis of the 'algorithmic management' provisions in the proposed Platform Work Directive, *Italian Labour Law e-journal*, 15 (1), 29–50

Anderson, B., Brynin, M., Raban, Y. and Gershuny, J. (2007), *Information and Communications Technologies in Society: E-Living in a Digital Europe*, London: Taylor & Francis

Bailey, D.E. and Kurland, N.B. (2002), A review of telework research: Findings, new directions, and lessons for the study of modern work, *Journal of Organizational Behavior*, 23 (4), 383–400

Barnard, C. (2012), *EU Employment Law*, Oxford: Oxford University Press

Beauregard, A., Basile, K. and Canonico, E. (2013), *Home Is Where Work Is: A New Study of Homeworking in Acas – and beyond*, London: ACAS

Becker, W.J., Belkin, L.Y., Tuskey, S. E. and Conroy, S.A, (2022), Surviving remotely: How job control and loneliness during a forced shift to remote work impacted employee work behaviors and well-being, *Human Resource Management*, 61 (4), 449–464

Bercusson, B. (2009), *European Labour Law*, Cambridge: Cambridge University Press

(1999), Democratic legitimacy and European labour law, *ILJ* 28 (2), 153–170

(1990), The European community's charter of fundamental social rights of workers, *MLR*, 624–642

Betten, L., (1998), The democratic deficit of participatory democracy in Community social policy, *ELRev*, 23, 20–36

Bruurs, S. (2023), Cross-border telework in light of the Rome I-Regulation and the posting of workers directive, *European Labour Law Journal*, 14(4), 588–608

Dean, J. (2020), Communism or Neo-Feudalism? *New Political Science*, 1–17

Della Porta, D., Chesta, R.E. and Cini, L. (2022), Mobilizing against the odds. Solidarity in action in the platform economy, *Berliner Journal für Soziologie*, 231–241

Derber, M. (1970), *The American Idea of Industrial Democracy, 1865–1965*, Chicago: University of Illinois Press

Di Martino, V. and Wirth, L. (1990), Telework: A new way of working and living, *International Labour Review*, 129(5), 529–554

Dorssemont, F. (2010), The right to form and to join trade unions for the protection of his interests under Article 11 ECHR: An Attempt "to Digest" the Case Law (1975–2009) of the European court on human rights, *ELLJ*, 185–235

Dorssemont, F. and Rocca, M. (2019), Article 28 – right to collective bargaining and action, in: Dorssemont F., Lörcher, K., Clauwaert, S., and Schmitt M. (eds), *The Charter of Fundamental Rights of the European Union and the Employment Relation*, Oxford: Hart, 465–504

Dukes, R. (2014), *The Labour Constitution: The Enduring Idea of Labour Law*, Oxford: Oxford University Press

(2008), Constitutionalizing employment relations: Sinzheimer, Kahn-Freund, and the role of labour law, *Journal of Law and Society Period*, 341

European Foundation for the Improvement of Living and Working Conditions and the International Labour Organization (Eurofound and ILO) (2017), Working Anytime, Anywhere: The Effects on the World of Work, Luxembourg: Publications Office of the European Union and Geneva: ILO, eurofound.link/ef1658 (accessed 25 September 2024)

Ewing, K. (2003), The implications of Wilson and Palmer, *ILJ*, 32(1), 2003, 1–22

Explanatory Memorandum to the Framework Agreement on the application of Article 16 (1) of Regulation (EC) No. 883/2004 in cases of habitual cross-border telework, https://socialsecurity.belgium.be/sites/default/files/content/docs/en/international/explanatory_memorandum_to_the_framework_agreement.pdf (last accessed 25 September 2024)

Forsyth, A. (2022), *The Future of Unions and Worker Representation: The Digital Picket Line*, Hart, 2022, 116–131, 146–164

Framework Agreement on the application of Article 16 (1) of Regulation (EC) No. 883/2004 in cases of habitual cross-border telework, https://socialsecurity.belgium.be/sites/default/files/content/docs/en/international/framework_agreement_on_cross-border_telework.pdf (last accessed 25 September 2024)

Franssen, E. (2002), *Legal Aspects of the European Social Dialogue*, Antwerp: Intersentia

Fredman, S. (1998), Social law in the European Union: The impact of the lawmaking process, in: Craig, P. and Harlow, C. (eds), *Lawmaking in the European Union*, London: Kluwer, 386 et seq

Golden, T.D. and Fromen, A. (2011), Does it matter where your manager works? Comparing managerial work mode (traditional, telework, virtual) across sub-ordinate work experiences and outcomes, *Human Relations*, 64 (11), 1451–1475

Golden, T.D., Veiga, J.F. and Dino, R.N. (2008), The impact of professional isolation on teleworker job performance and turnover intentions: Does time spent teleworking, interacting face-to-face, or having access to communication-enhancing technology matter?, *Journal of Applied Psychology*, 93 (6), 1412–1421

Graeber, D. (2018), *Bullshit Jobs: A Theory*, London: Penguin Books

Gschwind, L. and Vargas, O. (2022), Telework and its effects in Europe, in Messenger, J.C. (ed), *Telework in the 21st Century: An Evolutionary Perspective*, Cheltenham: Edward Elgar (in Association with International Labour Office), 36–75

Harris, D. and Darcy, J. (2001), *The European Social Charter*, 2nd ed., New York: Transnational Publishers

Hepple, B. (1993), *European Social Dialogue: Alibi or Opportunity?* London: IER

Hertwig, M., Holz, M. and Lorig, P. (2024), Solidarity and collective issues in remote crowd work: A mixed methods study of the Amazon Mechanical Turk online forum, *New Technology, Work, and Employment*, 39 (2), 281–302

Hill, E.J., Erickson, J.J., Holmes, E.K. and Ferris, M. (2010), Workplace flexibility, work hours, and work–life conflict: Finding an extra day or two, *Journal of Family Psychology*, 24 (3), 349–358

Hill, E.J., Ferris, M. and Märtinson, V. (2003), 'Does it matter where you work? A comparison of how three work venues (traditional office, virtual office, and home office) influence aspects of work and personal/family life', *Journal of Vocational Behavior*, 63 (2) 220–241

Hill, E.J., Hawkins, A.J., Ferris, M. and Weitzman, M. (2001), 'Finding an extra day a week: The positive influence of perceived job flexibility on work and family life balance', *Family Relations*, 50 (1), 49–58

Iannuzzi, F.E. and Campolongo, F. (2023), Transformed or transferred? How workers perceive managerial control over home telework: Some Insights from an Italian Case, Relations Industrielles; Quebec, 78 (*1*), *1*–*18*

International Labour Organisation (ILO, The Future of Work in Information and Communication Technology, GLO/17/20/JPN, www.ilo.org/projects-and-partnerships/projects/future-work-information-and-communication-technology (accessed 25 September 2024)

Kahn-Freund O. (1983) in: Davies, P. and Freedland M., *Kahn-Freund's Labour and the Law*, 3rd ed., London: Stevens

Kelliher, C. and de Menezes, L.M. (2019), *Flexible Working in Organisations: A Research Overview*, Oxford: Routledge

Kobrin, S. (1998), Back to the future: Neomedievalism and the postmodern digital world economy, *Journal of International Affairs*, 361–398

Kohler, T. (1995), Civic virtue at work: Unions as seedbeds of the civic virtues, *Boston College Law Review*, 36 (2), 279–304

Kurland, N.B. and Bailey, D.E. (1999), The advantages and challenges of working here, there anywhere, and anytime, *Organizational Dynamics*, 28 (2), 53–68

Kuttner, R. and Stone, K. (2020), *The Rise of Neo-Feudalism*, Princeton: The American Prospect

Levine, P. (2001), The legitimacy of labour Unions, *Hofstra Labor & Employment Law Journal*, 18 (2), 529–573

Lester, G. (2011), Beyond collective bargaining: Modern unions as agents of social solidarity, in: Davidov, G. and Langille, B. (eds), *The Idea of Labour Law*, Oxford: Oxford University Press, 329–343

Lo Faro, A. (2000), *Deregulating Social Europe: Reality and Myth of Collective Bargaining in the EC Legal Order* (R. Inston (trans.)), Oxford: Hart

Maffie, M.D. (2020), The role of digital communities in organizing gig workers, *Industrial Relations* 59 (1), 123–149

Mazzucato, M. (2019), Preventing Digital Feudalism, Project Syndicate, 2 October 2019, www.project-syndicate.org/commentary/platform-economy-digital-feudalism-by-mariana-mazzucato-2019-10 (accessed 25 September 2024)

Messenger, J. and Gschwind, L. (2016), 'Three generations of telework: New ICT and the (r) evolution from home office to virtual office', *New Technology, Work and Employment*, 31 (3), 195–208

Messenger, J.C. (2022), 'Introduction: Telework in the 21st century – An evolutionary perspective' in Messenger, J.C. (ed), *Telework in the 21st Century: An Evolutionary Perspective*, Cheltenham: Edward Elgar (in Association with International Labour Office), 1–34

Moriset, B. (2004), Télétravail, travail nomade: le territoire et les territorialités face aux nouvelles flexibilités spatio-temporelles du travail et de la production, Cybergeo, 2004 (257)

Morozov, E. (2022), Critique of techno-feudal reason, *New Left Review*, 89–126

Nelson, L. and Howell, J.H. (1993), *Industrial Democracy in America: The Ambiguous Promise*, Cambridge: Cambridge University Press;

Nilles, J.M. (1988), 'Traffic reduction by telecommuting: A status review and selected bibliography', *Transportation Research Part A: General*, 22 (4), 301–317

(1975), Telecommunications and organizational decentralization, *IEEE Transactions on Communications*, 23 (10), 1142–7

Nyberg, A.J., Shaw, J.D. and Zhu, J. (2021), The people still make the (remote work-) place: Lessons from a pandemic, *Journal of Management*, 47 (8), 1967–1976

Polanyi, K. (2001), *The Great Transformation: The Political and Economic Origins of Our Time*, 2nd ed., Boston: Beacon Press

Prosser, T. (2011), The implementation of the Telework and Work-related Stress Agreements: European social dialogue through 'soft' law?, *European Journal of Industrial Relations*, 17 (3), 245–260

Riesenhuber, K. (2012), *European Employment Law*, Cambridge: Intersentia. Cambridge

Ryan, B. (2003), The charter and collective labour law, in: Hervey, T. and Kenner, J. (eds), *Economic and Social Rights Under the EU Charter of Fundamental Rights – A Legal Perspective*, Oxford: Hart, 67–90

Schmidt Am Busch, H.-C. (2012), The legacy of Hegelian philosophy and the future of critical theory, in: Smith, N.H. and Deranty J.-P. (eds), *New Philosophies of Labour: Work and the Social Bond*, Leiden: Brill, 63 et seq

Sorian, C.R. and Cabanes, J.V.A. (2020), Entrepreneurial solidarities: Social media collectives and Filipino digital platform workers, *Social Media + Society* 6(2), 1–11

Sostero, M., Milasi, S., Hurley, J., Fernandez, Macias, E. and Bisello, M. (2023), Teleworkability and the COVID-19 crisis: Potential and actual prevalence of remote work across Europe, *IZA Journal of Labor Policy*, 13 (1)

Srnicek, N. (2017), *Platform Capitalism*, Cambridge: Polity

Supiot, A. (2017), *Governance by Numbers: The Making of a Legal Model of Allegiance* (S. Brown trans.), Oxford: Hart

(2013), The public-private relation in the context of today's refeudalization, *International Journal of Constitutional Law*, 129–145

Świątkowski, A.M. (2007), *Charter of Social Rights of the Council of Europe*, Alphen aan den Rijn: Kluwer Law International

Tassinari, A. and Maccarrone, V., (2020), Riders on the storm: Workplace solidarity among gig economy Couriers in Italy and the UK, *Work, Employment and Society*, 34 (1), 35–54

(2017), The mobilisation of gig economy couriers in Italy: Some lessons for the trade union movement, *Transfer*, 23 (3), 353–357

Van Den Abbeele, G. (2022), Can the precariat be organized?: The gig economy, worksite dispersion, and the challenge of mutual aid, *Telos*, (198) 67–89

Varoufakis, Y. (2023), *Technofeudalism: What Killed Capitalism*, London: The Bodley Head

Varoufakis, Y. (2021), Techno-Feudalism Is Taking Over, Project Syndicate, 28 June 2021, www.project-syndicate.org/commentary/techno-feudalism-replacing-market-capitalism-by-yanis-varoufakis-2021-06 (accessed 25 September 2024)

Vartiainen, M. and Vanharanta, O. (2024), True nature of hybrid work, *Frontiers in Organizational Psychology*, 2, 1448894

Veitch, K. (2013), Law, social policy and the constitution of markets and profit making, *Journal of Law & Society*, 137–154

Vergis, F. (2019), Back to the future: Rediscovering the role, value and scope of labour law and collective labour institutions in a changing world, in Blackham A., Kullmann M., and Zbyszweska A. (eds), *Theorising Labour Law in a Changing World: Edited Collection*, London: Hart Publishing, 81–105

Waldron, J. (1993), *Liberal Rights*, Cambridge: Cambridge University Press

Webb, S. and Webb, B. (1902), *Industrial Democracy*, 2nd ed., London: Longmans, Green and Co (1st ed. 1898)

Wells, K., Attoh, K. and Cullen, D. (2021), "Just-in-Place" labor: Driver organizing in the Uber workplace, *Economy and Space*, 315–331

Welz, C. (2008), *The European Social Dialogue under Articles 138 and 139 of the EC Treaty: Actors, Processes, Outcomes*, Austin: Kluwer

Wood, A.J., Graham, M., Lehdonvirta, V. and Hjorth, I. (2019), Networked but commodified: The (Dis)Embeddedness of digital labour in the gig economy, *Sociology (Oxford)*, 53 (5), 931–950

Zimmer, R. (2022), Solidarity as a central aim of collective labour law?, in Lopez-Lopez, J. (ed), *Inscribing Solidarity: Debates in Labor Law and Beyond*, Cambridge: Cambridge University Press, 43–62.

# 5

# Telework in Japan

## *A Game Changer for the Employment System and Labor Law Policy*

*Takashi Araki*

### 5.1 INTRODUCTION

This chapter examines how teleworking is changing traditional employment practices, and what legal issues it is raising, taking Japan as an example. It will also consider the possibility that telework could act as a game changer for future labor laws that realize the well-being of individual workers with diverse circumstances, considering new legislative developments in some foreign countries.

Remote work is commonly referred to and discussed as telework in Japan. Although not strictly defined, remote work broadly refers to performing work away from the workplace, while telework denotes work using information and communication technology (ICT). Telework in Japan encompasses three forms: work from home, satellite office work, and mobile work[1].

Since the 1990s, the Japanese government has implemented policies to promote telework[2]. However, until the COVID-19 pandemic, telework had not gained widespread acceptance in Japan. This limited adoption seems to stem from the characteristics of the Japanese employment system, which emphasizes teamwork-oriented work styles. Yet, with the outbreak of COVID-19 in 2020, the government declared a state of emergency, prohibiting workers from coming to work. As a result, even companies that had not introduced telework were forced to adopt it, and many workers were compelled to experience telework for the first time. Japanese employment relationships, which both companies and workers had believed could only function well with face-to-face collective working relationships, have experienced

[1] Kōsei Rōdō Shō [Ministry of Health, Labour and Welfare], 2021. www.mhlw.go.jp/content/000759469.pdf.

[2] Rōdō Seisaku Kenkyu Kenshu Kikō [Japan Institute for Labour Policy and Training], 2021. Sato, Koji, 2001, 153 suggests that Japan's telework efforts began in the 1980s to address the concentration in Tokyo, but that it was not until the 1990s, after the rapid development of information and communication technologies such as the internet, that telework really began to take off.

that with the development of ICT, telework can also function well if the appropriate systems and infrastructure are in place. Additionally, it has become increasingly recognized that telework requires different job and personnel management systems compared to those used in traditional workplaces. Moreover, telework has opened up the possibility of work styles that allow for a better work–life balance, which was previously considered unattainable.

After the COVID-19 pandemic subsided, Japan's proportion of companies implementing telework slightly decreased. However, many companies have shifted to a hybrid work arrangement, such as two days of telework and three days of in-office work per week, thereby accepting telework as a viable work style. In other words, telework has begun to take root as a normal way of working, rather than a special, exceptional one. In this way, telework has the potential to become a game changer, significantly altering Japan's traditional employment system, which has long been considered resistant to change.

As telework becomes a more common way of working, some countries are developing legislative policies that require employers to accept, in principle, workers' wishes to work flexibly, including telework (e.g., the Netherlands, the UK, and Australia). While there have already been legal systems that require employers to provide reasonable accommodations or special arrangements for specific workers, such as those with disabilities or family responsibilities, the flexible working laws in these countries now demand that telework and other flexible work options be made available to all workers, not just specific groups.

Telework is thus making us realize that a legal framework allowing workers to choose their preferred working style is necessary to achieve the well-being of an increasingly diverse workforce. In this sense, telework or remote work may be a game changer for labor law policies in many countries, prompting the need to envision new labor laws that provide individualized support focusing on diverse circumstances in addition to traditional labor laws that offer universal protection.

## 5.2 JAPAN'S TEAMWORK-ORIENTED EMPLOYMENT PRACTICES, MEMBERSHIP-BASED EMPLOYMENT, AND TELEWORK

The Japanese government established the Telework Promotion Council in 1996 and compiled its report in November. Since the beginning of this century, the spread of telework has always been a policy issue. However, telework has struggled to gain traction. One of the reasons lies in Japan's unique employment practices. Specifically, Japanese office workers traditionally form teams by arranging their desks face-to-face within their respective sections, creating a work environment known as the "large-room principle." This practice emphasizes teamwork, where everyone shares how their colleagues are doing their work and mutually helps each other. If one's work was finished and the colleague or supervisor next to him or her continued to work, leaving the office alone was considered a lack of loyalty to the team. There was a tendency to equate long hours spent at the company with contributions to the team and the organization. As a result, subordinates spent time sitting at their desks without work until their supervisors went home, resulting in unproductive long work hours[3].

This employment practice is closely linked to Japan's unique "membership-based employment" system. Under the well-known lifetime employment, Japanese workers agree to become employees of a particular company but do not agree on the specific job they will perform at that company. In other words, job descriptions are not specified in the employment contract. The employment contract is merely a contract to acquire a position as a company member. In contrast to the "job-based employment" prevalent in Western countries, where job descriptions are clearly defined, this Japanese employment practice is referred to as "membership-based employment" by Keiichiro Hamaguchi[4]. Since workers are employed as members of the company rather than for a specific job, even if a particular job is eliminated, they are reassigned to other departments, thus maintaining their employment. This has made the Japanese job security system known as Lifetime Employment possible.

Since workers' job descriptions are not clearly defined in the contract, even if they finish the task currently assigned, it does not mean they have no problem going home immediately. All the work assigned to the team can be one's task. Under such teamwork-oriented employment practices, telework, in which workers work individually at home, was considered impossible to work productively, and the introduction of telework has not progressed.

However, the COVID-19 pandemic prohibited commuting to the office and forced Japanese companies to adopt telework. The percentage of companies that had introduced telework rose dramatically from 9.3% in 2013 and 20.2% in 2019 to 47.5% in 2020 and 51.9% in 2021. Although this figure slightly decreased to 51.7% in 2022 and 49.9% in 2023, a high adoption rate of around 50% continues[5].

It should be noted that these figures represent the percentage of companies that have introduced telework, not the number of teleworkers. According to the government survey, the percentage of employed teleworkers nationwide was 14.8% in 2019, before the pandemic, and 19.1% in the Tokyo metropolitan area. By 2021, these figures had increased to 27% nationwide and 42.3% in the Tokyo metropolitan area. After the pandemic, in 2023, the figures slightly decreased to 24.8% nationwide and 38.1% in the Tokyo metropolitan area. Notably, a significant trend is toward

[3] Sōmu Shō [Ministry of Internal Affairs and Communications], 2021a points out the following: "In Japan, the seniority system is still maintained, so when middle-aged and older managers come to work, younger employees are forced to go to work, which tends to create a sympathetic pressure to come to work in vain. In addition, face-to-faceism is ingrained among middle-aged and older workers, who tend to view time spent present in the workplace as working hours and value those who work longer hours."

[4] Hamaguchi, Keiichiro, 2009, 2021.

[5] Sōmu Shō [Ministry of Internal Affairs and Communications], 2024.

expanding hybrid work, combining office work and telework. The percentage of hybrid work (those engaged in telework 1–4 days per week) rose from 40.7% in 2019 to 82.1% in 2023, nearly doubling[6].

### 5.3 PROMOTION OF TELEWORK AND ITS IMPACT ON THE EMPLOYMENT SYSTEM

Why has the Japanese government sought to introduce telework, which has been incompatible with the Japanese employment system since the end of the last century? In government discussions during the 1990s, various benefits of telework were highlighted. For companies, teleworking at home or in satellite offices can improve productivity and creativity because it provides a work environment suitable for tasks that require concentration; if teleworkers can use mobile terminals and other devices to communicate from outside the office, it will reduce travel time, improve sales performance, and increase customer satisfaction. For workers, telework was expected to allow for a more relaxed lifestyle and make it easier to balance family responsibilities, such as childcare and caregiving, with work. For society, telework was anticipated to eliminate commuting and travel, contributing to environmental protection and serving as an effective tool for maintaining corporate and socioeconomic activities during disasters[7,8].

In the 1990s and early 2000s, the primary focus in Japan was on satellite office-based telework. However, during the COVID-19 pandemic, the development and widespread adoption of web conferencing tools like Zoom, Webex, and Teams led to an explosive increase in home-based telework, which became the central topic in discussions about telework.

The recommendations compiled by "Task Force on the Future of Telework in the Post-Corona Era" in the Ministry of Internal Affairs and Communications (MIC) in August 2021 were subtitled "Aiming for the Well-Being of Individuals, Companies, and Society as a Whole." The task force's recommendations highlighted five characteristics of the "Japanese-style telework": (1) contributing to solving Japan's various social issues, (2) promoting the active use of ICT tools, BPR (Business process reengineering), and DX triggered by telework, (3) consideration of socialization, (4) devising ways to bridge the generational gap, and (5) improving well-being.

6 Kokudo Kōtsu Shō [Ministry of Land, Infrastructure, Transport and Tourism], 2024.

7 Description of telework circa 1998 by the Department of Posts and Telecommunications. www.soumu.go.jp/main_sosiki/joho_tsusin/whatsnew/telework9906.html

8 Incidentally, the Clinton administration of the United States, which developed the Information Superhighway (officially called NII, National Information Infrastructure) at the same time, cited similar reasons for promoting telework: (1) administrative reform; (2) improvement of citizen services; (3) increased motivation of employees (employment of the physically disabled and single mothers); (4) energy conservation; (5) elimination of air pollution and response to global warming; and (6) alleviation of traffic congestion. See Sato, Koji, 2001, 169.

These are closely related to the transformation of Japan's employment system. The advisory board established in the MIC to implement these recommendations examines the effects of introducing "Japanese-style telework" on Japan's employment system[9]. Regarding the issues of population aging and decline, telework is expected to support the continuous securing of labor by enabling flexible work styles not constrained by time or location. Telework can also enhance individual well-being by freeing workers from long commutes and crowded trains. As for the seniority-based employment system, introducing telework for middle-aged and senior management can eliminate unnecessary peer pressure on subordinates to come to the office. Furthermore, teleworking makes it possible to shift from analog work styles, characterized by face-to-face interactions, stamping documents, and printed papers, to new work modes with business process re-engineering and DX.

On the other hand, the advisory board pointed out that potential problems arising from the introduction of telework could be appropriately addressed. Regarding the relationship between telework and Japan's "membership-based employment" system, which emphasizes shared information and unity, the board noted that this can be maintained through the thorough use of ICT tools. Regarding the relationship with the practice of hiring new graduates with no work experience en masse on April 1 of each year, which is a characteristic of the Japanese employment system, the board emphasized the importance of face-to-face socialization during the training period.

In this way, the government's recommendations actively seek to transform aspects of Japan's employment relations that need revision through the introduction of telework while suggesting a gradual approach for areas where sudden changes might cause problems in Japanese society. This dual approach is why these recommendations are called "Japanese-style telework."

In any event, telework has the potential to become a game changer, bringing significant changes to Japan's employment system. The following section will analyze these changes from a legal perspective and examine the new legal challenges that arise, considering a comparative law viewpoint.

## 5.4 LEGAL ANALYSIS OF CHANGES IN THE EMPLOYMENT SYSTEM DUE TO TELEWORK

Telework is a labor-providing relationship that differs in many respects from the traditional employment relationship. If teleworking becomes widespread as a usual way of working rather than a special way of working, it may change the nature of the employment relationship.

9 Sōmu Shō [Ministry of Internal Affairs and Communications]. 2021b. Available at www.soumu.go.jp/main_content/000779401.pdf

### 5.4.1 *Self-Determination of Where and When to Work*

First, telework involves work performed away from the workplace, beyond the direct supervision and command of the employer. This could signify a work style free from the essential characteristic of employment relationships – subordination – which involves working under the employer's direction and orders, with fixed work hours and locations. Consequently, if workers can freely choose and decide when and where they work (working anytime, anywhere)[10], their work may be classified not as employment but as independent self-employment (self-employed telework).

However, with the advancement of ICT, monitoring workers even during telework is technically possible. Therefore, even if teleworkers are allowed to work outside the direct supervision of the employer, they would still be considered employees if they are subject to the employer's overall direction and control, such as being subject to disciplinary action. Under the current Japanese labor law system, even those who can make their own discretionary decisions regarding working hours and work location are not denied worker status (discretionary work scheme under Articles 38-3 and 38-4 of the Labor Standards Act). Teleworkers who are not given such complete discretion would, of course, be considered workers.

However, a significant legal issue arises in determining how to count hours worked during telework. If employers are strictly required to monitor working hours, they may impose more stringent and stressful conditions on teleworkers, such as requiring them to keep their computer cameras on at all times or frequently requiring online communication. This could lead to a work environment that is more restrictive than working within the company. Apart from the general regulations on working hours prohibiting exceeding statutory maximum hours (8 hours per day, 40 hours per week), the Labor Standards Act provides special working hour regulations, such as a presumed working hour system[11] for off-site work (Art. 38-2, LSA), a presumed working hour system for discretionary work (Art. 38-3 and 38-4, LSA), and exemptions for supervisory employees (Art. 41 No.2, LSA).

The government's Telework Guidelines suggest that telework can be implemented under any of these systems. As mentioned above, applying the general working hour regulations would impose an obligation on employers to objectively calculate working hours, and whether this makes telework a desirable work style for workers requires careful consideration. Telework encompasses a variety of forms, ranging from tasks like call center work performed at home, where actual working

[10] Joint ILO-Eurofound report, 2017.

[11] The presumed working hour system presumes the hours worked to be those stipulated in the labor-management agreement or labor-management committee resolution, rather than the actual hours worked. For instance, if the labor-management agreement specifies an eight-hour workday, then eight hours are presumed, regardless of whether the actual hours worked were six or ten. As to the details of the Japan's presumed working hour system, see Araki, Takashi, 2015.

hour management is appropriate, to types where workers intermittently care for family members while working. Therefore, it is worth thoroughly considering the introduction of new working hour regulations tailored to telework, distinct from the general actual working hour regulations, to accommodate the diverse nature of telework[12].

### 5.4.2 *Home as the Workplace*

Second, in the case of working from home, the home becomes the workplace. This has both positive and negative aspects for workers. On the positive side, it eliminates the need for commuting[13]. Additionally, for workers with childcare or nursing care responsibilities, telework is welcomed as a work style that facilitates a better work–life balance. It will also lead to greater employment opportunities for women, the elderly, disabled people, and others with difficulties to work outside. In Japan, employers have broad authority to transfer employees, often requiring relocation every two to three years, including to distant locations. However, telework has begun to allow employees to perform their duties through telework, even working from home, without having to relocate, marking a significant change in Japan's personnel management practices.

On the other hand, however, the fact that the private space of the home becomes the workplace also introduces various issues. For instance, turning on the camera during web meetings exposes private spaces and raises concerns about privacy protection. In addition, the traditional work–life balance discussion has been based on the separation of work and private life, but in the case of telework, these boundaries can become blurred, leading to a fusion of work and private life. Addressing how to manage such a state of work presents a new challenge.

#### 5.4.2.1 Ensuring Health and Safety

Ensuring health and safety in telework is also a critical issue. Since telework is conducted outside the direct supervision of the employer, there is a risk of workers engaging in prolonged work hours or irregular work patterns, leading to health

[12] Since the requirements for applying the presumed working hour systems to work outside the workplace or discretionary work are strict, many teleworkers do not meet these criteria. For example, the presumed system for off-site work can only be applied when it is difficult to calculate working hours, but it is not always difficult to calculate the working hours of telework. The presumed system for discretionary work requires that the employer gives no instructions regarding the allocation of working hours, leaving it entirely to the worker's discretion. However, there are many cases of telework that do not satisfy this requirement.

[13] In particular, workers would benefit greatly from being freed from long, crowded train rides to work, as is the case in the Tokyo area.

deterioration or mental health issues. As a general rule, occupational health and safety regulations also apply to telework. Therefore, employers must implement the following health measures for teleworkers, as required for all workers: establishing a system for health consultations (Art. 13-3, Industrial Safety and Health Act), providing safety and health education upon hiring or when changing work duties (Art. 59), conducting necessary health examinations and taking actions based on the results (Art. 66 to 66-7), providing medical interviews and taking actions based on the results for long-hour workers (Art. 66-8 to 66-9), monitoring working hours for the purpose of medical interviews (Art. 66-8-3), calculating overtime and holiday work hours for medical interviews and providing this information to the industrial physician (Art. 52-2, Industrial Safety and Health Implementing Regulations), conducting stress checks and taking actions based on the results (Art. 66-10, the Industrial Safety and Health Act), and providing health education, health consultations, and other measures to maintain and improve workers' health (Article 69). Safety and health education is critical when transitioning from workplace-based employment to telework.

Moreover, when working from home, the absence of supervisors and colleagues makes it difficult to detect changes in the worker's physical or mental condition. To address this, the Telework Guidelines suggest using tools like the "Checklist for Ensuring the Safety and Health of Teleworkers (For Employers)" and implementing measures to enhance the health consultation system and communication.

The Industrial Safety and Health Act imposes detailed regulations regarding the maintenance of work environments. However, in the case of telework, it is not appropriate for administrative oversight to directly extend into the private domain of an employee's home. Therefore, the Telework Guidelines specify that while health and safety regulations applicable to workplaces do not apply to home-based work, employers are expected to provide education and advice to teleworkers to ensure that their work environment is equivalent to the health standards of a typical workplace. A checklist titled "Checklist for Verifying Work Environment When Teleworking at Home (For Workers)" is provided, and teleworkers are encouraged to use it to report on their home work environment. The guidelines encourage cooperation between labor and management to improve the work environment if necessary.

If a work-related accident or disease occurs due to teleworking, workers' compensation insurance benefits are provided under the labor insurance compensation system, with the employer bearing all the insurance premiums. However, incidents caused by non-work-related activities, such as private acts, are not covered, making this determination crucial. In Japan, deaths from overwork (*Karoshi*) and suicides due to mental stress caused by overwork (*Karo-jisatsu*) are significant issues within the realm of work-related accidents. To determine work-relatedness, if overtime exceeding 40 hours per week exceeds 100 hours in a month or averages more than 80 hours over several months, the onset of the illness is recognized as strongly related to the work, and the worker is certified as having a work-related injury. In this regard, monitoring the status of working hours[14] in telework is critical.

#### 5.4.2.2 Right to Disconnect

The development of ITC puts teleworkers in a position where they can receive work-related instructions from their employer or supervisor at any time. This issue is particularly pronounced in telework. As a result, the "right to disconnect" has been discussed in many countries. The introduction of explicit provisions for the right to disconnect through the 2016 Labor Code amendment in France and the European Parliament's draft Directive on the right to disconnect, published in January 2021, has drawn attention in Japan as well[15].

Currently, Japan does not have regulations concerning the right to disconnect. The existing Guidelines merely suggest establishing voluntary rules to limit the sending of emails by managers or supervisors. However, since workers are not obligated to respond to work outside of their prescribed working hours, any disadvantageous treatment (such as disciplinary action) or dismissal for not immediately responding to emails after hours could be protected under the current laws prohibiting the abuse of disciplinary power (Art. 15, the Labor Contract Act) and the abuse of dismissal rights (Art. 16, the Labor Contract Act). In many countries, the implementation of the right to disconnect is often left to negotiations between labor and management. It is worth considering mandating such labor-management discussions in Japan as well.

### 5.4.3 *From Collective and Organized Work to Individual Work*

Third, telework, particularly when working alone from home, has forced a significant change in the perception of employment relations for Japanese labor and management, who have traditionally assumed that work is carried out collectively within the organization of a company.

There were concerns that Japan's team-oriented collective work system would not function in a telework environment, leading to a significant decline in productivity. Indeed, when telework was suddenly imposed during the COVID-19 pandemic,

[14] Even if a presumed working hour system (off-site work system or discretionary work system) is adopted, it is still necessary to monitor the status of working hours.

[15] According to Yamamoto, Yota, 2023, 485, legislative policies on the right to disconnect in foreign countries can be categorized into three: (1) prohibition of disadvantageous treatment for exercising or attempting to exercise the right to be disconnected, (2) clarification or restriction of the time during which employers can access workers, and (3) implementation of measures to ensure (more specifically, the implementation of mandatory labor-management negotiations).

without adequate ICT infrastructure, productivity naturally decreased. However, as the technological infrastructure has been developed, it became clear that contrary to expectations, it is possible to work quite efficiently by devising work styles compatible with the telework environment. In other words, it has become clear that Japan's employment management has simply not been prepared for individual, proactive ways of working.

Working at home has advantages for workers in that it allows them to work freely without having to conform to the workplace order, and it allows them to work free from stress and harassment caused by contact with other people. On the other hand, it can also lead to stress from working in isolation and concerns about whether employers will properly evaluate telework done in isolation. Additionally, in Japan's employment system, where education and training are typically provided through on-the-job training, telework could lead to a loss of such opportunities. Addressing these issues is also necessary.

The Guidelines, therefore, recommend that, regarding the issue of isolation, efforts be made to promote communication, such as introducing software that allows employees to communicate in the same manner as in the workplace. Regarding personnel evaluations, the Guidelines recommend that specific evaluation criteria be specified in advance and that flexible opportunities should be provided for labor and management to share a common understanding of the status of achievement of the criteria, as necessary. Regarding education and training, the report mentions online human resource development.

Now that the COVID-19 pandemic has subsided, many companies have adopted hybrid work models, such as working two days in the office and three days remotely per week, instead of complete telework. This can be seen as a practical approach to leveraging the benefits of telework while overcoming its challenges.

## 5.5 THE RIGHT TO ORDER TELEWORK AND THE RIGHT TO REQUEST TELEWORK

As described above, telework is a new form of work that brings advantages and certain disadvantages to both labor and management. This raises legal questions: Can an employer unilaterally order telework, and can an employee demand to work via telework? The EU's Framework Agreement on Telework (2002) emphasizes that telework should be voluntary for both parties. There are currently no laws or regulations on this issue in Japan, so it is left to interpretative discussions, but basically, the same idea prevails.

### 5.5.1 *Employer's Right to Order Telework*

Can an employer unilaterally order a worker to telework without the worker's consent? This should be considered separately for normal times and emergencies.

#### 5.5.1.1 Normal Times

If a worker does not voluntarily consent to telework, there must be a contractual basis in the employment contract to order telework unilaterally. When the rules of employment[16] establish the authority to order telework work as a reasonable system, this could be the contractual basis. Japanese employers generally establish the right to order transfer (the right to change the workplace as needed for business) in the rules of employment. Under membership-based employment, the transfer provision in the rules of employment is considered reasonable and becomes the contract content. Thus, the issue arises whether telework can be ordered by exercising transfer authority. Some scholars support this interpretation[17]. However, telework differs in quality from regular transfers because telework involves using the worker's home as the workplace. Therefore, with reference to discussions in Germany and France, a growing view among Japanese scholars holds that telework should not be ordered under transfer authority. In Germany, home-based work is seen as an intrusion on the inviolability of the home (Art. 13, the Basic Law) as a specific provision of general personal rights (Art. 2(1) and Art. 1(1), the Basic Law), and employers cannot unilaterally order it without the employee's consent. In France, the right to respect for private life (Art. 9, the Civil Code) and the right to refuse home-based work under the Labor Code (L1222–9 III, Labor Code) allow employees to reject such work. Similarly, under Japanese law, a prominent view argues that based on the protection of private life (Art. 13, the Constitution) and the inviolability of the home (Art. 35, the Constitution), employers cannot unilaterally order telework without balancing it against the disadvantages to private life[18].

#### 5.5.1.2 Emergencies

In contrast to the normal times described above, Germany and France have introduced legislation that allows workers to work from home without individual consent in crises such as the threat of infectious diseases like COVID-19[19]. It is, however, not clear what exactly constitutes a crisis. In addition to cases of infectious diseases, there is also the question of whether telework can be ordered, for example,

16 Rules of employment (shugyo kisoku) are rules concerning working conditions and workplace discipline that are uniformly applied to all workers at a workplace. Employers who employ ten or more workers at a workplace must draw up rules of employment (Art. 89, Labor Standards Act). If the rules of employment are made known to workers and their contents are reasonable, the working conditions stipulated in the rules of employment become the content of the employment contract (Art. 7, Labor Contract Act).

17 Tsuchida, Michio, 2021; Ishizaki, Yukiko, 2021. However, these scholars also emphasize that the abuse of the right to order should be strictly scrutinized.

18 Kono, Natsuki, 2020, 83; Hosokawa, Ryo, 2021, 31; Yamamoto, Yota, 2023, 479.

19 German Law for the Prevention of Infectious Diseases (Infektionsschutzgesetz), article 28b, paragraph 4, sentence 2; French Labor Code, L.1222-11. See Yamamoto, Yota, 2023, 480.

for the continuation of official duties of public servants or public works projects when office work is not possible. Article 33 of the Japanese Labor Standards Act permits overtime work when it is temporarily necessary due to a disaster or other unavoidable circumstances. One of the advantages of telework is that it allows work to continue even in emergencies like disasters or other unavoidable circumstances. However, the discussion has not fully considered whether or not telework obligations can be imposed on workers. This point should be discussed further in the future.

#### 5.5.2 *Workers' Right to Request Telework: As an Option for Flexible Working*

On the other hand, do workers have the right to request telework? The EU Framework Agreement on Telework, European national laws, and Japanese Telework Guidelines all state that telework is left to labor-management autonomy. Therefore, unless such a right is established in the employment contract, it is generally understood that employees cannot claim telework as a right. However, during the COVID-19 pandemic, individuals with underlying health conditions might be able to request telework as a form of "reasonable accommodation," similar to what is provided to individuals with disabilities. In such cases, it is also a question of whether allowing telework imposes an undue hardship on the employer[20].

Recently, some countries have begun developing legislative policies broadly recognizing the right to request flexible working arrangements. In the Netherlands, the Flexible Work Act, which came into force in 2016, grants workers who have been employed for twenty-six weeks the right to request a change to flexible working arrangements, and employers must grant such requests unless the refusal is justified. One of these flexible working arrangements includes remote work[21]. In the UK, a recent legal amendment has allowed employees to request flexible working (including working from home) from their first day of employment, removing the previous requirement of twenty-six weeks of continuous employment[22]. When such a request is made, employers must deal with the request in a "reasonable manner," such as assessing the advantages and disadvantages of the application, discussing possible alternatives, and offering an appeal process. If an employer does not handle a request reasonably, the employee can take the case to an employment tribunal[23].

In Japan, workers with childcare and nursing care responsibilities are guaranteed the right to shift to part-time work (Art. 23, the Child Care and Family Care Leave Act). In addition, disabled workers can request flexible work as part of reasonable

[20] Ishizaki, Yukiko, 2021, 23–24; Yamamoto, Yota, 2023, 476.
[21] Waddington, Lisa and Bell, Mark, 2021, 522.
[22] Explanation Notes, Employment Relations (Flexible Working) Act 2023. www.legislation.gov.uk/ukpga/2023/33/pdfs/ukpgaen_20230033_en.pdf
[23] Flexible Working: www.gov.uk/flexible-working

accommodation (Art. 36-3, Persons with Disabilities Employment Promotion Act). However, legislation in the Netherlands and the UK allows flexible work for all workers, not just those with childcare and nursing care responsibilities or those with disabilities. The right to request conversion to remote work and part-time work as a form of flexible work is noteworthy. This kind of legislative policy should be fully considered in Japanese law.

## 5.6 CONCLUSION: TELEWORK AS A GAME CHANGER IN LABOR LAW POLICY

### 5.6.1 *Reconsideration of Traditional Labor Law*

Although the Japanese economy remains stagnant, it is still the fourth largest economy in the world in terms of GDP, after the United States, China, and Germany. However, according to the results of the OECD's evaluation of the well-being of each country using the Better Life Index, Japan ranks 12th from the bottom out of 38 countries. In particular, the work–life balance index is among the lowest in the world[24].

It has been pointed out that the Japanese labor market lacks the freedom to choose one's job, to choose one's working hours and working style, and to choose where to work[25]. If the lack of freedom of self-determination in the labor market is one reason for the low level of well-being among the Japanese, then the concept of labor law policy needs to be fundamentally reconsidered.

Traditional labor laws, not just in Japan but also in other countries, have viewed workers as a collective group and have established systems to protect that group as a whole. Labor protection laws establishing minimum working conditions, such as minimum wages and maximum working hours, belong to the individual labor relations law, but the protective norms are set as norms that are applied uniformly to all workers in principle. The norms are set at the most centralized national level. In other words, the protective norms envisioned by labor protection laws have been norms with content deemed appropriate for all workers. It lacked, or at least was extremely weak in, the perspective of protecting individual workers from the diverse, individualized difficulties they face in continuing their employment.

Labor protective laws merely set the floor for minimum working conditions. Traditional labor law has assumed that higher working conditions than the minimum would be achieved through collective bargaining by labor unions, which could negotiate on an equal footing with employers.

Thus, traditional labor law has approached the content of protective standards and improving working conditions from a collective perspective. However, as

[24] Suzuki, Kyoko, 2020; OECD, 2020.
[25] Kamuro, Ayami, 2017.

workers have diversified, along with their values and working styles, it has become unrealistic to assume protective standards universally applicable to all workers. Furthermore, unionization rates are declining globally. In Japan, the union density in 2024 is 16.1%[26]. As a result, most workers are left to negotiate better working conditions on their own, which is exceedingly difficult[27].

Traditional labor laws protecting workers from a collective perspective will undoubtedly remain important. However, they alone are insufficient to ensure the well-being of individual workers. New mode labor laws that focus on individual workers' diversified needs and support how they want to work are needed. In other words, in addition to labor laws based on universal protection, there is a need to conceive of labor laws from the perspective of individualized support.

Workers in Japan who were forced to work from home due to the COVID-19 pandemic experienced, for the first time, a working style different from the traditional model of working long hours in an office alongside colleagues. They have also realized that being able to choose to work the way they want to work, while maintaining a work–life balance and taking advantage of the development of ICT, will improve their well-being. The recognition of the importance of choosing one's preferred way of working through telework is likely an experience shared by many countries beyond Japan.

In fact, as discussed below, legal systems that recognize the right or opportunity of workers to request flexible working arrangements, including telework, have been introduced in several countries. However, many countries, including Japan, have already adopted a system that requires employers to accommodate a working style requested by individual workers, depending on their circumstances. The following section examines the similarities and differences between existing legal systems and the right to request telework.

### 5.6.2 *Three Approaches to Realize Work Styles That Respond to the Actual Circumstances of Individual Workers and the Impact of Telework*

There are at least three types of approaches that require employers to respond to the diverse circumstances of individual workers and provide individualized support to workers. The first approach is to demand "reasonable accommodation" as long as it does not impose an undue hardship on the employer. The demand for reasonable

[26] In particular, more than 90% of Japanese labor unions are company-based, and collective bargaining occurs at the company level rather than at the sector or industry level. As a result, unlike in European countries where the coverage of collective bargaining agreements is high, even though the unionization rate is low, in Japan, the union density is almost identical to the coverage rate of collective bargaining agreements. See, Araki, Takashi, 2019, 375.

[27] In countries like the United States, where there is an active labor market and job changes are common, improving working conditions by changing jobs is possible. In Japan, however, where stable employment at a single company is common and the job market is less dynamic, improving working conditions by changing jobs is not easy.

accommodation originates in the prohibition of religious discrimination under Title VII of the Civil Rights Act of 1964 in the United States. The question arose as to whether it constituted religious discrimination to treat adversely a person who believed in a religion that prohibited work on the Sabbath on the basis of that belief. The 1972 amendments to the Act defined religious discrimination as the failure to provide reasonable accommodation for religious observance and practice to the extent that it does not constitute undue hardship[28]. The requirement for reasonable accommodation has since been adopted in the United States for people with disabilities under the Rehabilitation Act of 1973 and the Americans with the Disabilities Act of 1990, and Europe under the 2000 Equal Treatment Framework Directive (2000/78/EC). In Japan, it was adopted in the 2013 Act on Employment Promotion of Persons with Disabilities.

The second approach is found in various countries' work–life balance laws that grant workers with caregiving responsibilities the right to choose flexible work arrangements that enable work–life balance. In the EU, under the Work-life balance Directive (2019/1158/EU) adopted in 2019, all Member States must "take the necessary measures to ensure that workers with children up to a specified age, which shall be at least eight years, and carers, have the right to request flexible working arrangements for caring purposes. The duration of such flexible working arrangements may be subject to a reasonable limitation" (Art. 9, Para. 1). The "flexible working arrangement" in the Directive means the possibility for workers to adjust their working patterns, including through the use of remote working arrangements, flexible working schedules, or reduced working hours (Art. 3 Para 1 (f)). In Japan, Article 23 of the Child Care and Family Care Leave Act gives childcarers the right to convert full-time to part-time work. However, the right to request telework is not mentioned.

The third approach, unlike the aforementioned two approaches aimed at workers with specific statutory grounds (such as disability or caregiving responsibilities), does not limit the scope of eligible individuals and instead grants all workers the right to request flexible working arrangements of their choice. As we observed in Section 5.2, this approach has already been implemented in countries such as the UK, the Netherlands, and Australia. One typical example of such flexible working arrangements is telework or remote work. As telework has become a standard mode of working rather than an exceptional one, the desire to choose telework is no longer limited to workers with disabilities or caregiving responsibilities. In other words, the normalization of telework may have driven the need for the third approach, which seeks to allow all workers to choose diverse working arrangements that suit their individual circumstances.

Traditional labor protection laws establishing universal protection norms for all workers, such as minimum wages and maximum working hours, and collective

[28] See Rothstein, Mark A. et al., 2014, 656.

labor relations laws that strengthen bargaining power through collective negotiations, will continue to be necessary. However, these traditional approaches alone are insufficient to ensure the well-being of workers, who are increasingly diverse and facing various challenges. The widespread adoption of telework, a new working mode, has highlighted the need for a new approach to labor law that allows individual workers to choose the working arrangements that suit them, thereby enhancing their well-being.

We have entered a new era. In addition to traditional labor laws that ensure universal protection, we must conceive of labor laws that provide workers with new, individualized support focusing on concrete, diverse circumstances. In this sense, telework may not only be a game changer for the Japanese employment system but also for labor law policies in all countries.

## REFERENCES


Araki, Takashi. 2015. "Working hour regulation and its reform in Japan", in Zbigniew Hajn and Dagmara Skupien, eds., *Przyszlosc Prawa Pracy: Liber Amicorum w piecdziesieciolecie pracy naukowej profesora Michala Sewerynskiego [The Future of Labor Law: Liber Amicorum in Fifty Years of Scientific Work of Professor Michal Sewerynski]*, Wydawnictwo Uniwersytetu Lodzkiego, 655–673.

2019. "Japan", in Ulla Liukkunen eds., *Collective Bargaining in Labour Law Regimes*, Springer, 375.

Hamaguchi, Keiichiro. 2009. *Atarashii Rōdō Shakai: Koyō Shisutemu no Saikōchiku he [New Labor Society: Toward the Reconstruction of the Employment System]*, Iwanami Shoten.

2021. *Jobu-gata Koyō Shakai toha Nani ka: Seishain Taisei no Mujun to Tenkan [What Is a Job-based Employment Society: Contradiction and Conversion of the Regular Employee System]*, Iwanami Shoten.

Hosokawa, Ryo. 2021. "Shingata Korona Uirusu-ka niokeru Telework no Fukyu to sono Kadai [The diffusion of telework and its issues in the new coronavirus disaster]," *Rōdō Hōritsu Junpō*, 1975+76: 31.

Ishizaki, Yukiko. 2021. "Koyō-gata Telework ni kakaru Rōdō Hō jōno Kadai [Labor law issues related to employment-type telework]," *Kikan Rōdō-hō*, 274: 22.

Joint ILO-Eurofound report, 2017. *Working Anytime, Anywhere: The Effects on the World of Work*, Eurofound, ILO.

Kamuro, Ayami. 2017. "Establishment of 'self-determination' in employment and labor," in Naohiko Jinno et al., eds., *'Wakachi-ai' Shakai no Kōsō [The Idea of a 'Sharing' Society]*, Iwanami Shoten, 25.

Kokudo Kōtsu Shō [Ministry of Land, Infrastructure, Transport and Tourism]. 2024. "2023nen-do Telework Jinkō Jittai Chōsa [FY2023 telework population survey]" (available online).

Kōno, Natsuki. 2020. "Telework to Rōdōsha no Shiseikatsu no Hogo [Telework and protection of workers' private lives]," *Hōritsu Jihō*, 92: 12: 83.

Kōsei Rōdō Shō [Ministry of Health, Labour and Welfare]. 2021. "Telework no Tekisetsu na Dōnyu oyobi Jisshi no Suishin no tameno Gaidorain [Guidelines for promotion of appropriate introduction and implementation of telework]" (available online).

OECD. 2020, *Better Life Initiative: Measuring Well-Being and Progress*, OECD.

Rōdō Seisaku Kenkyu Kenshu Kikō [Japan Institute for Labour Policy and Training]. 2021. Telework: Korona-ka ni okeru Sei-Rō-Shi no Torikumi [Telework: government, labour and management initiatives in the corona disaster] Japan Institute for Labour Policy and Training.

Rothstein, Mark A et al. 2014. *Employment Law*, Vol. 1, 5th ed, Thomson Reuters.

Satō, Koji. 2001. "Telework Suishin no tameno Koteki Siensaku: Nichi-Bei-Ou no Seisaku Hikaku [Public support measures for telework promotion: a comparison of policies in Japan, the US, and Europe]" *Shoukei Ronso*, 36(3): 153.

Sōmu Shō [Ministry of Internal Affairs and Communications]. 2021. "Posuto Korona Jidai ni okeru Telework no arikata Kentō Tasuku-fōsu Teigen-sho [Proposal by the Task Force to study telework in the 'post-corona' era]" (available online).

2024. "Tsushin Riyō Dōkō Chōsa 2023 [Telecommunications usage trends survey 2023]" (available online).

2021. "' Posuto Korona' Jidai ni okeru Telework Teichaku Adobaizari-bōdo [Advisory board for establishing telework in the 'post-corona' era]," First Meeting of the Secretariat's Briefing Material (available online).

Suzuki, Kyoko. 2020. "Naze Well-being wo 'Shiawase' to yakusu no deha tarinai noka? [Why is translating well-being as 'happiness' not enough?]" JILPT Research Eye No. 79 (available online).

Tsuchida, Michio. 2021. "Shingata Korona Kiki to Rōdō Hō, Koyōshakai (1) [COVID-19 crisis, labor law, and employment society (1)]," *Hōritsu Jihō*, 73(5): 41.

Waddington, Lisa and Bell, Mark 2021. "The right to request flexible working arrangements under the Work-life Balance Directive – A comparative perspective" *European Labour Law Journal*, 12(4): 508.

Yamamoto, Yota. 2023. "Koyō-gata Telework no Hō to Seisaku wo meguru Kokusai Hikaku [International comparison on the law and policy of employment-type telework]" in Yoshimi Kikuchi et al., eds., *Hataraku Shakai no Hen-yō to Seikatsu Hoshō no Hō [Changes of Work Society and Law on Life Security]*, Junpō Sha, 475.

# 6

# Remote Working and Subordination

*Adalberto Perulli*

## 6.1 THE POLARIZATION OF THE REMOTE WORKING DEBATE: A CRITIQUE OF CRITICAL POSITIONS

During the COVID-19 pandemic many millions of people worked from home: the process of remotization of work, which had already begun in previous years thanks to telematic technologies, digitalization and the development of knowledge work, have undergone an incredible acceleration[1]. The pandemic has in fact imposed rigid social distancing: Remote working has taken place exclusively in the form of teleworking without the possibility of experimenting with more flexible and nomadic forms of remote working and, above all, without rethinking and redefining the organization of work but simply adapting the existing one to the needs of distancing.

Once the health emergency has passed, this vast experimentation has opened up a multiplicity of perspectives for new forms of work organization inspired by a new model of employment relationship: less hierarchical, more autonomous, based on the trust and responsibility of the worker. Scholars, legislators and the social partners have realized that remote working has an extraordinary transformative potential capable of bringing about a paradigm shift in the employment relationship, in the very concept of subordinate work, as well as in the configuration of managerial prerogatives, which are redefined to make them consistent with the organizational models of remote working.

As often happens when faced with potentially disruptive innovations, positions on this issue have become polarized. Critics argue that remote work could involve a trade-off (quid pro quo) between a greater use of remote labor (perceived as less controllable) and lower levels of employment protection (Countouris 2023). It is

[1] ILO, Report Global dialogue forum on the difficulties and advantages of television for workers and employers in the sectors of ICT and financial services (October 24–26, 2016).

clear that the risk of exchanging greater autonomy in the performance of the remote work for a reduction of protections can be envisaged. However, it seems that the opposite happens: on the one hand, the law and collective bargaining reiterate that the remote worker maintains all the rights of the standard employment relationship, without any exceptions and without any discrimination, from other new social rights created (such as the right to disconnect) in order to avoid new risk of exploitation. In essence, remote workers, at least in the systems I am considering here (in summary the EU systems) not only maintain existing rights but enjoy additional rights and benefits, suitable for the new working context.

Critics also argue that remote work triggers managerial and HR strategies, including the increasing recourse to bogus self-employment and on-demand arrangements that could have the effect of thinning down the responsibilities and obligations that employers typically take charge of when hiring labor under a standard contract of employment. In essence, according to this thesis, remote working would be a new form of job precariousness, which critics define as "contractual distancing."

The thesis in question tends to confuse remote work with other forms of work, those of the gig economy (such as platform work), and to assimilate remote-work strategies to work outsourcing strategies. In reality the two phenomena are very different. While outsourcing took segments of production outside the physical and legal confines of the company, and consequently expelled the workforce (which was then re-internalized through subcontracting), the phenomenon of organizational redesign with which the remote working does not involve any outsourcing of work, which remains perfectly integrated into the production cycle and organization of the company. The risk that remote working entails an increased trend of misclassification is also contradicted by the fact that it is often a priori classified by law and collective bargaining as *subordinate work*: Thus, for example, the Italian law on "agile working" states that this is a particular voluntary way of carrying out an employment relationship (see art. 18.1, Act. N. 81/2017), and the same is stated by the European Framework on Telework (art. 2: "in the contest of an employment contract"): Remote working is not a contractual type that can be misqualified but a method of carrying out an *employment relationship*.

Finally, critics argue that remote working "undoubtedly" involves increased managerial control and surveillance, with increasingly intrusive forms of control and surveillance. In this regard, critics invoke the risks of using AI to create Orwellian (or Foucauldian) scenarios of panoptic control and a massive algorithmic system of surveillance and discipline. This point is very delicate, because, in fact, remote control systems, for example through telematic or digital technologies, can be very penetrating and invasive. However, two considerations apply here. The first: It is not clear why these control systems should be used massively precisely in a work performance model that is based on the trust and autonomy of the worker and not on the command and control model. The second:

The scenario of panoptic control does not take into account the regulatory instruments of a national or supranational nature aimed at putting a stop to possible Orwellian drifts. Just think of the attraction within the scope of the European GDPR of all automated decision-making and monitoring systems at work, according to a very broad and flexible notion of "personal data" which naturally includes the algorithmic system (which implies automated processing of data) and with the employer's obligation to carry out an impact assessment on fundamental rights (art. 29 a of the GDPR). And just think, as regards domestic systems, that the Italian law on agile working not only provides (as we will see) an individual (and therefore adaptive) regulation of the employer's powers, including the power of control, but also reiterates the application of all legislative safeguards aimed at limiting managerial prerogatives.

Countouris and De Stefano, however, in the conclusion of their analysis, find an optimistic vision and agree – even after having listed all the possible risks – on the fact that the world of work can find remote working a formidable tool and a historic opportunity to free millions of workers from the excesses of managerialism and to move from an idea of work in which workers are controlled and subordinated to an idea of work in which workers are more autonomous, collaborative, and worthy of personal trust.

Rather than following one or another of the positions that polarize the debate on remote work, in this chapter I will try to clarify the possible effects that a real organizational redesign based on remote work is entailing and, above all, the effects that this redesign could result in the near future, modifying many dimensions of work and impacting the regulatory structure of the employment relationship and in particular the concept/notion of subordination. In doing this I will try to base myself, as far as available, on reliable and scientific organizational studies, as well as on the same virtuous and advanced practices of collective bargaining, with particular reference to the Italian experience, but not only.

## 6.2 ORGANIZATIONAL STUDIES AND EXPERIENCES OF COLLECTIVE BARGAINING

Organizational studies are of fundamental importance to understand the possibilities of developing an organizational redesign suitable for innovating the characteristics of the employment relationship and in particular the dimension of subordination and the subjection of the worker to managerial powers. The ability of remote work to modify the concept of subordination depends, in fact, mainly on the desire to design and develop a business system based not only on a new organizational philosophy, but also and above all on a new idea of work, which includes planning of roles, tasks, and professions integrated with new technologies, with a view to increasing the worker's capabilities, the quality of work, personal *autonomy in work* (understood as the worker's ability to control his own working life), and *freedom from work*, understood as the ability to move away from work to carry out one's life by exercising the ability to choose.

To be genuine, to produce socially appreciable results, this process of organizational redefinition must not be unilaterally directed by the company according to its exclusive productive interest, but the fruit of a process of adaptive and discursive transformation, in which all stakeholders participate (management, territorial and national public regulatory authorities, individual workers, workers' union representatives) (Butera 2020).

In the public and jurisprudential debate, the company is increasingly conceived as an actor that is not only economic but also social and political. In its complex axiological dimension, in which the economic function is accompanied by a social function, the company, regardless of its legal forms (joint-stock company, simple company, etc.), no longer tends exclusively toward profit, according to the model of maximization of capitalist utility embodied by the shareholders' value model – whereby company directors are the agents of the shareholders – but adopts other rationalities and other horizons of meaning. These further rationalities of the company embrace societal values, which range from the protection of the environment to the protection of work in all its forms and applications, from consumer protection to respect for commercial and industrial partners (against whom no abuse of power, abuses of economic dependence, etc.), thus guaranteeing an overall balance between interests and social purposes of a societal type. It is legitimate to think that the organizational design of remote work should be placed in this evolutionary scenario of the actor-company, which we could define in terms of Sustainability (Novitz in this Volume), in which remote work becomes part of a more complex process of neo-republican civilization of business and workplaces. A process in which environmental values, social values, and personal values re-orient the behavior of the company in the perspective in which the latter becomes increasingly conceivable as a "common good" (Deakin 2012).

In this open process of social transformation of the company, which cannot be reduced to a simple question of organizational/production technique, all the regulatory tools typical of labor law are valorized, such as social dialogue, collective bargaining, and co-determination[2]. The analysis will therefore have to take into consideration the experiences of collective bargaining, especially at company level, which took place in the post-pandemic phase.

[2] An example of this model is offered by the Italian National Protocol on agile working of December 7, 2021 (an inter-confederal agreement signed by the major workers' and employers' trade unions ) which intended to "lay the foundations for creating a climate of trust, involvement and participation, as a fundamental premise for the correct application of smart working in the private sector, providing guidelines that can represent an effective reference framework for future negotiations collective, at national and corporate and/or territorial level, without prejudice to existing individual agreements."

Collective bargaining has grasped the need for a transition toward forms of remote working based on the interests of the workers, and not just businesses. We read, for example, in a recent collective agreement of the *Benetton Group* (2021–2023):

> the place where work activities take place in recent years and especially with the outbreak of the COVID-19 pandemic, and the concept of the office /"fixed" desk is waning because it is incapable of meeting the needs of employees who, since the beginning of 2020, have increasingly been accustomed to carrying out their work in various places/workstations. The office must therefore change its face, no longer the classic "fixed" location based on work activity but only one of the many places where this can be carried out, this also allowing a better balance to be achieved between the private and professional spheres. The Company will therefore evaluate for the future technical-organisational solutions capable of encouraging and developing this activity also through the aid of modern organizational systems for booking stations with maximum flexibility/productivity.

In this agreement (but the theme is recurring in the generality of Italian collective bargaining on this topic), the interest of workers in carrying out the activity in a ubiquitous manner and in achieving a better balance between life and work times clearly emerges.

Changing "how" and "where" to work should not be the result of heteronomous rules imposed by company management, nor of managerial projects prepared on the drawing board and implemented top down. From this perspective, unilateral practices, where existing, should be corrected, thanks to the action of trade union organizations and collective bargaining, which can play a decisive role in the preparation of a framework of shared rules for the planning of remote work itself. According to the ILO, collective bargaining can be a good tool for design teleworking practices and inclusive hybrid work, reconciling the preferences of employers and those of workers in terms of flexibility and autonomy, on the one hand, and by guaranteeing decent conditions for remote work, on the other hand.

Also, in other European countries company bargaining has demonstrated dynamism in the shared planning of remote work. For example, in Germany, which does not have a law on remote working, there are many examples of good negotiation practices which demonstrate that company agreement leaves the specific design on mobile working to the teams and their managers and this leads to an increase in the loyalty of skilled workers and greater employee satisfaction (Junge 2021). Italian collective agreements also indicate joint planning with individual agreements that define the scheduling of "agile" working days between the worker and his direct manager, according to a planning that takes into account the needs of the worker and those of the organization: thus, for example, in the *Leonardo Group* agreement (March 8, 2022). The situation seems more problematic in France, where case studies in companies of different sectors and sizes show the diversity of the implementation of teleworking, and the negotiation is permanent, broken down into phases and punctuated by agreements and amendments (Giotto 2022).

This type of change can therefore only occur with transformative projects within individual organizations supported by public promotion and regulation and collective bargaining programs, which involve worker participation and which place workers at the center of organizational transformation processes. In particular, these projects must be guided by strategies for the valorization of work and people, and must be oriented toward the planning of quality work, professionalized and decent work, capable of ensuring equity, opportunities, quality of life both for a population of educated workers, and to that unfortunately very large portion of workers who find themselves in unsatisfactory working conditions.

## 6.3 ORGANIZATIONAL REDESIGN AND THE NOTION OF SUBORDINATION

Remote working is one of the forms that the employment relationship can take to adapt subordination to new organizational contexts. In this new organizational dimension, subordination, from a model rigidly placed in the hands of the owner of the means of production, can be socially redesigned: no longer a manifestation of the unilateral power of the employer, to be limited as much as possible in order to avoid abuses and excesses, but a different way, more democratic and participatory, with which the worker experiences his work in the company, a non-deterministically hetero-directed way relating to "how" to carry out the service and contribute to the results of the company.

First of all, remote working can increase the worker's autonomy, extend the worker's spaces of freedom, and increase the balance between the person's working and nonworking life. But before delving into this point, we must carry out a general reflection on the concept of subordination.

Legally speaking, in civil law legal systems subordination is the expression of the worker's subjection to the power of direction and control of the employer. In certain legal systems, such as the Italian one, this element of hetero-direction is expressly provided for by law (art. 2094 civil code). Thanks to the directive and control power that constitute devices of an administrative authority, the company reduces the transition costs typical of the market and allows the worker's activity to be conformed to the changing needs of the organization (to all possible states of the world, as scholars of the economic analysis of the contract say) (Coase 1937). The principle of subordination reflects the authority of the employer, which is expressed through acts of exercise of legal powers of a private nature, but provided for and regulated by law (or, in the absence of law, recognized and regulated by jurisprudence).

It is debated in economic theory whether this authority is truly an irreplaceable necessity for the capitalist enterprise or whether, instead, non-hierarchical forms of organization of production are possible and not based on the exercise of unilateral prerogatives. According to economic historian David S. Landes, hierarchy is a "technology" of capitalism that is absolutely irreversible in terms of historical evolution. We can try to improve the inherited structure, increase worker participation in management decisions, diversify tasks, and rotate tasks, but we will not be able to abolish the hierarchy of responsibility and authority. On the contrary, economic theorist Stephen A. Marglin argues that hierarchical authority is not essential for achieving high productivity. From this perspective, material prosperity is also possible with a non-hierarchical organization of production. The social function of hierarchical organization does not lie in technical efficiency but in the accumulation of capital. In modern capitalism the institution dedicated to accumulation is the joint-stock company. The essential social function of the joint-stock company is the mediation carried out by its hierarchy between the individual producer (and shareholder) and the income on the market of the product of the company itself, assigning a part of the relative income to the expansion of the means of production. In the absence of hierarchical control over production and work, the joint-stock company would be forced to equip itself with egalitarian institutions for the accumulation of capital, or be satisfied with the level of accumulation already achieved. In this perspective, the parcellation of labor is not functional to efficiency but to hierarchical control, and the latter is in turn functional to justifying the indispensability of the production process.

The question of hierarchy and its more democratic alternatives has always been at the center of organizational science that studies the governance of work transactions. According to this perspective, the company can rely on market mechanisms, hierarchical-organizational mechanisms, clan mechanisms, and mixed mechanisms, in which market and hierarchy merge and form sub-models of quasi-market or quasi-hierarchy.

In the market model (typical of self-employment) information is ensured by prices and output and the level of collaboration is minimal, because the exchange is contextual and reciprocal. The alternative to the market (and its transaction costs) is hierarchy, where relationships with the worker are governed by the principle of authority. The logic of the market is therefore replaced by the action of managerial hierarchies, which is a source of "use of the organization" costs (e.g., loss of control as the size of the company increases). A third form of governance of work transactions is the clan, which by some is placed as an alternative to both the market and the hierarchy, while by others it is placed in connection and interaction with them. In this configuration, working relationships are regulated by the principle of loyalty, that is, adherence to certain values of solidarity or ideal principles that are spontaneously accepted and create a climate of collaboration (Hirschman 1970).

The level of communication and cooperation is high. It is therefore a relationship based on trust. The clan enhances and develops values of shared references, common languages and meanings, sense of belonging, and loyalty toward the corporate community and professional groups within the company (Ouchi 1980).

A nonhierarchical organization model, which focuses on trust, such as that of the clan, can be compared to the remote working scheme, especially in the agile version of Italian legislation, but not only. This clan model enhances the perspective, advanced by Marglin, of overcoming the hierarchy and the system of control and discipline of work typical of the company born from the Industrial Revolution. In that historical model the factory was created not so much for the advantages offered by new technologies based on water and steam, but for the advantages in economizing the costs of discipline and surveillance. In fact, the genealogy of subservience takes us back to a system of rules that are justified by the distrust that one party has toward the other. Labor law contains within itself the seeds of this mistrust which permeates the employment relationship on both sides (De Stefano et al. 2024). Labor law therefore seems ambiguously to be nourished by this "no-trust" paradigm which undermines the possibility of developing a more balanced, more democratic, less asymmetrical, equitable relationship between the parties. At the same time, however, labor law cannot help but enhance trust as a typical element of the bond that binds the parties of the employment relationship together, so much so that dismissal for personal reasons is conceived as a consequence of the breaking of the bond of trust ~~(in common law: damage~~ (the implied term of trust and confidence) that must necessarily exist within a relationship marked by personalistic and cooperative elements.

Now, the organizational transformations that underlie the remote working model represent an opportunity to rethink this distrustful model to replace it with a cooperative paradigm, based on trust and, consequently, on the autonomy of the worker.

## 6.4 TRUST: A RESOURCE FOR REMOTE WORKING

Trust, understood in the broadest sense of relying on one's expectations regarding the behavior of others, is an elementary situation in social life. For everyday life, trust is an essential component of the human horizon, an essential element of the world, whose alternatives are fear and chaos. Personal trust, which is offered to human beings, is possible because it is assumed that they are in possession of a personality, that they are the ordered and non-arbitrary center of a system of action, with which it is possible to come to terms. The recognition of the freedom of the other is implied in the fiduciary relationship. In fact, trust is the generalized expectation that the other will juggle his own freedom, with the mysterious potential of the actions made possible by his personality, with the personality he has presented and made socially visible.

Now, it is clear that remote work, by the very fact that it takes place outside a physical space (the office, the factory) marked by the continuous control of the worker by the employer, develops an implicit trust potential and latent in the employment relationship to the extent that it simultaneously enhances the worker's freedom with respect to his work activity and the constraints that subordination provides, both from a spatial and temporal point of view (where and when to work) and from the point of view of way of working (how to work). It is true that, as the most critically perceived doctrine of the possible risks induced by remote working points out, companies sometimes intensify remote control, rather than reduce it. But this intensification of control, if it really exists, must be considered as a truly perverse effect, as a true social pathology of remote working, contrary to the culture of organizational change and, therefore, as toxic and illegitimate, to be countered in the shared and participatory planning of organizational change.

Remote work cannot be based on the same distrustful schemes that we have mentioned. If this were the case, remote working would lose its very raison d'être and would be reduced to a form of pure and simple "distancing" of contractual performance, governed by the same systems of command and control of the more reactionary Taylor-Fordism, strengthened from technological surveillance tools. But this is not the remote working that the social partners are planning[3]. This is not what emerges from the social dialogue nor from the many collective agreements at company level which underline the managerial style that the profound organizational change is triggering. The trend in collective bargaining highlights the transformative aspect of remote working, stating that it is based on a cultural change, whose center of gravity is represented by trust and responsibility. In an Interconfederal Agreement on agile working for artisan businesses and SMEs in Italy, the social partners state that they want to

> experiment with organizational solutions to foster a culture organizational work-oriented for objectives and results, promote ways of working that can support the worker in specific moments of their personal and family life, promote a better balance between life and work times, improving organizational and individual sustainability, strengthen the autonomy and responsibility of the worker in managing working time and achieving results, promoting sustainable mobility by reducing travel.

The valorization of trust as a decisive factor in organizational redesign also emerges from the analysis of HR management guidelines[4]. These declared and shared purposes demonstrate that, in the planning intention of the social partners as well as in the stated HR objectives, the organizational method of remote working actually marks a decisive change in the conception (theoretical and practical) of the employment relationship, which is finally recognized and identified by elements, so

3 See ILO Report on Social Dialogue 2022, p. 190.

4 According to a 2021 Randstad report, conducted in Italy by interviewing 15,385 professional figures in the sector, including HR managers, General Managers, CEOs, CFOs, and owners, what is required of leaders is ability to motivate and inspire others; ability to adapt to new business needs; and ability to build *trusting relationships*.

far mostly denied in the work organization of the Taylor-Fordist enterprise, such as *autonomy* and *personal trust*.

## 6.5 FREEDOM AND TRUST

Freedom, as an expression of personality, is at the origin of the need for trust: freedom is the complex of actions for which one is personally responsible and is the source of the ability to learn trust. Now, that action which we recognize as the effect of a binding directive given to us by a hierarchical superior cannot be attributed to the personality. Hierarchical subordination, in which continuous orders and directives are expected, does not require particular trust: The subordinate slavishly carries out commanded activities, without freedom of action. The subordinate, who instead wants to show himself worthy of trust, must be put in a position to express his personality with an industriousness and conscientiousness that go well beyond the diligent execution of an order given; the worker must enjoy freedom of action, and in this way carry out tasks with a loyalty that corresponds to the trust placed in his person and his freedom (Luhmann 1979).

Now, this fiduciary model, in which elements of the person, of trust and of freedom are connected in a circle which, to be virtuous and to be credible, and to be taken seriously, must be institutionalized; that is, it must be generalized within legally established frameworks and with clear and enforceable rules. One of the vectors of this juridification of remote work is therefore collective bargaining, which in this matter also operates in harmony with a third source, individual negotiation (individual negotiation is in fact provided for by the law on agile working, as we will see, but it is, however, at the center of remote working in many legal systems as a voluntary provision). Perhaps for the first time not two, but three regulatory sources are at work with equal dignity in the discipline of the institute: law, collective bargaining, and individual autonomy.

In an Italian Group agreement (*Leonardo*), the parties established that "agile working is a model of work organization that combines greater autonomy, within the context of a relationship of trust between employee and manager, allows for greater orientation toward objectives already set at the beginning of the activity."

The survey conducted by the Committee established at the Italian Ministry of Labor in 2021/2022 found that agile-remote working can promote the balance between personal and work spheres, but also autonomy and individual responsibility toward achieving objectives, also favoring a saving in terms of costs and a positive impact on productivity. Likewise, the analysis conducted by the study group also made it possible to detect some critical issues, including those linked to the dimensions of coordination of the agile worker with the overall organization of work, the sharing of information, the reduction of response times, to the correct balance of pauses. The conclusions of the Ministry's working group state that:

> The social partners seeing as a great boost to the achievement of personal and organizational objectives, functional, effective and modern, a new conception of work organization, less pyramidal and more oriented towards objectives and work phases, such as to allow both a better conciliation of work and lifetimes, in the interests of the worker, and a more productive and streamlined organization, in the interests of the employer.

## 6.6 AUTONOMY AND FREEDOM

There is no doubt, for the reasons we have expressed so far, that these elements of autonomy, on the one hand, and trust, on the other, are connected to the modification of the how of work, of how the worker experiences his professional activity and the margins of action he has at his disposal to make his work an activity with meaning, not alienated (as far as it is possible to de-alienate work in a capitalist productive system of production).

The connection between autonomy, trust, and objectives is the heart of the model, and implies a necessary transformation of the traditional approach to legal subordination as a necessary and typical condition of the employee. It is known that this normative notion of subordination represents the fulcrum around which labor law was built as a discipline for the protection of the worker against the power of the employer. The power of the employer is not simply the expression of an imbalance of negotiating power between the parties, and it is not simply a private power of the company, attributable to the need that every company has to organize the means of production. The employer's power is foreseen (and legitimized) by the legal system in the very definition of employment relationship or the subjective figure of the employee, be it of a legal nature or jurisprudential.

This traditional paradigm of labor law can, however, be modified by the same legislator who, at the origin of labor law, effectively legitimized the social and economic power of the capitalists. The Italian law on agile working has started this journey. While qualifying the relationship as subordinate, and without abolishing the powers of the employer, the law has introduced changes that cannot be traced back to the traditional model, even allowing the worker to be able to *negotiate* those powers to create a set of interests consistent with the purpose of the law. But subordination is undergoing some transformation processes also at the level of the concrete organization of work, increasingly guided by an organizational rationality no longer focused on hierarchy and control but on autonomy and trust. These elements of autonomy must be specified and can also be modeled. Starting from the idea of personal autonomy proposed by Joseph Raz as "the vision of people controlling, to some degree, their own destiny, fashioning it through successive decisions throughout their lives" (Raz 1986), it was proposed to relate the worker's autonomy to work itself through job satisfaction and job security that derives from the personal experiences at the workplace, or arise from the worker's ability to control his or her working life (Lofaso 2007). In this perspective, the worker's autonomy presupposes a plurality of conditions, such as the mental ability to identify and know how to resolve issues that affect his working life, the access to information sufficient to generate a range of options to workers, the independence from coercive power, and the modes of participation that empower the worker to effect changes in his working life. By applying this scheme to remote work, we can verify the worker's degree of autonomy and the deviations from the command-and-control paradigm typical of the status of subordination.

It is first of all clear that, with reference to the definition proposed by Raz, the remote worker controls his own (working) destiny in a much more meaningful and effective way than a traditional worker, subjected to a rigid hierarchy, to a fixed working time, to spatial limits and to assiduous, direct and continuous controls by management. Being able to achieve objectives in relative autonomy, being able to manage working time autonomously, enjoying a much greater level of trust and recognition than the standard worker, the remote worker can to a certain extent be considered the actor and author of his own working life. Voluntarily deciding to work remotely, consensually defining the patterns of remote work (which days to be present and which days to be remote) and being able to balance, with greater breadth than the standard worker, the needs of the company with personal needs also in terms of place and time of performance, being responsible for the achievement of objectives without being subjected to slavish control of work performance, the remote worker can certainly be said to be more independent from the employer's coercion than the standard worker. Naturally, to these dimensions of autonomy, typical of remote work, we must add all the other elements of work autonomy deriving from legislative labor rights, collective bargaining, and systems of participation or industrial democracy, where existing, which concern the entire group of company workers.

Another theoretical framework that can be usefully used to evaluate the morphogenesis of subordination in the context of remote work is that of the freedom (positive, not negative) of the worker, in the different theoretical declinations that this freedom can take. Also in this case, the worker's autonomy constitutes a countervailing force to capital in the workplace (Lofaso 2007), but the theoretical presuppositions of this autonomy are part of broader theories of moral philosophy and political philosophy that must be adapted to the context of work, to the workplace, to the logic and rationality of the company.

The three main theories on positive freedom are neo-republicanism, which preaches an idea of freedom different from the liberal one (understood as simple non-interference) and which allows active participation of the citizen in the decisions of public power; the capabilities approach, which focuses on the guarantee of a decalogue of fundamental rights and on the possibility of the subject to acquire different functioning alternatives; and social freedom based on recognition, that is, on an intersubjective relationship between parties who recognize each other, and mutually attribute the dignity of autonomous and self-conscious persons.

The command-and-control model, the exercise of directive and control powers, and the strict and invasive direct surveillance that management can exercise within the walls of the factory or office are all factors that prevent the worker from freely exercising alternative functioning and enjoying recognition as an autonomous and self-conscious person. The idea of business presupposed by the principle of authority, the lack of fiduciary openings toward a worker-subject who must be continuously monitored, and the presence of a management that prescribes and punishes are the antipodes of the principle of positive freedom, and are instead entirely consistent with the idea of negative freedom, which is not interested in the spaces of positive freedom and is not concerned with removing the economic and social obstacles and constraints that limit or prevent the enjoyment of this positive freedom. In a word, subordination is the basis of a condition of alienation of work which prevents people from acquiring his own self-awareness through work and from realizing the desire for recognition which is the basis of social freedom. And this is even more true as the conflict with positive freedom risks increasing exponentially due to an increasingly invasive technological innovation that reduces the margins of discretion and autonomy of work (Supiot 2017), and by legislative developments aimed at strengthening managerial prerogatives in order to consolidate employer's capacity to determine the terms of the contract of employment.

To achieve positive freedom in the workplace it is necessary to redefine the legal concept of subordination, reducing the potential for domination that it presupposes and which in fact takes place within the employment relationship. If positive freedom is not the mere absence of constraint on the subject but is autonomy, that is, the positive ability to determine one's own choices by oneself, that ability needs a "training" process that makes it mature and robust: That is, it will have to go through the various articulations of recognition. In fact, both within the neo-republican and neo-Hegelian perspective, individual freedom may not be exercised subjectively, but only intersubjectively (Cabrelli and Zahan 2017), that is in the social and institutional dynamics of recognition and to the extent that subjects enjoy protection and resources available to exercise their functions (Schuppert 2014), as also suggested by the capabilities approach (Sen 2007; Pettit 2015; Del Punta 2019).

Remote work, with its potential for liberation from the stringent constraints of the Taylor-Fordist work organization, makes it possible to address in a new way the issue of subordination and the democratic deficit that characterizes the employment relationship. This is possible only when remote work is not identified with teleworking, if it does not fall flat on the scheme of externally directed work from home, as happened in the COVID-19 period (Sostero et al. 2020). In other words, the perspective cultivated here requires moving to trust-based remote working models and forms of organization which do not bind the worker to a "fixed and predetermined" place and which do not electronically or digitally reproduce the constraints of management and control typical of the work performance carried out within the physical perimeter of the company.

## 6.7 A FORM OF HYBRID REMOTE WORKING: THE "AGILE" WORKING

In this perspective, a comparative reference to Italian legislation may be useful. Law N. 81/2017 introduced a peculiar form of remote work, which is called *agile work* and which differs from the more classic telework. While teleworking constitutes a form of organization and/or performance of work where the work performance is *regularly carried out outside the premises of the company* (as stated in Article 1 of the European Framework Agreement on Telework), agile work is a *hybrid form* of work, which provides for the performance partly in the company premises and partly outside, *in any other place*. Agile work is defined as "a mode of execution of the employment relationship established by an (individual) agreement between the parties, also with forms of organization by phases, cycles and objectives and *without precise obligations of working hours or workplace*, with the possible use of technological tools in order to carry out the work activity" (Art. 18, Law N. 81/2017). Work is performed partly within the company and partly outside without a fixed workstation, only within the limits of the maximum duration of the daily and weekly working hours imposed by law and by collective bargaining.

What is remarkable about this definition is the flexibility it entails in terms of work execution: (1) there is no legal obligation to respect working hours (but there is, in order to protect the worker, a constraint not to exceed the maximum limits set by law and by collective bargaining); (2) there is no legal constraint of the place of work performance; (3) there is no legal obligation to carry out a simple work activity, because the concept of work refers to goals (as well as phases or cycles), therefore to measurable results (this seems to bring the employment relationship closer to the paradigm of self-employment, which is normally an obligation of result, namely the execution of the work as an "opus" agreed in the contract, and not an obligation of means); (4) there is no obligation to use technological tools to perform the work, but this is only a possibility.

Another decisive aspect to be highlighted concerns the purpose of agile work. Normally, the employment relationship is carried out in the exclusive interest of the company. The law does not direct the employment relationship (or the methods of carrying out the work activity) toward an objective recognized as being of interest to the worker. If anything, there may be individual/collective legal institutions that serve an interest of the worker in the context of the work performance (e.g., the regulation of parental leave). However, in the case of agile work, the Italian law establishes that such flexible working method has a specific end within the interest of the worker: facilitating the reconciliation of life and working time. It is true that alongside this end, the law also provides for the goal to increase the competitiveness of the company. However, while the increase in productivity seems to be a (hoped for or expected) *effect* of agile work – due to the improvement of the worker's personal situation in terms of satisfaction and of well-being – the social purpose, in order to make the worker able to reconcile work with private life, is the real objective of the regulation.

This social aim of reconciling life and work is particularly relevant in the public sector. The Guidelines of the Ministry of Public Function on agile work in Public Administrations (2017) provide the right key to interpreting the legislation on agile work, establishing that Public Administrations identify "the innovative methods, alternatives to teleworking, most suited to the needs of work-life balance for workers" and that "measures for reconciling working life and family life can increase individual and organizational productivity." A monitoring system is also advocated for, in order to verify "the impact that the conciliation measures have in terms of organization and the quality of the services provided." In essence, the guidelines clearly indicate that the purpose of agile work in the public sector is to reconcile the life and working time of employees and in this way increase productivity and improve services, to be understood as a secondary effect of the increase of worker satisfaction and well-being.

The Italian legislator has therefore seemingly supported, even before this emerged in the post-pandemic period, a clear subjective option for new forms of work activity that are closely related to people's well-being. In empirical research this social propensity is described as the sum of three components: the "subjective" (or hedonic) well-being focuses on the aspect of experiencing a pleasant life a combination of positive emotions, satisfactory working life, lack of negative effects, and so on; the "eudaimonic" well-being is focused on flourishing, self-realization, or positive psychological functioning; the "social" well-being focuses on the quality connections that are seen as sources of energy, social contribution, and integration (Microsoft New Future of Work Report 2022). The interplay between work and personal life fits into this complex dimension of well-being at work, activating a series of subjective transformations that have yet to find a precise legal formalization, but which, nonetheless, can be linked to the positive effects of flexible work in the interest of the worker. In this perspective, work–life balance represents an overcoming of work–life conflict. While such model sees work and life as competing factors, in a zero-sum game where the time dedicated to one of the two spheres is subtracted from the needs of the other, in the work–life balance model the focus shifts toward acknowledging equal importance of both work and life in the work–life relationship. In the work–life balance model, satisfaction arises from the possibility of performing and controlling multiple roles, and of being able to carry out activities compatible with the priorities emerging from the vital world. The next step leads to the work–life integration model where work and life demands are dynamic and transactional, with fluid and always balanced priorities between one sphere and the other.

## 6.8 THE DISCIPLINE OF THE MANAGERIAL PREROGATIVES IN THE "AGILE" MODE

As we have seen, in the agile work scheme the methods of exercising the employer's powers (the directive power, the control power, and the disciplinary power) are defined in the individual agreement with a purpose that is not only productive but social, that is, to make the worker able to reconcile work and lifetime. Using the language of the capabilities approach, the purpose of the law is to make the powers of the employer consistent with the worker's life needs and thus make him acquire a real alternative of functioning (Langille 2019). Agile work therefore affects the very autonomy of organizational power, which must be rethought according to an objective of conciliation. It can be argued that even if an employee is working away from the employer's premises it is still the employer who determines the purpose and the means of the work. However, this observation cannot be applied to the scheme of agile work, which functionalizes the directive power for a conciliation purpose and above all requires that the methods of exercising power be negotiated to be adequate with respect to the purpose set by the law. On the other hand, the range of work activities that can be carried out remotely and in a hybrid form such as agile work are not only that of data processing, but potentially any activity that has the content of technical analysis, study, design, and implementation of projects. This new management philosophy is therefore based on giving people back flexibility and autonomy in choosing spaces, hours, tools to use, and the operating methods in order to achieve objectives, with a greater accountability concerning results.

The agreement related to agile work regulates the exercise of the employer's directive power. From a theoretical point of view, negotiating the modalities of exercising a power means making this power less unilateral: It means reducing this power to a consensual element of the contract. The rationale for this provision is twofold. On the one hand, considering the specific purpose of agile work (reconciling life and work time), the parties must identify the methods of exercising the directive power that are most consistent with the purpose to be achieved. Indeed, it would be inconsistent with the purpose of the law if the employer exercised the directive power in such a way as to prevent conciliation (by ordering continuous changes in the place of work, by ordering compliance with a rigidly predetermined working time, etc.).

In the public sector, the Guidelines suggest that instead of traditional controls, the individual agreement on the exercise of the power of control could provide for availability periods according to general needs, in order to ensure coordination of the work performance with the overall organization of the employer. Given the purpose of reconciling working activity with the need for protection, the Guidelines state that the control power must be exercised with regard to the results of the work performance, in both quantitative and qualitative terms, in relation to the priorities defined by the manager. The verification of the achievement of the objectives also adapts to this new scheme, and is carried out through a report agreed between the manager and the worker, or through moments of discussion during the days the worker is on site. As can be seen in the Guidelines on agile work, there are no indications for the exercise of the control power in an authoritative form, but in a completely consensual one. This cannot fail to have important theoretical and practical consequences on the redefinition of the concept of subordination that emerges from this regulatory model.

## 6.9 FINAL OBSERVATIONS

The analysis carried out attempted to clarify in what terms the post-pandemic remote working model can actually contribute to evolving the concept of subordination in a new direction, based on the trust and autonomy of the worker. Although inserted in a process of capitalist valorization of human work, the organizational redesign of the organization of work guided by a genuine desire to make the worker freer, more autonomous, able to acquire a degree unprecedented control of a production process in which it participates in a not completely externally directed way, can be an achievable objective. This perspective is based on normative elements that we believe we have identified in the most recent trends of collective bargaining and social dialogue, which mark a until recently unexpected transition toward quality forms of work organization, centered on autonomy and trust, and designed to facilitate the reconciliation of work and lifetimes.

## REFERENCES

Butera, F., Le condizioni organizzative e professionali dello smart working dopo l'emergenza: progettare il lavoro ubiquo fatto di ruoli aperti e di professioni a larga banda, *Studi Organizzativi*, Vol. 1, 2020, p. 143.

Cabrelli, D., Zahan, R., Theories of domination and labour law: An alternative conception for intervention?, *The International Journal of Comparative Labour Law*, vol. 33(3), 2017, p. 339.

Coase, R., The nature of the firm, *Economica*, Vol. 4, 1937, p. 386.

Countouris, V. De Stefano, Out of sight, out of mind? Remote work and contractual distancing, in Nicola Countouris, De Stefano, V., et al. (eds.), *The Future of Remote Work*, ETUI, The European Trade Union Institute, Brussels, 2023.

De Stefano, V., Durri, I., Stylogiannis, C., Wouters, M., Does labour law trust workers? Questioning underlying assumptions behind managerial prerogatives, *Industrial Law Journal*, Vol. 53(2), June 2024, p. 206.

Deakin, S., The corporation as commons: rethinking property rights, governance and sustainability in the business enterprise, *Queen's Law Journal*, Vol. 37(I.2), 2012, p. 373.

Del Punta, R., Is the capability theory an adequate normative theory for labor law?, in B. Langille (ed.), *The Capability Approach to Labor Law*, Oxford University Press, Oxford, 2019, p. 82.

Giotto, T., Thoemmes, J., La négociation du télétravail: dynamique, variété et fragilité, *Negociations*, Vol. 38 (2), Feb 2022, p. 35.

Hirschman, A.O., *Exit, Voice, and Loyalty. Responses to Decline in Firms, Organizations, and States*. Harvard University Press, Cambridge, MA, 1970.

Junge, K., *The Impact of Teleworking and Digital Work on Workers and Society*, Policy Department for Economic, Scientific and Quality of Life Policies, Directorate-General for Internal Policies, European Parliament, April 2021.

Langille, B., *The Capability Approach to Labour Law*, Oxford University Press, Oxford, 2019.

Lofaso, A.M., Toward a fundamental theory of workers' rights: the autonomous dignified worker, *UMKC Law Review*, Vol. 75, 2007, p. 39.

Luhmann, N., *Trust and Power: Two Works*, Jon Wiley & Sons, Chichester-New York-Brisbane-Toronto, 1979.

Ouchi, W.G., Markets, bureaucracies, and clans, *Administrative Science Quarterly*, Vol. 25(1), 1980, p. 125.

Pettit, P., A brief history of liberty and its lessons, *Journal of Human Development and Capabilities*, Vol. 17 (1), Jan. 2015, p. 12.

Raz, J., *The Morality of Freedom*, Oxford University Press, Oxford, 1986.

Schuppert, F., *Freedom, Recognition and Non-Domination. A Republican Theory of (Global) Justice*, Springer, Heidelberg, New York, London, 2014.

Sen, A., *Individual Freedom as a Social Commitment*, Laterza, Bari-Roma, 2007.

Sostero, M., Milasi, S., Hurley, J., Fernandez-Macías, E., Bisello, M., *Teleworkability and the COVID-19 Crisis: A New Digital Divide?*, European Commission, Seville, 2020.

Supiot, A., *Governance by Numbers: The Making of a Legal Model of Allegiance*, Hart Publishing, Oxford, 2017.

# 7

# Cross-Border Remote Workers and the Virtual Place of Work

## *New Pressure on the Territorial Application of Labour Law*

*Alexandre de le Court*

### 7.1 DIGITALISATION AND REMOTE WORK: NEW OPPORTUNITIES FOR THE DEMUTUALISATION OF RISKS TO WORKERS

Remote work and, more specifically, telework have risen to the foreground since the pandemic. Even if post-pandemic figures point towards a decrease in telework, the transformation of jobs and the possibilities given by new technologies have created new realities centred around the remote performance of work. Its significance as an instrument in the context of work–life balance[1] or the appearance of the concept of digital nomad[2] are but two examples among others. Remote work has thus not only become more important because of its greater weight between the different modalities in which work is organised. It has also come to the foreground of social, political and academic interest.

One of the different notions it challenges is the notion of workplace through its virtual extension from the premises or establishment of the employer (or the employers' client) to the home of the worker or even any other place allowing the connection with the employers' organisation. In Labour Law, the workplace is a legal concept which has significance in different ways. While through the right of ownership, as a means of production, it enables the powers of the employer, it serves as a concept limiting the scope of application of the exercise of those powers, even if new technologies involve a relativisation of this spatial limitation[3]. It also serves as a reference for the exercise of employers' responsibilities, above all in terms of health and safety[4]. The workplace is also generally taken as a reference for the recognition

1 Eurofound 2020 at 13–26; Atkinson 2022; Arabadjieva 2022.

2 Rasnača 2023.

3 See, for example, the use of position trackers or the question of employer control through cameras or other technological means when working from home.

4 See, for example, in the EU context, the mentions of the 'workplace' in Directive 89/391 – OSH 'Framework Directive' of 12 June 1989 on the introduction of measures to encourage improvements in the safety and health of workers at work, or Directive 89/654/EEC of

of rights of representation of workers, sometimes translated through the concept of establishment of the employer[5]. Finally, as developed hereunder, the workplace is an important notion in establishing the applicable law in cross-border employment situations.

The surge of remote work involves some disruption in the application of the rules depending on the concept of workplace and their function of guaranteeing workers' rights and interests and defining responsibilities of employers. This surge also changes the framework within which employer responsibilities are exercised. The diffusion of the notion of workplace increases the possibilities for employers to evade their responsibilities and decrease individual and, above all, collective response through invisibilisation, atomisation and the shifting of costs in terms of means of production, health and safety, and so on, a process that amounts to the demutualisation of the risks surrounding work[6].

But when remote work has a cross-border character, that is, when worker and employer find themselves in different legal jurisdictions, the diffusion of the notion of workplace (and correlative rights and responsibilities) acquires an additional dimension, which is the possibility to apply to the worker an employment and social protection regime which can be more beneficial to the employer than the regime applicable to the worker if she were working at the premises of the employer or if she were working remotely, but in the same jurisdiction. Generally, the surge in technologies and new types of jobs increase the easiness with which remote work can happen in a cross-border situation and creates new possibilities for companies to delocalise the workforce, without delocalising physically themselves, opening new establishments abroad or extending supply chains internationally through subcontracting. Delocalisation happens thus without almost any movement of capital or workers, escaping more classical modes of migration, and shifts the legal perspective from the provision of services or the sale of goods towards the contract of employment.

While this phenomenon does not seem generally extended yet, it cannot be dismissed as purely potential, given already existing practices and the awareness of companies to the new management techniques it offers[7]. Some states have recently

30 November 1989 concerning the minimum safety and health requirements for the workplace.

5 See, for example, again in the EU context, article 1.1 of Council Directive 98/59/EC of 20 July 1998 on the approximation of the laws of the Member States relating to collective redundancies; Barreda 2023 cites the *Unifor* decision of the Tribunal Administratif du Travail of Quebec, where the notion of establishment was reinterpreted teleologically and extended to the workplace of teleworkers to ensure prohibition of strikebreaking by workers 'of the establishment' where the strike is taking place.

6 On the concept of demutualisation of risks to workers, see Countouris and Freedland 2013.

7 Barreda 2024; Baldwin and Dingel 2021; Boulay-Esperonnier et al. 2021.

started to provide special visa regimes for 'digital nomads'[8]. While virtual delocalisation, also coined 'telemigration'[9], does not necessarily aim to decrease labour costs or the demutualisation of risks[10], it is undeniable that those possible consequences can be seen as strong incentives to have recourse to that practice. Also, as shown in the different court decisions analysed hereunder, legal problems and conflicts of laws in cross-border remote work are not as much a 'sleeper' as a few years ago, when recent literature on the matter started to appear[11].

Some forms of demutualisation through legal means taking advantage of disparities between jurisdictions can affect general labour conditions (salary, working time, etc.), or the legality of arbitration clauses[12], but it would not be unreasonable to imagine that status of employment can become a central concern. As an important range of labour rights depend on the recognition of that status, offshoring work to jurisdictions allowing for easier application of the status of independent contractor might become an important demutualisation practice[13]. And considering that telework or remote work might involve a certain relativisation of the notion of subordination, as argued by Adalberto Perulli in his chapter in this book, doubts about a consistent recognition of the status of employee across borders cannot be dismissed.

Moreover, employers have not only more choices of jurisdictions under which the working conditions of their employees could be regulated, but they start also having a larger workforce from which to recruit. They can 'enlarge the labour pool' to workers located in other countries. This does not only in itself put pressure on wages of certain sectors because of the increase in competition, but also by enlarging possibilities to employ workers in countries with lower labour protections, without the need to physically relocate[14]. As such, this increases the possibility for social dumping. Not only social dumping in its 'lighter' meaning, as used, for example, by

8 For Spain, see the recently introduced chapter V BIS on 'International Teleworkers' in *Law 14/ 2013 of 27 September supporting entrepreneurs and their internationalisation.*

9 Baldwin and Dingel 2021.

10 Barreda 2024 cites as an example the practice of 'nearshoring' workers not able to acquire residence rights in the United States and thus working remotely for US companies while acquiring residence rights in Canada.

11 Cherry 2020 at 23.

12 Garden 2018.

13 Grušić 2023; Countouris and De Stefano 2023 write about the heightened risk for 'contractual distancing' in the context of telework. Forum shopping to avoid recognition of employment status could also reduce the effects of the goal of the Platform Work Directive, as voted in the European Parliament on 24 April 2024 to extend the status of employee to platform workers offering services that can be done remotely through Technology in two ways: firstly, within the EU, by contracting workers established in EU Member States leaning towards a model of independent contracting, like France, given the 'lighter version' of the presumption of employment in the current draft compared to the Commission's proposal; and, secondly, by offshoring the tasks to countries where the Directive does not apply, due to its limitation to 'platform work performed in the EU'. Concerning this question, see also Golub 2023.

14 Grušić 2023; Kakkad et al. 2021, 35; Althoff et al. 2022.

Catherine Barnard when she refers to the possibility to replace workers by cheaper ones[15] and increase the probability of movements keen to races to the bottom. But it increases also the possibility of social dumping as defined by the European Parliament in its Resolution of 14 September 2016 on social dumping in the European Union, according to which 'the concept covers a wide range of intentionally abusive practices and the circumvention of existing European and national legislation (including laws and universally applicable collective agreements), which enable the development of unfair competition by unlawfully minimising labour and operation costs and lead to violations of workers' rights and exploitation of workers'.

One could argue that the possibility to offshore new types of jobs towards countries with lower standards of living is not to be seen as something negative, above all from the perspective of the countries seeing job opportunities grow, and generally of jobs which could be considered as being of a higher quality[16]. However, one has also to consider the disrupting effects this might have in the offshoring countries, without guaranteeing perfectly proportional corresponding benefits in the receiving countries. Moreover, possible benefits might not offset the potential problems caused by the lack of physical link between employer and worker abroad, and the consequent precarious situation of isolated workers. And this above all when considering that the work provided might be 'gig work' or crowdwork in an important number of cases[17]. Another dimension to be considered is the imbalance existing between the (legal or real) possibilities of employers to virtually delocalise abroad and the right of workers to perform cross-border remote work. Most court decisions until now seem to refuse recognising such right[18]. Also, the international element adds to the deficit and difficulties for solidarity between workers. The possible application of different national laws might have a negative impact on representation and collective bargaining and might involve a fragmentation of that representation[19]. Moreover, the surge in cross-border remote work has also brought forwards

[15] Barnard 2009, 311.

[16] See Bercusson and Estlund (2008), who speak about the 'race to the rising bottom'.

[17] Cherry 2020.

[18] In Germany: *Arbeitsgericht München*, judgment of 27.08.2021 (12 Ga 62/21), given, inter alia, the risks for the employer in terms of shifting legal and financial consequences, and Landesarbeitsgericht Köln, judgment of 07.03.2024 (9 TaBV 6/24); in France: *Cour d'Appel de Toulouse*, judgment of 8 September 2023 (RG 22/00680) citing legal, social and tax concerns as well as time zone differences; in Canada, see Barreda 2023, 101. In a different register, the French Cour de Cassation, in its judgment of 27 November 2003 (12–24.880), considered that the lack of express authorisation from the company to continue to partially telework from France instead of the UK was an element to consider that the habitual place of work could not be France.

[19] Grušić 2023; for example, to what extent could remote workers be excluded from the number of employees of an establishment needed to grant specific collective rights to the workers of that establishment.

problems in terms of adscription to social security systems[20], and this might also be another factor incentivising delocalisation, or hampering performance of cross-border telework as a right of workers. Finally, the new cross-border situations that are created by the surge in remote work present challenges to legal certainty in terms of the laws applicable to the different relationships[21], as well as where possible actions can be brought in case of conflict[22].

All those problems are increased by the diversity in remote work situations with a digital component. The determination of the applicable law to permanent cross-border remote workers, digital nomads[23], workers teleworking only partly abroad[24], posted teleworkers, cross-border crowdworkers[25] or platform workers[26], as well as their vulnerabilities, differs greatly.

The following section contains a brief discussion of the existing rules determining the applicable law on the contract of employment in cross-border situations and argues that they are not adapted to the new realities of the enhanced digitalisation of remote work. The third section is dedicated to analysing how the existing framework could be reinterpreted to bring it more in line with those new realities, starting from the discussion of existing cases where new approaches were proposed in litigation. The last section briefly argues that remote work is another field where we must think about new techniques for the extraterritorial application of labour law.

## 7.2 CROSS-BORDER REMOTE WORK AND THE INADEQUACY OF THE TRADITIONAL CONFLICT OF LAW RULES CONCERNING EMPLOYMENT CONTRACTS

According to Article 8 of the Rome I Regulation, which defines the conflict rules when a case is brought before the courts of the Member States of the EU, the applicable law to an employment relationship is that which has been contractually chosen by the parties. This connecting factor has only a relative importance,

[20] During the pandemic and the temporal surge in cross-border telework, the Administrative Commission for the Coordination of Social Security Systems (EU) 'clarified' existing rules, based on the place of performance of work as provided by enshrined in Article 11 of EU Regulation 883/2004, through guidance notes, to avoid that cross-border teleworkers working above 25 per cent of the time at their residence abroad would see a change in the applicable social security law. Since the 1 July 2023 EU a new (definitive) guidance note clarifies the possible exceptions to the rule of the place of performance of work and a voluntary Framework Agreement exists to avoid the application of the law of residence when telework is performed there in some cases (up to 49 per cent of the time) which would not be covered by the exceptions to the principle of art. 11 of Regulation 883/2004.

[21] Barreda 2024, 100.

[22] Barreda 2023.

[23] Rasnača 2023.

[24] Rosin 2024.

[25] Cherry 2020; Carinci and Henke 2021.

[26] Golub 2023.

however, because (i) in the absence of choice, other connecting factors apply and (ii) in any case, provisions which can only be waived to the profit of the worker (mandatory provisions) which would apply according to those other connecting factors have precedence on the applicable law chosen by the parties[27].

According to Article 8(2) of Rome I Regulation, thus, in the absence of choice of law, the 'main' applicable law is the 'law of the country *in* which or, failing that, *from* which the employee habitually carries out his work in performance of the contract', being understood that this law will not change in case the worker is temporarily employed in another country. Therefore, in a situation where a worker is hired to work remotely from the country where she resides for an employer in another country, the law of her country of residence would apply[28]. According to the CJEU, it is the place where the worker fulfils her economic and social duties and where the business and political environment affects employment activities[29].

On the other hand, it would be less clear if cross-border hybrid forms of work, where the worker works remotely in one country and works part of the time at the employers' location in another country, would involve the application of the law of the former. According to the jurisprudence of the CJEU, the 'habitual place of work' is the one where the worker carries out the 'essential' part of her duties, which would be a question of importance[30], even if according to earlier jurisprudence the amount of time worked at one physical place, or another, is not to be ruled out[31].

Furthermore, when the applicable law cannot be determined with reference to the 'habitual place of work', the 'contract shall be governed by the law of the country where the place of business through which the employee was engaged is situated'. While the CJEU has interpreted that alternative criterion in a restrictive way[32], it seems that this definition might be applicable in the case of digital nomads, because their moving between different places without being possible to distinguish in which of the places the essential part of their duties is performed makes it impossible to ascertain the habitual place of work.

Also, Article 8 of the Rome I Regulation contains an 'escape clause', according to which 'where it appears from the circumstances as a whole that the contract is more closely connected with [another] country [...], the law of that other country shall apply'. In application thereof, another law than the habitual place of work or the place of engagement could apply if it is showed that the centre of gravity of the relationship is situated in another country. For this, elements like the place where

[27] CJEU, judgment of 15 July 2021, cases C-152/20 and C-218/20 (*Grüber Logistics*); see also Carinci and Henke 2021, 138 or Rosin 2024.

[28] Bruurs 2023; Grušić 2023; Rosin 2024.

[29] CJEU, judgment of 15 March 2011, case C-29/10 (*Koelzsch*), at 42.

[30] CJEU, judgment of 14 September 2017, cases C-168/16 and C-169/16 (*Nogueira and others*), at 58–59.

[31] Carinci and Henke 2021, 139.

[32] Carinci and Henke 2021, 140.

taxes are paid or where social security coverage is given, or the parameters relating to salary determination and other working conditions, have to be taken into consideration, applying a qualitative, and not quantitative, approach[33]. In 2020, the Dutch *Rechtbank Midden-Nederland* applied the escape clause in a case where the worker was habitually (tele)working in the Netherlands for a company situated in London, after having worked 'hybridly' in England[34]. The plaintiff considered that the termination of her contract was not valid under the law of the Netherlands and, thus, claimed the payment of salary. The court deemed the law of England and Wales applicable to the contract, despite the fact that taxes and social contributions were paid in the Netherlands, because (i) the decision to move to the Netherlands was made by the worker to allow her to stay with her husband, and was 'only' tolerated by the company which had no interest in such a move; and (ii) the company had no establishment or any activity in the Netherlands. The court recognised that, while Article 8 of the Rome I Regulation had as an objective the protection of the weaker party, given the circumstances of the case, the worker could not claim such protection. While this decision can be criticised for not interpreting restrictively the escape clause and asking for 'interest' of the company in cross-border remote work for worker protection[35], it shows that other considerations can be taken into consideration, like the location of the activity of the company.

The Rome I Regulation only operates within the sphere of the EU, but the Private International Law rules to establish the law applicable to the contract of employment in the rest of the world tend to follow the same principles. As a few examples found in the literature, one can cite Canada[36], countries of North-Eastern Asia[37], Togo[38] or India[39,40].

Even if the overall logic of those connecting factors is the protection of the workers as a weaker party in a contract, this is not done directly, but only through the application of a logic of proximity with the physical place of work or the close connections with the place where the relationship is principally embedded. The logic of protection and the logic of embeddedness coincide in case of work performed at the premises of the employer but can diverge in case of cross-border remote work, contrary to what the CJEU seems to understand in *Koelzsch*[41].

33 CJEU, judgment of 12 September 2013, case C-64/12 (*Schlecker*), at 40–41.

34 Rechtbank Midden-Nederland, judgment of 27.08.2020 (8627715 MV EXPL 20–84).

35 Carinci and Henke 2021, 7, advocate a restrictive interpretation to avoid that the employer can choose the applicable law through its control of the elements justifying a closer connection to the forum of its choice.

36 Barreda 2023, who treats the problem posed by telework on the Federal and Provincial PIL rules.

37 Suk 2015.

38 Avegnon 2023.

39 Cherry 2020, at 22.

40 According to Cherry 2020, the US approach based on the concept of 'governmental interest' seems to amount also to the application of the habitual place of work, at least in California.

41 CJEU judgment of 15 March 2011, case C-29/10.

The application of the habitual place of work as general connection factor and the strict interpretation of the exceptions have as consequence that, in case of cross-border remote work, and above all telework, the presumed link between the place of work and the activity of the company can be severed[42]. As such, the 'habitual place of work' is not necessarily the place where, according to the CJEU, 'the business and political environment affects employment activities'.

Therefore, the territorial character of the application of norms, which seems to be confirmed by the principle of the habitual place of work as connecting factor, allows employers to delocalise employment in countries with less strict protection through permanent or at least long-term remote work, without the necessity to have any activity in those countries (nor in the country of the business or establishment, for that matter). This also raises the question of equal treatment between employees of a same company, who might see applicable different regimes in function of their place of work, while possibly being part of the same 'virtual' team. And this runs contrary to the principle of equal treatment between teleworkers and 'presential' workers enshrined in most of the recent legal frameworks regulating telework[43].

There is also a question of unequal treatment between the application of the habitual place of work in the absence of choice of applicable law in the contract and the application of the same connecting factor when parties have chosen to apply the law of the employers' location to the contract. In the second case, according to Article 8 (1) of the Regulation, the choice of law expressed by the parties "*may not, however, have the result of depriving the employee of the protection afforded to him by provisions that cannot be derogated from by agreement under the law that, in the absence of choice, would have been applicable pursuant*" to the connecting factors applicable in the absence of choice of law. The system of the most favourable provisions between the forum of the business of the employer and the forum where the worker habitually works will only apply in case the law of the former has been chosen contractually, but not if no choice has been expressed[44].

Another problem is to be found in the fact that overriding the choice of applicable law expressed in the contract is only available if the contract is an individual contract of employment. Those protective rules therefore do not generally apply in relations between self-employed and their clients. Here, technology connecting workers with their 'employers' could be used to 'hire' workers in forums which make it more difficult to detect bogus self-employment. Also, the existence of self-employed status makes it easier to impose conflict resolution agreements which might avoid the application of the judicial forum rules, making it also more difficult to bring

[42] Barreda 2023, 38.
[43] Ibid.
[44] Carinci and Henke 2021; Barreda 2023, 5; Bruurs 2023.

proceedings to the courts of the location of the employer, which renders more difficult to apply possible solutions as proposed in the next section[45].

Within the EU context, the application of the EU-notion of worker to Article 8 of the Rome I Regulation involves, however, some harmonisation in this matter, so some authors do not see great risks in that respect[46]. But this leaves the rest of the world out of the picture, as well as those categories which are situated between the EU notion of worker, which has been criticised to leave out problematic forms of personal work and genuine self-employed[47], and which might involve different levels of protection in different countries, so that some 'applicable law shopping' might be done by employers.

### 7.3 REMOTE WORK AND THE RECONSTITUTION OF THE FRAGMENTED CROSS-BORDER PLACE OF WORK

Litigation in matters of conflict of laws in cross-border remote work situations in their new context is quite recent and jurisprudence is scarce. However, some rulings have already addressed the attempts to reconstitute the workplace in cross-border remote cases based on the proposal of new interpretations of existing locational factors, mainly the place of work or the establishment of the employer.

A first example can be found in cases, related to German social law, where companies without establishment in Germany tried to have their remote workers in Germany receive benefits in application of the short time working arrangements system (*Kurzarbeit*), during the suspension of activities of those companies for reasons related to the COVID pandemic. Even though the workers in question were registered with the German social security system (because they were residing and working in Germany), both the *Landessozialgericht* Berlin-Brandenburg[48] and the *Landessozialgericht* München[49] refused to recognise the extension of the right to benefits to those workers by allowing a broad interpretation of the notion of establishment or branch of the employer, to include home offices or co-working spaces. The appeal courts overturned the decisions of the lower courts by relying on the territoriality principle, rooted in the need for the state to be able to control the conditions of access to social benefits. This control would not be possible if the employer would be physically situated outside the German borders. There was thus no reason to depart from the classical interpretation of the notion of branch or establishment, according to which there must be a separate, operationally independent part of the company to which commercial, technical and personnel measures are assigned exclusively instead of to the overall organisation. The mere physical

45 Grušić 2023.

46 Ibid.

47 Countouris 2018; concerning status of employment for platform workers, see note 13.

48 *LSG Berlin-Brandenburg* 15.02.2023 – L 18 AL 46/22 R.

49 *LSG München* 09.08.2023 – L 10 AL 167/21 and L 10 AL 56/21.

distance from the employing company cannot be considered as a criterion, especially in times of modern means of communications which allow to work away from the physical offices.

Another recent example, already discussed by Barreda[50], concerns litigation on the application of Quebec labour norms on the cross-border remote work situation. The most recent case concerns a worker, Mrs Marchetta, with residence in Quebec who worked for a US company both from her home and in the United States. The company was active on the US market, but not in Canada. The worker sought to apply the Quebec law and its provisions concerning protection against dismissal, instead of the fire-at-will system of the United States. According to section 2 of *the Loi sur les Normes du Travail*, the provisions of the law apply to workers (i) when they have their place of work in Quebec, (ii) when they work both outside and inside Quebec (with a substantial part inside) for an employer established in Quebec, and (iii) when they have their residence in Quebec and work in another jurisdiction, but for an employer established in Quebec[51].

The idea that it should be the physical place of work which determines the application of the Quebec Labour Act under rule i) had already been challenged in cases where remote work was performed in Canada, but outside of the province of Quebec, with the argument that with new technologies, the physical place from which the employee performs the work is of a secondary order and could thus be considered to be done at the employers' premises, situated in Quebec. The courts, however, while recognising that fact (and invoking even the possibility of legislative changes) refused to depart from the classic interpretation involving the need of physical presence at the place of work[52].

Central in the *Marchetta* case was the interpretation of the notion of establishment of a company under rule ii), necessary for it to be in Quebec for the law to apply to situations where a worker works both in and outside the province. According to existing interpretation, the employer must have its residence, domicile, enterprise, registered office or office in Quebec and must provide, with a certain character of permanence, services in Quebec through one or more employees. In previous cases, the fact that a sales manager worked for an American company from its home in Quebec, attending to clients in both Quebec and the United States, while the equipment (internet, computer, etc.) was provided by the employer, was deemed sufficient for the notion to apply. In the case discussed here, following this jurisprudence, the *Tribunal Administratif du Travail* found that the

[50] Barreda 2023; the article was written before the final decision of the Cour Supérieure du Quebec in the case.

[51] The 'general' conflict of law rule contained in sections 3118 of the Civil Code of Quebec is similar to the EU principles, reason for which the case analysed here is also (and above all) a problem of coordination between conflict of law rules (contained in the Civil Code) and the rules of territorial application of a substantive law; see Barreda 2023, 108–111.

[52] Barreda 2023, 102–103.

home of the worker could be considered as an office or establishment of the employer. However, the decision was overturned by a second ruling of the *Tribunal Administratif du Travail.* The *Cour supérieure du Quebec* confirmed the second judgment and found that having a computer and a phone provided by the employer was not sufficient, as other elements were needed to show 'a certain degree of organisation of the place where the employee worked, which allows to conclude that it forms a point of contact of the employer in Quebec, for some of its activities'[53]. Having an activity in the forum seems thus to be an important factor of connection, present in the case of sales representatives, but absent in this case, despite the fact that the worker seemed to exercise a substantial part of her activities in Quebec.

Moving to the EU context, would there be no space to argue that, in some circumstances, when teleworking, the place of performance of the work could be the employers' premises, as the technological environment sufficiently relativises the place where work is performed? Or conversely, if the application of the law of the forum of establishment of the employer involves weaker protection than the law of another jurisdiction to which the situation is also connected with through remote work, could this establishment be extended to the place of work in that other jurisdiction? Considering the reasoning of the court in *Koelzsch*, this seems to be difficult. However, one must not forget that the judgment is permeated with the objective of protecting the weaker party (in the case at hand, as an argument to not allow too easily the application of the second alternative criteria of Article 8, the place of engagement, i.e. the establishment of the employer). At point 46, the Court refers to recital 23 in the preamble to the Regulation to find that the interpretation of Article 8(1) 'must be prompted by the principles of *favor laboratoris* in that the weaker parties to contracts must be protected by conflict-of-law rules that are more favourable'.

Some authors argue in favour of the use of the 'place of engagement exception' (place of business of the employer) to try to solve the problems that might involve the application of the habitual place of work in case of remote work, above all when the employer has no real activity in the country from which work is provided. The argument would be based on the reconstitution of the fractured workplace through the idea that the worker would be virtually present at the place where the business of the employer is established, which is the place from which control on the worker is exercised as well as the destination of the provision of the work and the services which are sold by the employer[54], or to use a similar concept, where beneficial ownership is exercised[55].

53 *Cour Supérieure du Quebec*, judgment of 17 July 2023, 2023 QCCS 3254 at 120.
54 Martín-Pozuelo López 2020.
55 For the idea of beneficial ownership as justification of extraterritorial application of labour law, see Mundlak 2009.

However, firstly, it would be difficult to admit that this argument could amount to the idea that the habitual place of work cannot be established, which is a precondition for the application of the place of engagement exception. Secondly, such an approach does not fit within the existing systematicity of the instruments determining the applicable law, which defines the habitual place of work as the general rule, and the place of engagement as an exception to be interpreted strictly. Thirdly, and again, it is not guaranteed that the establishment of the employer is also the place of beneficial ownership.

Another possibility would be the use of the 'escape clause' to attain the same objective. Is it possible to consider that a situation where a remote worker working habitually in one country can have a closer connection with the country where the employer is established, based on the idea that establishment is to be considered as an extension of the workplace abroad? This approach could be seen as more ideal, in the sense that it provides more flexibility to consider different factors for the application of the law of the 'better' forum. The decision of the Dutch court commented above shows that the reach of the employers' activity could also be considered. The corporate motivation behind the creation of the cross-border situation could be used as an element of analysis, conducing to the application of the escape clause when the habitual place of work has been chosen to evade responsibilities or leads to social dumping. The principle of equality between on-site workers and remote workers could also be considered in this context.

Another mechanism, complementary to the first, would be the use of Article 9 of the Rome I regulation, which provides that the 'overriding mandatory provisions' of the law of the forum will apply no matter the applicable law pursuant to Article 8. As a premise, this would require that the worker would bring proceedings against her employer in a forum in the EU which would be more favourable to her. The CJEU confirms that the court of the forum cannot, in principle, apply overriding mandatory provision of another law than that of the forum, even if it is the applicable law to the contract[56]. This impedes thus, within the EU, application of the most favourable 'overriding mandatory provision' (except if, pursuant to Article 9(3) the application of mandatory provisions of the law of the place where the obligations arising out of the contract are performed render the contract unlawful). According to the Lugano Convention, as well as the Rome II regulation, a worker can always bring proceedings before the courts of the location of the employer, so this would cover the situations of delocalisation through remote work. The problem resides, however, in the uncertainty of the notion of 'overriding mandatory provisions' of labour law that would apply.

According to Article 9(1) of the Rome I Regulation, 'overriding mandatory provisions are provisions the respect for which is regarded as crucial by a country for safeguarding its public interests, such as its political, social or economic

[56] CJEU, judgment of 18 October 2016, case C-135/15 (*Nikiforidis*).

organisation, to such an extent that they are applicable to any situation falling within their scope, irrespective of the law otherwise applicable to the contract under this Regulation'. There is a lot of uncertainty concerning the interpretation of the concept, and a wide margin of appreciation seems to be given to the courts[57]. According to the CJEU, which bases its opinion on recital 37 of the Regulation, 'this exception has the purpose of enabling the court of the forum to take account of considerations of public interest in exceptional circumstances'[58]. According to the same recital, the concept 'should be distinguished from the expression "provisions which cannot be derogated from by agreement" and should be construed more restrictively'. In this context, the question arises whether a rule protecting a weaker party in a contract, like the employee, could be considered as overriding. It seems that this might be the case, among other reasons, because the CJEU has accepted that the social protection of workers involved a public interest[59]. It could also be argued that there is a recognised public interest in applying certain provisions protecting the employee working remotely from another jurisdiction (and, in the EU, above all when working from a third country), which would be combatting social dumping in the sense this chapter understands it. Having recourse to such cases of remote work has a negative impact on the labour market of the state where the employer is situated and would give those employers a competitive advantage regarding employers using the local workforce[60].

Some authors suggest that the concept of overriding mandatory provisions could be interpreted as including the minimum provided by the posted workers' directive, which would thus be applicable to telework provided from third countries[61]. They argue that the directive corrects the social dumping that the Rome I Regulation allows in case of temporary change of the place of work, and could thus be applicable in other cases where the anti-dumping function of the Rome I Regulation is thwarted by its shortcomings, and does it by selecting a series of standards which it considers essential[62]. However, one could argue that the Directive addresses an explicit exclusion of the Rome I rules, contained in the last sentence of Article 8(2), the temporary modification of the place of work of the worker. This exception was introduced not to hamper the freedom to provide services, in the context of the building of the single market. Nevertheless, EU Member States should remain free to combat social dumping operating from outside the EU and make remote work from third countries conditional on the respect of certain standards without this going against EU single market rules.

57 Van Bochove 2014, 148.
58 CJEU, judgment of 18 October 2016, case C-135/15 (*Nikiforidis*) at 43.
59 Van Bochove 2014, 150.
60 Golub 2023, 340.
61 Houwerzijl and Van Hoek 2016; Orlandini 2012; Carinci and Heke 2021.
62 Carinci and Heke 2021, 144.

In any case, the overriding mandatory provision approach is a mechanism that allows for the simultaneous application of the laws of different jurisdictions to one and the same cross-border situation, an approach which is not generally pursued by the standard conflict rules, which tend to the application of the law of a sole jurisdiction to all the conflicts arising out of the same employment relation. As such, all the circumstances surrounding a cross-border situation are considered for a solution applicable to all aspects of the relation, and no distinction is made between the types of claims made before the court. The reference to the word 'contract' as object of the closer connection analysis of art. 8(4) of the Rome I Regulation, instead of 'conflict' or a more open work like 'situation', is an example of that uniform approach. And that uniform approach, even under less 'territorial' interpretations, can favour workers when such fora offer better protection (and, in some cases, avoid social dumping practices), but might also be to their disadvantage (or encourage social dumping practices) when they are regulated by less protective labour norms[63].

Therefore, the problem is not only about which connecting factor would be better as an overall solution, but also how several objectives and interests, which can be different in each case, can be reconciled. In this context, it is important to point out that extraterritorial application of labour law does not need to be comprehensive. Some conditions, like wage rates, can be modulated in function of local realities, but others, related to health and safety, protection against dismissal or fundamental rights could be considered to have a vocation to apply universally, answering thus possible reservations against extraterritorial application[64]. Therefore, a diversified approach to the determination of the applicable law might be a step towards more adapted solutions to the complex problems posed by cross-border remote work and the conflicting interests in play, alluded to in the first section. The application of more favourable provisions in case of choice of law, the 'governmental interests' approach or the application of overriding mandatory provision of one forum together with the law of another shows that such diversified approaches exist. And in that context, the question of the status of employment, the lifting of the corporate veil and the respect of basic labour rights are paramount to finding a just balance between the different interests and could justify extraterritorial application of more favourable laws.

Finally, this section cannot be concluded without mentioning the role which can be and must be played by unions and worker representatives in the matter. An important function they could fulfil is helping remote workers located abroad to bring claims before the courts of the forum of establishment of the employer. Most possibly, lack of funds and knowledge make it virtually impossible for an individual abroad to pursue the application of more favourable norms or mandatory

63 See also Barreda 2023, 114.

64 Mundlak 2009, 214.

provisions to their contract of employment (or to assess their status of employee for the purpose of benefitting from weaker party protection). Even if the lack of conflict rules on the application of collective rights might question the formal representativeness by those agents of workers abroad, they should have the knowledge and the resources to organise formal representation for bringing cases before the courts. Another question is the introduction, through collective bargaining, of clauses in individual contracts with a cross-border element that would favour the application of the most favourable norm. Given the actual system, pressuring employers to introduce a choice of law clause applying the law of the employers' forum would already be a good way forward, as it involves the application of 'the best of both worlds' to employment contracts with a cross-border element.

## 7.4 CONCLUSION: ANOTHER BATTLEFIELD FOR THE EXTRATERRITORIAL APPLICATION OF LABOUR LAW

The enhanced virtuality of the place where remote workers provide their labour eases the way towards worker management strategies taking advantage of the existing rules defining the applicable law in a cross-border situation, while those same rules limit the freedom of workers to work remotely from other jurisdictions than the one decided by or agreed with their employer. The territorial character of those rules and their interpretation does not consider the cross-border character of the growing labour market which the increased virtuality of the place of work creates, and in which the employer enjoys much greater freedom than the worker to act.

New avenues to promote extraterritorial application of labour laws to cross-border remote work situations, to protect workers' rights and to limit social dumping, must be explored. Some advocate for specific instruments on cross-border remote work or specific categories of remote workers[65]. But the fact that the proposed Platform Work Directive does not seem to consider cross-border situations further than legislating a mechanism to ensure a coherent application of employment status across the EU and providing no extraterritorial reach shows that policymakers have not given real thought to the problem. But the GDPR shows that EU instruments can have extraterritorial effect[66].

Most authors discuss possible interpretations of existing rules, as has been done here as well. However, it is not only for the courts to address the problem through innovative interpretations, given existing limitations. Legal instruments should be revised to take the new realities into account. And the discussion which precedes the revision should not so much be centred on which legal order should apply, but

[65] Cherry 2020, 233–237, writes about an international sectoral instrument on crowdworkers on the model of the regulation of maritime workers; limited to the EU; Carinci and Heke 2021, 137; Bruurs 2023, 607 on remote worker instruments on the model of the Posting of Workers Directive.

[66] Cherry 2020, 233.

which would be the adequate connecting factors. A better (but nevertheless complementary) approach would be to discuss which labour law institutions or rights should be given extraterritorial reach in the different configurations in which cross-border remote work manifests itself currently, and to what extent. The existing system of 'overriding mandatory provisions' can be a starting point or inspire new norms, so as to protect not only the interests of the parties to the contract but also those of the community in general[67]. And this should be done considering, firstly, the different situations of vulnerability in which remote workers can find themselves; secondly, the limitation of the incentives for the employer to have recourse to social dumping through remote work; and thirdly, the difficulties that the current system of determination of applicable law has on the workers' right to cross-border telework.

## REFERENCES

Althoff, Lukas, Eckert, Fabian, Ganapati, Sharat and Walsh, Conor. 2022. 'The geography of remote work' *Regional Science and Urban Economics* 93: 1–20.

Arabadjieva, Kalina. 2022. 'Reshaping the work-life balance Directive with Covid-19 lessons in mind' ETUI.

Arthurs, Harry W. 2010. 'Extraterritoriality by other means: How labor law sneaks across borders, conquers minds, and controls workplaces abroad' *Comparative Research in Law & Political Economy*. Research Paper No. 25/2010.

Atkinson, Christopher L. 2022. 'A review of telework in the COVID-19 pandemic: Lessons learned for work-life balance?' *COVID* 2, 10: 1405–1416.

Avegnon, Koffi Edem. 2023. 'Le droit du travail applicable au télétravail à l'étranger' *AFRILEX. Revue d'étude et de recherche sur le droit et l'administration dans les pays d'Afrique*. https://afrilex.u-bordeaux.fr/2023/11/17/le-droit-du-travail-applicable-au-teletravail-a-letranger/ (accessed 10.09.2024).

Baldwin, Richard and Dingel, Jonathan I. 2021. 'Telemigration and development: On the offshorability of teleworkable jobs' *NBER Working Papers* 29387. National Bureau of Economic Research.

Barnard, Catherine. 2009. 'Fifty years of avoiding social dumping? The EU's economic and not so economic constitution' in Michael Dougan and Samantha Currie, eds., *50 years of the European treaties: Looking back and thinking forward*. Hart Publishing: 311–341.

Barreda, Naivi Chikoc. 2023. 'Le télétravail transfrontalier face aux défis de coordination des regles de conflit et des normes minimales d'emploi' *Mc Gill Law Journal* 68, 1: 89–122.

2024. 'Jurisdiction over cross-border employment contracts in Canada and its implication for teleworking' in Alfonso Ortega Giménez, dir., and Lerdys Heredia Sánchez, coord., *Nuevos problemas y nuevas soluciones en el teletrabajo transfronterizo*. Thomson Reuters Aranzadi: 431–460.

Bercusson, Brian and Estlund, Cynthia. 2008. 'Regulating labour in the wake of globalisation: New challenges, new institutions' in Brian Bercusson and Cynthia Estlund, eds., *Regulating labour in the wake of globalisation: New challenges, new institutions*. Hart Publishing: 1–13.

[67] On the justification for and limits to the extraterritorial application of Labour Law, see Mundlak 2009; Arthurs 2010.

Boulay-Esperonnier, Céline et al. 2021. '8 questions sur l'avenir du télétravail, vers une révolution du travail à distance?' *Rapport d'information* n° 89 (2021–2022). Sénat. www.senat.fr/rap/r21-089/r21-0891.pdf (accessed 10.09.2024).

Bruurs, Stan. 2023. 'Cross-border telework in light of the Rome I-Regulation and the Posting of Workers Directive' *European Labour Law Journal*, 14, 4: 588–608.

Carinci, Maria Teresa and Henke, Albert. 2021. 'Employment relations via the web with International elements: Issues and proposals as to the applicable law and determination of jurisdiction in light of EU rules and principles' *European Labour Law Journal* 12, 2: 134–155.

Cherry, Miriam A. 2020. 'A global system of work, a global system of regulation? Crowdwork and conflicts of law' *Tulane Law Review* 94: 183–245.

Countouris, Nicola and De Stefano, V. 2023. 'Out of sight, out of mind? Remote work and contractual distancing' in Nicola Countouris et al., eds., *The future of remote work*. ETUI: 147–161.

Countouris, Nicola and Freedland, Mark. 2013. 'Introduction: The myths and realities of social Europe' in Nicola Countouris and Mark Freedland, eds., *Resocialising Europe in a Time of Crisis*. CUP: 1–16.

Eurofound. 2020. 'Telework and ICT-based mobile work: Flexible working in the digital age' New forms of employment series. Publications Office of the European Union.

Garden, Charlotte. 2018. 'Disrupting work law: Arbitration in the gig economy' *University of Chicago Legal Forum* 2017: 205–234.

Golub, Jura. 2023. 'Contemporary forms of work with a digital feature in private International law' *EU and Comparative Law Issues and Challenges Series (ECLIC)* 7: 316–345.

Grušić, Uglješa. 2023. 'Remote work in private international law' in Nicola Countouris et al., eds., *The future of remote work*, ETUI: 185–199.

Houwerzijl, Mijke and van Hoek, Aukje. 2016. 'Where do EU mobile workers belong, according to Rome I and the (E)PWD' in Herwig Verschueren, ed., *Residence, employment and social rights of mobile persons: On how EU law defines where they belong* Intersentia: 215–235.

Kakkad, Jeegar, Palmou, Cristina, Britto, David and Browne, James. 2021. *Anywhere jobs: Reshaping the geography of work*. Tony Blair Institute for Global Change.

Martín-Pozuelo López, Ángela. 2020. 'El teletrabajo y el Derecho Internacional Privado: el régimen particular del teletrabajo transnacional' in Tomás Sala Franco, coord., *El teletrabajo*. Tirant lo Blanch: 101–144.

Mundlak, Guy. 2009. 'De-territorializing labor law' *Law & Ethics of Human Rights* 3, 2: 188–222.

Orlandini, Giovanni. 2012. Il rapporto di lavoro con elementi di internazionalità. Working Paper CSDLE "Massimo D'Antona" 137/12. www.academia.edu/43256845/Il_rapporto_di_lavoro_con_elementi_di_internazionalit%C3%A0 (accessed 10.09.2024).

Rasnača, Zane. 2023. 'Enforcing the rights of remote workers: The case of digital nomads' in Nicola Countouris et al., eds., *The future of remote work*, ETUI: 201–2019.

Rosin, Annika. 2024. 'Cross-border telework and the applicable labour law: The role of different connecting factors in determining objectively applicable law' *European Labour Law Journal* 15, 4: 755–772. https://doi.org/10.1177/20319525241251435 (accessed 10.09.2024).

Suk, Kwang Hyun. 2015. 'Harmonization of private international law rules in Northeast Asia' *The Journal of International Law and Diplomacy* 114, 1: 1–26.

Van Bochove, Laura M. 2014. 'Overriding mandatory rules as a vehicle for weaker party protection in European Private International Law' *Erasmus Law Review* 7, 3: 147–156

# 8

# Remote Work and Redistribution of Responsibility

## *The Korean Case in Perspective*

*Choi Sukhwan*

### 8.1 REMOTE WORK IN KOREA: THE SOCIAL CONTEXT

There was a remarkable increase of Unionization rate recently at a company in Korea. A company named Kakao (the most famous corporation for its mobile instant messenger in Korea) ordered its employees to come back to the office after the pandemic is at its stable situation. When it made it clear to go for a change in the working environment, from home to work, it faced huge resistance from its employees[1]. Just a week after Kakao ended the remote work system and announced a change into the office-oriented work system, the union membership rate, which had been below 10% for several years, dramatically soared, exceeding 50% in an instant (Park 2023). It achieved the majority of unions, and got the position of representative for the collective bargaining (Choi 2024a)[2]. This was really news, considering the recent nationwide union membership rate, about 14%, which has increased in these 4–5 years but still not that high (Kwon 2023). Employees who newly joined the union insisted that there was not enough communication between management and employees in the process of transitioning the working system from telework to the office centered work. They were members of an instant message company, very much accustomed to working without facing people even before the pandemic, and sudden transition into face-to-face work was a huge change for them. In the IT industry, there was an atmosphere that conflicts were inevitable due to the withdrawal of remote work, when many companies were getting back to the office

1 www.donga.com/news/Economy/article/all/20230105/117301094/1 [in Korean].

2 Trade Union and Labor Relations Adjustment Act (TULRAA) of Korea Art.29-2. Para.1. Nr.1. Where at least two trade unions established or joined by workers exist in one business or one place of work regardless of the type of organization, trade unions shall determine a bargaining representative trade union (including a representative bargaining organization, the constituent members of which are members of at least two trade unions; hereinafter the same shall apply) and request the same to bargain. For a more detailed explanation about the system, see Choi 2024a: 412.

from "Work Anywhere" policy. During the pandemic age, a lot of work which was originally accomplished at the office was performed without actual contact, which a Korean scholar named the age of "untact" (Kim 2017). With the end of the story, increase in union membership rate among the IT industry, we realize that we can still utilize traditional labor law as a tool for improving issues occurring with the new types of work, including remote work.

Before the pandemic, we had tried to introduce remote work in Korea, which was not that successful (MOEL 2020c: 206)[3]. For example, for the public officials, "Smart work center" was set up by administrative offices and courts, as an attempt to make satellite offices so that some part of the workday could be done outside their original workplace. This is a kind of work–life balance by place, a welfare for the employees. Because many government offices moved to the rural side in the name of "balanced development of the nation," this space has become an alternative workspace when officials come to Seoul, the place where they worked before, to join their families, or submit all the data requested by the National Assembly which is still in Seoul. In this case, it was far from the type of remote work which workers could entirely determine where to perform their work.

However, in Korea, the type of remote work rapidly spread amid changes in the environment caused by COVID-19. Many companies have introduced remote work and telework, which was welcomed by workers who had to live far away from their companies because of high housing costs. In particular, restrictions on gathering together and requests for "social distance" during the COVID-19 period accelerated the fast proliferation of telecommuting. Remote work soon became a preferred option for both labor and management. IT companies expanded recruitment and increased the size of their companies, to build and maintain such infrastructure.

In addition to the pandemic, there is one more critical issue about remote work in Korea: fertility rate. Koreans spend more time on paid work than workers in most of the OECD countries. With annual hours worked, South Korea has been one of the longest working countries in the OECD (Kim 2023a), with the average of 1740 hours in 2023[4]. Korea's fertility rate is the lowest level in the OECD, 0.81 in 2021[5], and Korea's long working culture is pointed out as one of the main reasons for the low birth rate (Kim 2023b). This is such a critical issue that recently the "Presidential committee on ageing society and population policy" has launched as a new governmental organization[6]. In this situation, remote work is actively supported, in terms of contributing to the tackling the low birth rate by making women's working environment family-friendly, mainly supporting childcare.

3 Only 3.5% of the whole enterprise introduced remote work system in 2019, 4.5% work at home.

4 www.oecd.org/en/data/indicators/hours-worked.html?oecdcontrol-d7f68dbeee-var3 = 2023.

5 www.oecd.org/en/data/indicators/fertility-rates.html?oecdcontrol-00b22b2429-var3 = 2021.

6 www.betterfuture.go.kr/index.do;jsessionid = 3615F3D9246F42211A6AB1BD64A6081E.node20.

In this chapter, I'd like to describe the situations and institutional reply concerning remote work from the perspective of distribution of responsibility. The employment contract is a mutual contract, a structure in which each party bears related obligations and is responsible for it. This structure necessarily requires distribution of responsibility. From the traditional perspective of employment law, subordination has been the most important essence of the employment contract. Face-to-face direction and close supervision by the employer, usually with sharing spaces, have been thought of as an important basis for the subordination, which brings about a lot of unique obligations to the employers in labor relations. We can raise a question that, if we do not have these factors any more by remote work, in some part we have to reconsider the distribution of the responsibilities; in other parts, we still have to keep the traditional structure of the distribution of responsibility, maybe in a different way.

Surveys about the experiences of remote work in Korea show pros and cons. It was reported (MOEL 2020b: 8) that the biggest hurdle from the employers' side was difficulty in communication (62.6%). Hurdles in fair management compared with employees carrying out jobs not familiar with working at home (44.1%) and difficulty in performance evaluation (40.0%) were also problems indicated with the introduction of remote work. The answer mentioned that the cost burden for the infrastructure was only 9.0%[7]. From the workers' side, the ambiguous boundary between working hours and breaks was reported as the biggest problem (45.8%), which made workers hesitate to go for the remote work. Decreases in efficiency due to non-separation of workspaces (44.8%) and alienation due to lack of interaction with the colleagues (30.4%) were also main reasons.

However, both sides are basically positive about remote work, especially work at home. Work efficiency was to be expected to improve with less unnecessary meetings and reports, and job satisfaction increased through self-directed work performance and efficient goal achievement. Evaluation of workers' satisfaction with work at home reached 91.3%, contrary to 8.7% dissatisfaction (MOEL 2020b: 7). It has contributed greatly to the protection of workers' health during COVID-19 as the most effective social distancing method. It greatly helped to protect workers of vulnerable groups, especially pregnant women and those with underlying diseases. Working at home allowed work–life balance, relatively free from time and place constraints, with the expanded choices of working time and places, being able to participate in family care. The disabled, the elderly, those in care, or pregnant or childbirth who prefer to work at home could have the chance to continue to work without quitting their jobs by using telecommuting. From the employers' point of view, working at home or any other place could reduce the cost for workspace,

7 This is the answer from the employers who are actually having remote work as working style in the company. At the same survey, 34.2% of the employers who did not introduce remote work system answered the reason as "the cost for newly building infrastructure."

prevent skilled personnel from changing jobs, and expect long-term service. It helped to attract excellent human resources by enhancing job satisfaction, customer service satisfaction, and corporate image that supports workers' work and life balance. Also, working from home could have a positive impact on the environment, reducing traffic congestion and pollution during commuting hours. Increasing demand for IT infrastructure, such as collaborative tools and video conferencing systems, could boost non-face-to-face industries and create jobs.

In Korea, we had been experiencing a highly work-oriented society through industrial development for many years, and this apparently had been influencing regulations as well. For example, there are many cases that admitted an employee's death as an industrial accident covered by public insurance during or after the company dinner (Han 2015)[8]. Traditional features of Korean working culture like close human relations at work and company dinner as part of work (Choi 2024a; Chang 2015) were influencing regulations too, but as remote work doesn't necessarily suppose these types of relations, it is changing the way of working and consequently regulations for our working life too, consequently suggesting redistribution of responsibility.

## 8.2 REMOTE WORK IN KOREA: THE FRAME OF REGULATION

For the regulation, under the current Labor Standards Act (herein after LSA), employees' workplaces are based on their contract and employers' work rules (art. 15 and art. 93). In general, workers' homes are recognized as private spaces, away from the direction and supervision of employers, so telecommuting is an unfamiliar way of working from the traditional perspective of the labor law. However, the recent development of digital devices and communication technologies created an environment where people can work regardless of time and place, and the COVID-19 situation accelerated this transition.

Current LSA does not distinguish regulations on remote work, so in principle, it would be reasonable to assume that workers have no right to request or implement it. However, if there is a basis for remote work in contracts, work rules, and/or collective agreements, it can be interpreted that, with the consent of workers, the employer can start it. However, in the event of a disaster like COVID-19, in order to continue the business and secure the life and safety of workers, they can be ordered to work from home without the consent of workers, which cannot be disadvantaged for not agreeing to work from home.

Even at this time, regulations for working hours (Article 50), restrictions on overtime work (Article 53), rest (Article 54), and holidays (Article 55) should be applied. Working at home without real-time supervising technology will inevitably lead to legal issues like the initiative for the introduction and implementation of

8 As one of the leading cases, Supreme Court of Korea 2008. 10. 9. 2007du21082.

remote work, the way to decide important working conditions such as wages and working hours when working at home, responsibility about health, privacy, and industrial accident protection of remote workers. From the perspective of LSA, remote work without supervising by employer is rather similar to the discretionary work (art. 58 para.3), in that employees can decide allocation of working time[9]. In this way, even if there are no legislations related to remote work under the LSA, there have been efforts to deal with the situation of appearance of remote work, and in principle, labor standards for ordinary employees apply to remote workers.

However, there was a need to regulate remote work in more clear ways, and another type of regulation was sought, resulting in two "guidelines" by the Ministry of Employment and Labur (herein after MOEL), in 2011 and 2020 respectively. These were in the form of "soft law," not a binding law with strong enforcement, but with a more flexible way of regulation, rather close to the recommendation by the administrative authority. They clarified the application of existing laws and regulations to some ambiguous matters caused by remote work. Instead of the traditional method of imposing penalties for violations, they provided support and incentive by the government. They attempted to visualize the responsibilities of employers and employees in very specific situations with examples, and pointed out that it would be better to have an agreement between the parties regarding each specific matter that was not imagined before remote work became the main role on the stage.

First, the 2011 smart work guideline by MOEL defined smart worker as "a worker works all or part of his or her working hours at home, in a separate office provided by the employer, or in an unspecified place" (MOEL 2011). It also described smart work as "a flexible working method that works regardless of location or time, such as using information and communication devices, unlike working in a fixed working place according to a predetermined working time." The 2011 smart work guideline made it

[9] In case of works designated by Presidential Decree as those works which, in the light of their characteristics, require leaving the methods of performance to a worker' discretion, it shall be deemed that the works have been provided for such work hours as determined by a written agreement between the employer and the labor representative. In this case, such written agreement shall specify the matters falling under the following subparagraphs: (1) Work to be provided subject to such written agreement. (2) Statement that the employer would not give specific directions to the worker regarding how to perform the work, how to allocate work hours, etc. (3) Statement that the calculation of work hours shall be governed by the written agreement concerned. Works designated by presidential decree here are as follows: (1) Research work in the field of research and development of new products or new technologies or humanities and social sciences or natural sciences. (2) Design or analysis of information processing systems. (3) coverage of articles in newspapers, broadcasting or publishing businesses, organizing or editing work. (4) Design or design of clothing, interior decoration, industrial products, advertising, etc. (5) Producers or directors' duties in the production business of broadcasting programs, films, etc. (6) Other duties prescribed by the Minister of Employment and Labor (business that provides counseling, advice, appraisal, or agency under the delegation and commission of others in the affairs of accounting, legal cases, tax payment, legal, labor management, patent, appraisal, financial investment analysis, investment asset management, etc.).

clear that smart workers should be under the regulation of current labor laws such as the LSA, Minimum Wage Act, Workers' Retirement Benefit Guarantee Act, Occupational Safety and Health Act, and Industrial Accident Compensation Insurance Act.

According to the guideline, when hiring workers to use the smart work method, the place of work must be specified, whether regular or occasional. In other words, it should be stated that in the normal case, the place of work is the home or satellite office of the worker, and in the occasional case, a certain frequency and time can be worked in different places along with the main place of work. The place of work had not been highly specified before remote work; only abstract wording of "the location determined and directed by the employer" had been used. The 2011 guideline made it more distinct and articulated that home of the worker could be a pace of work on the basis of contracts, work rules, or collective agreements. If there are no regulations on smart work, and no changes in working conditions other than the place of work between smart work workers and ordinary workers, it is sufficient to obtain individual consent from workers who want to do smart work, but with a change in working conditions such as working hours and wages as well as the place of work for all workers, then work rules need to be changed. The guideline also deals with working hours management of smart work, depending on the possibility of command orders for working hours. If there are information and communication devices to make employers be able to connect with the workers all the time, it is just the same as the regulation for ordinary workers. If it is difficult to calculate working hours because the information and communication device is not in a state of connecting at all times and the employer does not give specific work instructions, then art. 58 of LSA can be applied. At the same time, however, the employer is recommended to check and manage the working hours of the workers periodically, in the sense of the responsibility to take care of workers' health. The standards about the responsibility can be adjusted in consideration of the privacy of the workers, but still employers are required to take regular education for safety and health. The worker must prove whether an accident that occurred to the smart worker is work-related. The guideline suggests making a consensus between labor and management on smart work, documenting or setting up in advance about what to do, how to perform it, how to contact with each other, and how to take fair performance evaluation and personnel management.

But in September 2020, the MOEL suggested a "Comprehensive Manual on Work at Home," mainly focusing on the situation caused by COVID-19, in which work at home was inevitable. The main objective lies in giving support to companies considering the introduction of work at home system, and this is also an important difference with the smart work guideline 2011. Here "work at home" is defined as the type of work performed by a worker in a designated place, such as home. It is mentioned here, too, that when companies attempted to introduce a work at home system, if there provisions don't exist about work at home or somewhere else, in the employment contract or work rules, then individual consent from the workers is needed. However, it also says that when there appear situations like epidemic disease, then the order to work at home can be justified only with consultation, even without consent. It also stipulated that the government could support indirect labor costs, telecommuting infrastructure construction costs, and cost for consulting services to promote telecommuting. Next, in order to collect information on the location of telecommuters, like using GPS tools, consent from workers is required. In principle, the cost of expendable office supplies generated by telecommuting is borne by the employer. In particular, the guideline speaks to the principle that injuries or diseases that occur in relation to work at home are occupational accidents. Governmental support for telework entailed a multifaceted approach, encompassing diverse measures aimed at promoting the introduction and settling down of flexible work practices. It also recommends a more clear way of job description, a more detailed standard setting about performance evaluation, and making a system of eliminating the fear of discrimination with the persons who work at the office.

### 8.2.1 *Uncomfortable Cohabitation with Traditional Labor Law*

Two guidelines mentioned above are in the form of "soft law," not binding laws that have strong enforcement. The use of soft law contrasts with the fact that Korea's labor law, especially the LSA and unfair labor practice system, has been a hard law regulation with criminal punishment. The use of soft law can be highly evaluated in two perspectives. First, in the time that requires optimized regulatory response when hard law is a little too tight, it can be easy to perform a rather flexible way of regulation (Kang 2014: 539). Second, we are still in the way of forming regulations with these new situations and unfamiliar technology, where soft law regulation can leave much room to be decided by autonomy of the parties concerned, especially collective autonomy. This can also be evaluated as an attempt to reconsider the nature of these working conditions and shift from the public order to the agreement between private parties. The fundamental question of what should be dealt with the regulation of labor law is here, when working people seem to have more freedom and less control and domination by the employers with remote work.

However, with this possibility of flexibility by soft law, we still need to be careful about the limit of minimum working conditions (e.g., maximum working hours). The approach that soft law is searching for about remote work, it certainly gives more discretion to the employees and maybe to the employers, so easy to deal with this new phenomenon. But even with remote work, we still have area that traditional regulations still presides, especially about OSH issues. The responsibility to protect workers from unhealthy and a dangerous working environment is a kind of duty that should not be easily transferred to the employees' side, even if they are not visible right in front of the employer.

What is more, among the changes in values caused by the COVID-19 era, a key element of remote work that does not share space can be found to be used as a reason to avoid employers' traditional labor law responsibilities. This raises the question of whether remote work is accelerating the fragmentation of labor relations, outsourcing the labor force, which can bring about the blurring of employer responsibilities. Certainly, technological advances seem in a way to enlarge discretion and independence of employees. But as seen in the *MES* case[10] and portable devices workers carry at all times, unlike what they look like, the relations do include commands and directions disguised with technologies, especially when connected with GPS. This is the very situation where labor law finds its original place to be applied. Anyway, it is clear that remote work is at least a catalyst that requires a review of the distribution of responsibilities between employers and workers, between multiple users or stakeholders.

### 8.2.2 *Redistribution of Responsibility in Contract*

Remote work seems to make it easier to have multi-jobs for the employees. Exclusivity, which traditionally has been main feature of the employment and the very essence of managerial prerogative (De Stefano et al. 2024), is getting more and more difficult to be guaranteed (Countouris & De Stefano 2023: 153). Here we can approach from a new perspective about safety and health. Exclusive domination by the employer necessarily requests the whole responsibility about the OSH of the workplace. However, there are attempts to limit this responsibility because of the discretion that employees have when he/she works apart from the face-to-face supervision of the employer. In Korea, we have discussion about working hours as public order with multi-job workers, and burden of proof concerning industrial accidents.

Traditional labor and employment law presuppose the sharing of space. The fact that the employer who manages his or her facility and the employee who works in

[10] Supreme Court of Korea 2022. 7. 28. 2021da2221638. This is a case whether a production management system (Manufacturing Execution System, hereinafter referred to as MES) can be recognized as control and order of employers. This computer-based process management system is widely introduced in various manufacturing process to support various activities such as work schedule, work instruction, quality management, and work performance aggregation at the production site of a company. Although the details of the MES may vary from company to company, it is common for data at the production site to be collected, processed, and provided in real time through MES. In this case, the production process and operation system were planned and managed by a MES, and the subcontractor's employee performed cooperative work according to what was designated through the MES. Most of the tasks performed were simple, repeated job according to the manual standard, did not require a high degree of expertise and skills. The reward paid by the company to the subcontractor was calculated mainly based on the number of workers and working hours input by the subcontractor, not the quantity of the work. The court said that worker control by MES was recognized as the command and supervision typically performed by the employer.

the employer's facility are located within the same space enabled a strong command without any other external factor's intervention. The employer's direction and order were both the essence of the employment contract and the basis for various responsibilities. The employer's authority to place a worker in a particular place entails his or her responsibility for risks arising from that place at the same time. The basic principle of the employers' responsibility for occupational health and safety lies in this presumption.

The LSA mandates a 40-hour weekly working limit but lacks provisions about working more than 40 hours with multiple employers. Traditional employment contracts involve one employer and one employee, and exclusivity has been one of the main factors to decide whether a service provider is an employee or not. But the focus has shifted to individual contracts with multiple employers, raising concerns about health and self-determination in working time regulation. Combining total hours across employers could address the working hour ceiling, but calculating total working hours by an employee – whether by the employers or public authority – raises privacy concerns. The emergence of new work models, such as "Coupang Flex" in Korea, where individuals work as independent contractors in delivery services, presents challenges despite flexibility. The increased demand for delivery services during the pandemic has led to more participants for this job. Addressing health and safety in this context requires new regulations to handle prolonged working hours for both workers and independent contractors. When we take a perspective that views maximum working hours as a public order everyone – not only employers – should observe, it may offer a comprehensive approach to the issue (Choi 2021: 120–121). The problem here with the multi-job worker is also meaningful with the remote workers. If surveillance by employer is widespread with the technology and consequently exclusive subordinate characters of the relation is still unavoidable[11], then it is back to the traditional regulation, with the full package of responsibility by employer.

However, if there is much discretion available to the employees, including setting standards of working hours, orders, safety, and health, then the shift and reallocation of responsibility can be considered. Of course, we should be careful about the attempt that an employer tries to avoid his/her responsibility with, by highlighting factors that can backup employee's ability to decide his/her own working conditions. When employees are forced to take this type of relation, it is highly possible to lead to misclassification. When different types of supervisions and commands, like directions to the employee by algorithms and AI, are combined with remote work, it also suggests the possibility of transferring the employer's duty of consideration to the employee side.

[11] Where communication is possible at all times through information and communication devices, and so on, and it is possible to manage the start and end time of work, rest time, and so on determined by the user, the usual working hours system may be applied.

Along with the distribution of responsibility between employer and employee, the role of government, at least part of its responsibility for health and safety, also needs to be considered. We can get inspiration from the role of government described in the Comprehensive Guideline 2021, to support financial allocations earmarked for the establishment of telework infrastructure.

With the traditional Bismarck model (Esping-Andersen 1990) for social security, Korea has been categorized as a model in the middle of the corporatist-statist and liberal model. Health insurance is tremendously close to the statist model, while much of the role of safety net for the employed persons and their family has been the burden of the company, that is, the market. Facing remote work and thinking of the changes in the labor law, it may be the time to make a switch. At least part of the things that were thought that the employer should take care of, things that were regarded as the area of contractual rights and duty, can be shifted to the area of public order, when a strong tie that classical mutual relations persisted becomes weaker. Governmental support about setting infrastructure and financial support for the employment, prescribed in the recent work at home guideline (MOEL 2020a), suggests that when introducing remote work was the result of the social issues like epidemic disease, then it is not only the responsibility of contractual parties' anymore, but the public's too. If so, when we think of remote work not just for productivity, but also for the fertility rate, childcare, and climate issues (reducing pollution by commuting), then traditional mutual contractual duties may need to be redistributed, including society as the one to take responsibility.

At the same time, burden of proof required in the industrial accident is another issue. In Korea, industrial accidents must be proved by the employee who argues that he or she met with an accident. But a recent minority opinion of the Supreme Court ruling[12] separated "work-related characteristics" and "causal relationships," suggesting the redistribution of responsibilities that the former must be proved by workers and the latter by employers. For remote work, the smart work guideline stipulated that in the case of home-type smart work, "in principle, there is no need to implement the safety and health standards prescribed by the Occupational Safety and Health Act" (MOEL 2011). In addition, the smart work guideline stipulated that

[12] Supreme Court of Korea 2021. 9. 9. 2017du45933. "Most methods of evidence or information exist in the workplace in lawsuits related to industrial accident insurance benefits, making it difficult for workers to prove without the absolute cooperation of the employer. In many cases, the working conditions or working environment in which the worker worked are not disclosed because it is a trade secret. In the case of a professional accident, the cause of the accident is complex and technical due to the specialization or modernization of the work, so a high degree of professional knowledge is required to determine the cause of the accident, and it may be difficult for workers to scientifically prove the cause of the accident themselves. In the case of occupational diseases, it is often impossible to determine medical causal relationships due to a lack of medical expertise or limitations of epidemiological investigations. In particular, for diseases whose cause has not been medically identified, it is contrary to the principle of fairness and the notion of justice to have workers who cannot afford it bear the burden of proof even though epidemiological investigations take a lot of time and cost."

if it is to be admitted as an industrial accident covered by OSHA, then the worker himself must prove that the accident is caused by the smart work. About the same issues, the recent work at home guideline (MOEL 2020a) states that in principle, the Occupational Safety and Health Act applies to telecommuting, but it is limited in that only some regulations can be applied because work is provided in places where it is difficult for employers to actually control and manage. It is positive that the obligation of employers to protect and consider the safety and health of workers is recognized in remote work too. At the same time, it is necessary to set and comply with standards for the working environment so that remote workers can work in an environment where they can maintain their health, and to provide measures such as supporting the cost of improving the working environment if necessary. While acknowledging that accidents during performing smart work are also recognized as industrial accidents, it is said that telecommuters themselves must prove it, and the person who works alone at home may have more difficulty to prove causality with work in the event of an accident than the person who works at the workplace with the employer and colleagues. Remote work regulation seems to limit the responsibility of the employer, including the burden of proof. Will this be a fair distribution of burden, or will this make it more difficult for the employee to prove and be covered by public insurance? Remote work may suggest who will be in charge of the responsibility, instead of freedom. We should be careful who really enjoys and benefits from this freedom.

### 8.2.3 *Collective Bargaining in the Age of Remote Work*

Even with the progress of remote work, there are some points that we still feel reluctant to be changing our stance. The status of employer to take responsibility of collective bargaining is another issue in Korea. Labor unions can be organized based on company, industry, or occupation as desired, basically based on the freedom of association articulated by the Constitution of Korea, art. 33. But when the unions wish to start a collective bargaining process, a bargaining unit should be set by a group of workers with common interests toward certain employers, and they choose a representative to negotiate. It has been criticized for limiting the constitutionally guaranteed rights of collective bargaining to some extent. Korean labor law enhances these limitations by enforcing the duty of fair representation and facilitating the negotiation process[13].

However, two problems arise because both the work at home guidelines (2020) and the smart work guidelines (2011) target employees under the LSA[14], that is,

[13] Constitutional Court of Korea, 2012. 4. 24. 2011hunma338; 8; Constitutional Court of Korea, 2024. 6. 27. 2020HUNMA237, etc. For a more detailed description about the bargaining system in Korea, see Choi (2024b: 90–91), and Choi (2024a: 412–413).

[14] The term "employee" means a person who works in a business or workplace for the purpose of wages, regardless of the type of occupation (LSA art. 2.nr.1.).

employees who have signed employment contracts with employers and are employed by specific employers. For them, these guidelines provide new protection or extended protection under the remote work environment. The first issue is about the independent self-employed people with ambiguous worker characteristics, working by remote work. If the command and supervision of the employer is not that directly designated and is hard to distinguish from the direction of civil contract, this functions as an element that can weaken the protection of law because the status as an employee under the LSA is questioned. Second, for this reason, it has been argued mainly on the workers' side that collective bargaining should be allowed at least on those conditions even if there is no direct contractual relationship if the working conditions can be substantially and concretely controlled and determined. Considering this trend, the collective bargaining system in Korea may be described as at the point of expanding employers (users)' responsibility, if they have decision-making power about the working conditions (Choi 2024b:93). Sometimes command seems to have been excluded by having distance, not sharing common physical space; however, when the location gap is compensated with technology, it inevitably requires the resurrection of traditional labor laws. This can be another insight to deal with the field of global supply chain and transnational collective bargaining. By extension of the notion of the employer on one hand, and multinational corporation and GSC on the other hand, we can broaden the actors and contents of the collective bargaining, or at least conversation among the stakeholders, though we have the hurdle of jurisdiction. In the end, there is a wide spectrum of discussions on how far to extend "responsibility" of communication, to hear about what the workers request, whether it is the scope of the person responsible for ensuring a safe environment, whether it is the subject to ensure the payment of adequate wages, or whether it is a position and obligation as a counterparty to collective bargaining.

### 8.2.4 *Orthodox Question: The Notion of Employee and Employment Contract*

Here we come back to face the classical question of whom to protect with employment and labor law, in the special situation of remote work. Remote work often tries to exclude employees and marginal workers from the category of employee, with the ground of physical distance and rather loose direction from the employers; consequently, some of the remote workers cannot be covered by the protection of employment and labor law (Countouris and De Stefano 2023: 152–153). When we see the distance of remote work over the borderline, the principles of legal regulation under the current private international law regulations are also concerned with remote work and the notion of employment contract. In Korean international private law, if there is an agreement on the designation of the governing law, it is determined accordingly (art. 45), and even in this case, the protection granted to employees under the legal regulations of the country that provides labor habitually, or the country where the employment office is located, cannot be deprived (art. 48 (1) and (2), domestic mandatory regulations). On the other hand, if there is no agreement on the designation of the governing law, it shall be subject to the law of the country that provides labor on a daily basis or the country where the employment office is located (art. 48 (2)), and if the place of daily labor provision is only slightly related to the employment contract relationship, it shall be subject to closely related laws (art. 21). In light of legislative purposes, the mandatory regulations of the Republic of Korea, which must be applied to the relevant employment contract relationship regardless of the governing law, also apply to cases where foreign laws are applied as the governing law (art. 20, international mandatory regulations).

On the premise of the current status of these regulations, it is a matter related to the scope of "employment contract" referred to in private international law. There is also a question of determining the governing law to determine the existence of an employment contract by which law to judge it as an employment contract, but at a subsequent stage, a review of which contract is an employment contract to which the special cases referred to in this Act apply is required. In particular, this is of great significance considering the circumstances when the person who did not sign the employment contract but is a member of a trade union. If the union takes a collective agreement with the employer, then the problem of normative effect or expansion effect of that collective bargaining can be controversial without specific current regulations. When the question that who should have the duty to sit at the collective bargaining table and the issue of remote work are combined, we do face multinational collective bargaining issues, rarely experienced until now in Korea. Problems that may arise from the failure of private international law to provide clear regulations or criteria for judgment on employment contracts are more clearly contrasted with those detailed in art. 42 of the LSA. Art. 42 limits the scope of consumer contracts that need protection while prescribing it as "a contract concluded by a consumer for purposes other than his or her job or business activity." There are many discussions on the above provisions that provide certain expected protection in relation to consumers' residences, but if the purpose of acknowledging the special case is clarified and identified as an attempt to reflect it, improvement from this perspective will also be appropriate for employment contracts too. This seems to be a circular logic, but a purposive approach for this legislation and cases can help to clarify the idea of remote work and persons to be protected in that area.

### 8.2.5 *Future of Remote Work and Institutional Response*

Responsibilities shift from employer to government, labor law's characteristic from private law to public law, technology and possibility of collective autonomy, and the democratic basis of organization will also be remaining questions arising from remote work. All these questions will also be related to raise the question of redistribution of the responsibility, that of employer, user, employee and the government, even international institutions. From these perspectives, remote work should not be just a temporary phenomenon to deal with. It should be a resurrection of traditional labor law, its fundamental values, and contemporary application for all.

## REFERENCES


Chang, Kangmyoung (2015), *Fired* (K-Fiction Series 13), translated by Teresa Kim, Asia publisher. https://library.ltikorea.or.kr/translatedbooks/22367.

Choi, Sukhwan (2021), Better Opportunity or Extended Sweatshop? — Labor Law and Policy in the Age of Digitalization in Korea, Japan Labor Issues, vol. 5, no. 32. www.jil.go.jp/english/jli/documents/2021/032-10.pdf.

(2024a), Labor and employment law, in SNU Asia-Pacific Law Institute (ed.), *Understanding Korean Law*, SNU Press.

(2024b), Diversification of working people and voices at work in Korea, *Japan Labor Issues*, vol. 8, no. 50. www.jil.go.jp/english/jli/documents/2024/050-08.pdf.

Countouris, Nicola & De Stefano (2023), Valerio, out of sight, out of mind? Remote work and contractual distancing, in Countouris, Nicola et al. (eds.), *The Future of Remote Work*, ETUI. www.etui.org/publications/future-remote-work.

De Stefano, Valerio et al. (2024), ¿Does labour law trust workers? questioning underlying assumptions behind managerial prerogatives, *Industrial Law Journal*, vol. 53, no. 2. https://doi.org/10.1093/indlaw/dwad022.

Esping-Andersen, Gøsta (1990), *The Three Worlds of Welfare Capitalism*, Princeton University Press.

Han, Byung-Chul (2015), *The Burnout Society*, Stanford University Press.

ILO (2021), *Working from Home: From Invisibility to Decent Work*, ILO. www.ilo.org/global/publications/books/WCMS_765806/lang–en/index.htm.

Kang, Seong-Tae (2014), Application of labour law for smartwork (Telework), *Hanyang Law Review*, vol. 31, no. 1 [in Korean]. www.kci.go.kr/kciportal/ci/sereArticleSearch/ciSereArtiView.kci?sereArticleSearchBean.artiId = ART001865989.

Kim, Minsub (2023a), *OECD Average Annual Hours Worked: Comparative Analysis and Implications*, KDI Focus. www.kdi.re.kr/eng/research/focusView?pub_no = 18199.

Kim, Nando (2017), Trend Korea 2018, Miraebooks. [in Korean]

Kim, Taewook (2023b), The impact of working hours on pregnancy intention in childbearing-age women in Korea, the country with the world's lowest fertility rate, *PLoS ONE* vol.18, no.7. https://doi.org/10.1371/journal.pone.0288697.

Kwon, Hyunji (2023), Recent Trends in Increasing Unionization Rates and Generation-specific Perception of Unions, Korean Social Trends 2023. https://kostat.go.kr/board.es?mid = b10104000000&bid = 12046&act = view&list_no = 432649.

López López, Julia (ed.) (2019), Collective bargaining and collective action: Labour agency and governance in the 21st century? Hart.

MOEL (2011), Guideline about labour related laws for the expansion of smart work [in Korean]. www.korea.kr/briefing/pressReleaseView.do?newsId = 155738756.

(2020a), Guideline for work at home [in Korean]. www.moel.go.kr/news/enews/report/enewsView.do?news_seq = 10851.

(2020b), Comprehensive Manual for work at home [in Korean]. www.moel.go.kr/policy/policydata/view.do?bbs_seq = 20200900802.

(2020c), Survey on work life balance 2019 [in Korean]. www.moel.go.kr/news/enews/report/enewsView.do?news_seq = 11450.

(2024), Manual for flexible working with work life balance [in Korean]. www.moel.go.kr/local/uijengbu/info/policydata/view.do?bbs_seq = 20241001018.

Park, Jae-hyuk (2023), Kakao employees decry end of remote work, *The Korea Times*. www.koreatimes.co.kr/www/tech/2024/10/129_343413.html.

WHO & ILO (2021), Healthy and safe telework technical brief. www.who.int/publications/i/item/9789240040977.

# 9

# Telework and Digital Surveillance

## *Legal Challenges on the Interface of Labour and Data Protection Law*

*Elias Felten*

### 9.1 INTRODUCTION

The rapid acceleration of digitalisation in industries and services over the past decade has had a direct impact on the organisation of labour. While telework is now primarily associated with the COVID-19 pandemic, it is fundamentally a result of the growing significance of information technology in both our professional and personal lives. Today, even manual labour is frequently supported by digital technologies, making data processing an integral part of virtually every employment relationship. This applies not only to employees working on-site but particularly to those working remotely. In fact, the rise of remote work as a widespread phenomenon is largely due to the use of modern information technologies.

However, the organisational changes in work resulting from digitalisation challenge the functionality and effectiveness of labour law. Data protection is becoming increasingly important in the labour context, and in many instances, labour protection and data protection can no longer be considered separately. Despite this, the law has not adequately evolved to reflect these changes.

This chapter will therefore at first analyse the existing shortcomings and gaps in the law also from a human rights perspective, using the issue of digital surveillance in telework as an example. In its second part, it aims to explore potential legal mechanisms to establish or even enhance the interaction between labour and data protection law.

### 9.2 TELEWORK AND CONTROL

Telework is nowadays the key for employees by which they can perform tasks remotely, outside of the employer's premises, in most cases (in the aftermath of the COVID-19-pandemic) at home. One potential benefit of combining telework with remote work is that it can help improve the balance between work and family responsibilities. Employees who can work from home are able to respond more flexibly to family needs, such as caring for sick children. The elimination of commuting, furthermore, creates additional time that can be used for caregiving duties within the family. This view is shared by the European legislator, as reflected in the Work-Life Balance Directive 2019/1158/EU, which promotes flexible working arrangements, explicitly including remote work[1].

Remote work is, of course, only made possible in most cases by modern communication technologies. That is why remote work and telework usually go hand in hand. This is already expressed in the legal definition of telework, as defined by the framework agreement between European social partners[2]. The agreement defines telework as a 'form of organising and/or performing work, using information technology, in the context of an employment contract/relationship, where work, which could also be performed at the employer's premises, is carried out away from those premises on a regular basis'. Analysing this definition, the notion of 'telework' is characterised by a crucial criterion which distinguishes this so called 'flexible working agreement' from traditional organised work: It is not merely the use of information technologies to perform tasks; after all, many employees working on their employer's premises use such technologies as well. The defining feature is that employees provide their services 'away from the employer's premises'. Even though employees working off-site, such as at a client's office or home, have long existed, they represented a small minority. Since the COVID-19-pandemic, however, the number of employees working at home has increased significantly.

### 9.2.1 *Monitoring Measures: An Integral Part of Telework*

The organisational impact of telework, namely, the separation of employer and employee by location, has gained greater importance and introduced one specific new qualitative challenge: employers are no longer able to personally verify whether their employees are fulfilling their contractual obligations. This marks a shift in the approach to human resource management. Employers are increasingly aiming to encourage employees to work more independently and to focus on results, with the goal of boosting productivity. Management by objectives is perhaps the most well-known expression for this management style. This increase in independence, however, is naturally accompanied by a loss of control on the employer's side. That is the reason why in many cases technical control measures, sometimes disguised as mere performance evaluation tools, come into play when it comes to telework[3].

Some might argue that the situation on the employer's premises is not significantly different, given the large number of employees. No employer can personally

1 Cf Article 3 (1) lit f Directive 2019/1158/EU.
2 https://eur-lex.europa.eu/EN/legal-content/summary/teleworking.html.
3 Vitak and Zimmer (2023, 1).

supervise every individual. This is true to a certain extent. However, on-site, the limitations of direct supervision are often compensated for by 'social pressure' exerted by management and colleagues[4]. If a division manager fails to report an employee's unexcused absence, colleagues are likely to do so. This is the key distinction between working remotely, such as from home, and working on-site. At home neither the social pressure exerted by colleagues nor any other compensatory control mechanisms, such as clients noticing an employee's tardiness to a meeting, apply to close this gap. As a result, the employer's understandable concerns that an employee may focus on personal matters rather than work-related tasks serve to justify, in practice, the implementation of more stringent monitoring measures. These measures are designed to ensure that employees perform their duties in both the required quantity and quality.

However, the scope of monitoring measures extends even further: to a certain degree, they replace the employer's direct authority. While the employer may not be physically present in the employee's home, the sense of their presence can actually be stronger due to pervasive surveillance measures enabled by AI-driven collaboration platforms commonly used in telework. This creates a significant paradox: although teleworkers appear to enjoy greater autonomy by working remotely free from the employer's immediate physical oversight, they are simultaneously subjected to greater dependency[5]. The employer's authority becomes more dispersed yet concentrated through digital control mechanisms.

This trend is reinforced by the fact that monitoring tools can be easily, inexpensively and highly effectively implemented, as they are now an integral part of modern, especially AI-based, communication and collaboration technology[6]. In fact, the provision of digital workplace monitoring tools has evolved into a distinct business sector, with a growing number of software vendors offering such solutions in recent years[7].

### 9.2.2 *Monitoring Measures: The Impact of Data Protection Law*

The justification for implementing monitoring software, however, is not limited to the employer's legitimate interest of ensuring the employee's compliance with the labour contract and maintaining managerial authority beyond the workplace. Data protection law can also support this rationale, because telework is inconceivable without data processing. However, even when an employee works remotely and processes data from home, the employer still determines the purpose and means of data processing. This is because the employer's role as a 'controller' in the sense of

4 Goricnik (2021, 150).
5 Jervis (2018, 449).
6 Jervis (2018, 448); Nurse et al. (2021, 5).
7 Aloisi and De Stefano (2022, 298); Auer-Mayer (2020/88).

Article 4 (7) GDPR does not depend on the location where the employee is working.

As the data controller, the employer is responsible under Article 24 (1) GDPR for implementing appropriate technical and organisational measures to ensure, and demonstrate, that data processing complies with the GDPR. In other words, the employer is required to establish a data protection policy. In accordance with Article 32 GDPR, this policy must include specific measures to address the risk of accidental or unlawful destruction, loss, alteration, unauthorised disclosure of or access to personal data that is transmitted, stored or otherwise processed. It is the responsibility of the controller, that is, the employer, to decide which measures are appropriate to achieve these objectives. However, when determining these specific measures, the 'nature, scope, context, and purposes of processing, as well as the risks of varying likelihood and severity for the rights and freedoms of natural persons' must be considered, as explicitly outlined in the GDPR. In summary, the greater the risk of a potential data breach, the stronger the need for effective measures to ensure data protection and security.

Given the strict standards of European data protection law, there is no doubt that remote telework conducted from an employee's home poses a significant risk to the data protection rights of individuals. The employer is typically unable to ensure that other individuals, particularly family members, do not have access to sensitive data, nor can the employer guarantee that this data is stored securely[8]. The mere fact that family members share the same living space, or even the same room, as the employee must already be considered a risk. Additionally, the home infrastructure used to perform work-related tasks, such as internet access, falls outside the employer's control. This, in turn, may justify the implementation of extensive digital monitoring of teleworkers[9].

## 9.3 THE EMPLOYER'S RIGHT TO CONTROL: FOUNDATIONS AND BOUNDARIES

Considering the relationship between telework and monitoring, one must acknowledge that control is, of course, an integral part of any employment relationship. Even if it is not explicitly outlined in the employment contract, the employer's right to exercise control is implicitly agreed upon by both parties. It is, in fact, a reflection, and more importantly, a fundamental aspect, of the personal dependency that defines the employee's legal status under labour law. Since employees agree to provide services of a certain quantity and quality under the employer's direction, the employer has the right to monitor and verify whether the employee is fulfilling their contractual obligations. However, the employer's right to control is inherently linked

[8] WP29 (2017, 16).

[9] Ibid.

to the employee as a person. This is a logical consequence of the nature of an employment contract, where the services provided cannot be separated from the individual providing them. As a result, control of the services inherently involves control of the individual performing those services.

### 9.3.1 *The Role of Fundamental Rights*

Nevertheless, the mutual agreement that the employer has a right to control does not imply that the employee has consented by these means to waive their personal rights. This statement is of central importance because individual personal rights are recognised and protected as human rights. The European Court of Human Rights recently made clear, that the right to respect for everyone's private life according to Article 8 includes also the legal obligation to take care of the employees' personal rights and their legitimate interests at the workplace[10]. That imposes the positive obligation to safeguard respect for private life in the relations between individuals, and therefore also between the labour parties, by setting up a legislative framework taking into consideration the various interests to be protected in a particular context[11]. That applies especially to monitoring measures set up by employers at the workplace, as the European Court of Human Rights pointed out: the right to respect for private life contains the obligation to ensure that the introduction of measures to monitor employees, irrespective of the extent and duration of such measures, is accompanied by adequate and sufficient safeguards against abuse[12]. One of these safeguards, according to the European Court of Human Rights, is the employer's obligation to provide legitimate reasons to justify monitoring employees. More invasive methods, therefore, require weightier justification[13].

The enshrinement of the right to respect for private life as a human and thus as a fundamental right would generally lead one to expect that it imposes effective limits on employers using technical measures to control employees, particularly at home. Although the human rights impact has been explicitly recognised by the European Court of Human Rights, the Court has also clarified that the scope and extent of such control measures depend on the employer's legitimate interest in monitoring their employees. In effect, this means that individual personal rights are not absolute but are contingent on the competing interests of the employer. What is noteworthy in this context is that these interests do not necessarily need to be backed by fundamental rights; rather, purely economic interests seem sufficient to justify intrusions into the right to respect of private life.

[10] Cf ECHR Barbulescu vs Romania Rc 70 ff.
[11] Cf ECHR Barbulescu vs Romania Rc 115.
[12] Cf ECHR Barbulescu vs Romania Rc 120.
[13] Cf ECHR Barbulescu vs Romania Rc 120.

This is indicated by the case law of the European Court of Human Rights who concluded in a landmark case that GPS tracking of vehicles to monitor the distances driven by employees during work activities is consistent with Article 8 ECHR, provided the employer uses it to verify the accuracy of recorded daily, weekly and monthly activities, visits made, absences and business travel expenses. The Court recognised that by evaluating geolocation data related to distances travelled, the employer is pursuing the legitimate aim of monitoring the company's expenses which justifies GPS tracking of employees[14]. Or in other words: mere economic interests are sufficient justification for allowing significant interference with employees' personal rights.

This approach which makes the extent, duration and intensity of control measures contingent upon the employer's economic interests is on closer look highly problematic as data protection comes into play.

### 9.3.2 *The Role of Data Protection Law*

The conclusion that the employer can rely on legitimate interests in relation to employees working remotely is crucial for the introduction of digital monitoring measures, particularly from a data protection law perspective. Since digital surveillance of teleworkers inherently involves data processing, the requirements of data protection law, harmonised across the European Union through the regulatory instrument of a regulation, must also be fulfilled. According to the GDPR, any processing of personal data must be 'lawful' under Article 6 and, depending on the sensitivity of the data involved, under Article 9 as well. This could again serve as an effective limitation on invasive control measures by the employer, especially since the possibility of individual consent to monitoring measures is mostly not available at the time of entering into the employment contract. Article 7 GDPR requires 'freely given consent' to data processing. However, the element of voluntariness is notoriously absent in the employment relationship due to the structural imbalance between employee and employer and the resulting dependency[15].

Nonetheless, the GDPR provides other grounds under which data can be lawfully processed. In this context, Article 6 (1) lit f is particularly relevant, as it permits data processing if the processor again can demonstrate a legitimate interest. Although Article 6 (1) lit f GDPR does allow for the consideration of the employee's interests as well, especially when shaped by a fundamental right like the right to respect for private life, it is also true that these rights and freedoms must 'override' the interests of the data controller to prevent the processing of personal data. It is not sufficient if the employee's interests or fundamental rights are merely impacted; they must outweigh the controller's legitimate interests to limit data processing.

[14] Cf ECHR Florindo de Almeida Vasconcelos Gramaxo vs Portugal – 26968/16.

[15] Kotschy (2020, 330); Van Ecke and Simkus (2020, 1234).

The possible consequences of this highly problematic legal approach to legitimate data processing by an assessment of interests shall be illustrated by the following example: Taking screenshots hourly with the purpose to check whether teleworkers are sitting and working at their desk is obviously striking the employee's personal rights. But at the same time, one could raise the question by which other means the employer shall control whether a teleworker is in fact fulfilling his or her duties to perform services in person at home? Would it not be lawful as well, if the employer enters the employees' offices at the employer's premise every hour to check whether they are present? Are the interests of the teleworkers in respecting their private lives indeed 'overriding' the employer's legitimate interests to check compliance with the labour contract in this case?

The GDPR does not give a concrete answer to these questions. That is the point where Article 8 ECHR might come into play. The enshrinement of the right to respect for private life as a human right would again lead one to expect that it imposes effective limits on employers processing personal employees' data considering that Article 6 (1) lit f GDPR is explicitly referring to the 'interests' and 'fundamental rights or freedoms' of the data subject. However, Article 8 ECHR does not seem to be the appropriate lever to strengthen employees' interests within this weighting, at least according to the interpretation of the European Court of Human Rights who stated that the employer's reliance on merely economic interests shall already be sufficient to justify close-knit geo-tracking of the employees' activities[16]. It is not to be expected that a stricter standard will be applied in data protection law. This is particularly true in light of the common legal doctrine on Article 6 (1) lit f GDPR which accepts every 'visible' interest not necessarily explicitly recognised by law as a legitimate interest of the controller, respectively, the employer[17].

Therefore, the importance of the GDPR setting up additional general principles for the processing of data must not be underestimated in practice, because they give at least certain guidelines for the concrete design of monitoring measures: Article 5 (1) lit a safeguards that the employee must be informed in advanced about the implementation of measures monitoring his or her activities. Furthermore, the obligation to delete data, which are no longer serving a legitimate purpose, can be extracted from Article 5 (1) lit e. However, once again, the general principles do not address the question to what extent the interests of the data subject must be considered for data processing to be considered lawful. And this once more is a loophole because it led the European Court of Human Rights to come to the conclusion that close-meshed geo-tracking serving the legitimate aim to monitor the company's expenditures is lawful as long as it was notified to the employee in advance and as long as the collected data gets deleted after checking the reported and registered activities[18]. Applied to the initial example of

[16] ECHR Florindo de Almeida Vasconcelos Gramaxo vs Portugal – 26968/16.
[17] Kotschy 2020, 337.
[18] ECHR Florindo de Almeida Vasconcelos Gramaxo vs Portugal – 26968/16.

monitoring teleworkers through screenshots, this ruling leads to the following result: screenshots taken automatically every hour might be lawful in the light of the jurisdiction of the European Court of Human Rights as long as the employee has been informed in advance and as long as the screenshots get deleted after having checked that the employee is in fact present in his or her home office, which must be considered a legitimate employer's interest comparable to the interest of monitoring the company's expenses.

## 9.4 A LABOUR LAW APPROACH

This mechanism of Article 8 ECHR as well as of the GDPR allowing to weigh up every possible employer's interest – even merely economic interests – with employee's fundamental rights without setting standards for a proper balance is apparently a fundamental loophole of our existing set of laws which will probably cause even more problems in the near future. It seems evident that modern information technologies, particularly AI-driven systems, will increasingly permeate the organisation and execution of economic activities. These technologies will become even more crucial as means of production and operational resources for employers than they are today. Soon there will be no alternative, less intrusive measures that employers could use[19]. Consequently, the employer's interest in utilising them will also grow[20]. This is a reality that judges cannot ignore when balancing the conflicting interests of employers and employees. Therefore, it is very likely that the 'collateral damage' caused by these technologies, which enable comprehensive surveillance, will be accepted due to the lack of viable alternatives. In summary, the growing digitalisation will shift the balance of interests in favour of employers, which, under current regulations, will likely render even highly intrusive surveillance measures lawful[21].

However, this scenario of new technologies having unforeseeable and at the same time inevitable impacts on the personal rights of employees is not totally new. Only the dimension is probably unprecedented[22]. In fact, on the level of national labour law specific mechanisms were already designed in the past to safeguard that the personal rights of employees are respected properly and not overridden by the economic interests of the employer[23]. A central role in this context is played by collective representation of interests. From the outset, its function has been to balance the structural inequality between employees and employers. And, indeed, it has been shown that this approach can ensure fair working conditions for employees. This has ultimately led to the right to collective bargaining finally being

[19] Cf with regard to the 'least intrusive means test' Molè and Mangan (2023, 699).
[20] Cf also Van Ecke and Simkus (2020, 1236).
[21] Molè and Mangan (2023, 700).
[22] Aloisi and De Stefano (2022, 300).
[23] Aloisi and Gramano (2019, 108 f.)

constitutionally protected by both the ECHR (Article 11) and the EU Charter of Fundamental Rights (Article 28).

In Austria[24] as well as in Germany[25] for instance, an employer's right to exercise control is contingent upon a collective agreement between the employer and the works council, the democratically elected and mandatory representative of all employees at the workplace. The involvement of the works council, along with the ability to apply collective pressure, aims to ensure that the personal rights of individual employees are adequately protected and that the specific control measures implemented are not overly intrusive[26]. In this way, collective labour law seeks to limit the employer's control to a legitimate purpose, ensuring it does not exceed what is necessary to achieve that aim. In other words, employees' participation shall prevent that personal dependency results in a system of total personal surveillance.

In practice, employers will need to offer specific commitments or guarantees to safeguard personal rights in order to reach an agreement with the works council. Without such an agreement, the employer is not permitted to introduce or implement monitoring measures. The obligation to engage in collective bargaining and reach an agreement is in fact a powerful tool to ensure that employees' interests are properly considered. To prevent the misuse of this bargaining power, German law provides employers with the option to apply for conciliation if an agreement with the works council cannot be reached[27]. Austrian labour law does not provide this possibility but requires the employer to reach an agreement, at least with regard to control measures which 'touch human dignity'[28]. So, for example, the introduction of new AI-based information technologies, enabling the employer to monitor the performance and activities of teleworkers in a very granular way, requires the involvement of the works council and therefore a consideration of the employees' interests under Austrian as well as under German law. The idea behind this legislation is that collective negotiations about the introduction and implementation of monitoring measures serve as a very effective legal instrument to safeguard the respect for employees' personal rights.

## 9.5 LABOUR LAW AND DATA PROTECTION LAW: FRIENDS OR FOES?

A comparable structural imbalance and thus the need to balance interests can be observed in relation to the processing of personal data for control purposes. On the one hand, employees are often unaware of or do not fully understand the monitoring capabilities associated with the use of digital information and communication technologies. On the other hand, there is a risk that employees may accept intrusive

[24] Cf Sect 96 para 1 no 3 and Sect 96a para 1 no 1 Arbeitsverfassungsgesetz (ArbVG).
[25] Cf Sect 87 para 1 no 6 Betriebsverfassungsgesetz (BetrVG).
[26] Krause (2020, 361).
[27] Sect 87 para 2 Betriebsverfassungsrecht (BetrVG).
[28] Sect 96 para 1 no 3 Arbeitsverfassungsgesetz (ArbVG).

monitoring simply to secure the opportunity to work remotely. In this context, protecting individual privacy rights through collective representation in negotiations with the employer could be a viable approach.

However, implementing this mechanism, which ties an employer's authorisation to collect and process employees' personal data to the existence of a collective agreement, means that standards for protecting employees' individual interests may vary from company to company, depending on the specific agreement in place. The ability to develop tailored solutions through this process is undoubtedly a benefit. From a data protection law perspective, however, one might question whether the GDPR aligns with the Austrian and German approach, as the GDPR aims to establish a uniform and binding standard for the legality of data processing across all Member States. That is why the European legislator chose the legal instrument of a regulation whose introduction was justified by the need to ensure the proper functioning of the internal market[29]. Or to put it in the words of the CJEU: the regulation seeks to ensure the harmonisation of national legislation on the protection of personal data which is, in principle, complete[30]. As a consequence, according to the Court, Article 6 GDPR sets out an exhaustive and restrictive list of the cases in which processing of personal data can be regarded as lawful[31]. The consent of employees' representatives through a collective agreement is not explicitly mentioned in this list, which is unsurprising given that the approach of data protection law is individualistic rather than collective.

### 9.5.1 *Data Protection through Collective Agreements*

However, the GDPR includes an important exception that allows Member States to introduce 'more specific rules', which can lead to deviations from the general standards established by the GDPR. According to Article 88 (1) Member States may, by law or by collective agreements, provide for more specific rules to ensure the protection of the rights and freedoms in respect of the processing of employees' personal data in the employment context. In other words, Member States may introduce specific employment data protection provisions which do not necessarily have to follow one single common European standard. These 'more specific rules' can be based on 'laws' as well as 'collective agreements' according to the explicit wording of the GDPR. Article 88 (1) GDPR thus provides an opportunity for employee participation in finding a fair balance between the employer's and employees' interests regarding the processing of personal data.

[29] Cf Rec 13 of the GDPR 2016/67/EU.

[30] CJEU C-34/21, Hauptpersonalrat der Lehrerinnen und Lehrer beim Hessischen Kultusministerium, Rc 51.

[31] CJEU C-34/21, Hauptpersonalrat der Lehrerinnen und Lehrer beim Hessischen Kultusministerium, Rc 70.

Thus, Article 88 (1) GDPR appears to be a suitable legal basis for integrating the labour law approach of protecting individual interests through collective means with the general principles of data protection law, especially concerning the lawfulness of monitoring measures. Article 88 (2) GDPR points out that those 'more specific rules' shall include suitable and specific measures to safeguard the data subject's human dignity, legitimate interests, and fundamental rights, with particular regard to (among others) monitoring systems at the workplace. At first glance, Article 88 GDPR appears to facilitate a connection between data protection law and labour law mechanisms, such as those in Austrian and German law, which require employers to negotiate the introduction and implementation of monitoring measures with the works council[32].

A closer examination of the so-called 'opening clause' in Article 88 GDPR, however, may raise concerns about the interplay between labour and data protection law. Specifically, a range of complex legal questions emerges: Are only trade unions permitted to negotiate such 'more specific rules', or can works councils at the shop level, as foreseen in Austrian and German law, also engage in this process? The term 'collective agreement' in Article 88 (1) GDPR is not sufficiently clear in this point. Additionally, a works council in contrast to a trade union cannot invoke the right to collective bargaining guaranteed by Article 11 ECHR and Article 28 EU Charter of Fundamental Rights in this context, because their role is based on a legal obligation rather than the free will to participate. Moreover, the purpose of the GDPR to establish a common and coherent standard for data processing could support a restrictive interpretation as well. However, there is a strong argument that shop agreements are also included: Recital 155 of the GDPR refers explicitly to 'works agreements' explaining the consideration behind Article 88.

Another important question is whether the negotiating parties have complete freedom in shaping these specific measures to safeguard data subjects' human dignity in the context of monitoring systems, or if it is up to the legislator to define these measures? The CJEU recently stated that the Member States' discretion in adopting rules under Article 88 (1) GDPR is constrained by paragraph 2[33]. Hence, in order to be classified as a 'more specific rule' within the meaning of Article 88 (1) GDPR, the measures designed to protect employees' interests must meet the conditions outlined in paragraph 2 of that Article[34]. According to this provision, those more specific rules shall include 'suitable and specific measures to safeguard the data subject's human dignity, legitimate interests and fundamental rights, with particular regard to the transparency of processing [...] and monitoring systems at

[32] Goricnik (2023, Tz 41).

[33] CJEU C-34/21, Hauptpersonalrat der Lehrerinnen und Lehrer beim Hessischen Kultusministerium, Rc 72.

[34] CJEU C-34/21, Hauptpersonalrat der Lehrerinnen und Lehrer beim Hessischen Kultusministerium, Rc 74.

the work place'[35]. It may be questioned whether these requirements are met if the Austrian or German legislator only mandates employee participation in introducing monitoring measures without specifying parameters for the social partners on how to safeguard employees' human dignity and fundamental rights. Or, in other words, is it in line with Article 88 (2) if the legislator leaves it entirely up to the social partners to define the appropriate measures?[36] If this is not the case, would that not again infringe upon the autonomy of social partners and the right to collective bargaining protected by Article 11 ECHR and Article 28 EU Charter of Fundamental Rights? These questions clearly indicate that Articles 88 (1) and 88 (2) GDPR do not adequately account for the specific mechanisms and functioning of collective labour law. However, an interpretation that does not adequately recognise the bargaining autonomy of the social partners risks undermining the potential of the opening clause to serve as an effective interface between labour law and data protection law.

### 9.5.2 *Balancing of Interest through Collective Agreements*

Against this background, it is particularly important that there is another strong legal rationale for collective bargaining as a key instrument to protect employees' personal interests when they are subject to the processing of their personal data. According to Article 6 (1) lit f GDPR processing of data is lawful if the processing 'is necessary for the purposes of the legitimate interests pursued by the controller or by a third party, except where such interests are overridden by the interests or fundamental rights and freedoms of the data subject which require protection of personal data'. To put it simply, the lawfulness of data processing depends on the balancing of interests. How this balancing of interests is to be carried out is, of course, left open by the European legislator. This is a big advantage, because it allows for the incorporation or application of labour law standards in this assessment. Referring again to Austrian legislation, it can be argued that within a system of collective negotiations, which does not provide for compulsory arbitration, the balance of interests required by Article 6 (1) lit f GDPR is achieved by the mere fact that the employer and employees' representatives reach a mutual agreement on the conditions and extent of personal data processing in the context of monitoring measures, provided that this agreement contains specific provisions to safeguard employees' personal rights as outlined in Article 88 (2). In other words, the fact that social partners have reached an agreement confirms in the sense of Article 6 (1) lit f GDPR that employees' fundamental rights and interests are considered properly and do not override the employer's interests in processing data[37]. This interpretation of Article 6 (1) lit f

[35] Cf also Van Ecke and Simkus (2020, 1234).

[36] Goricnik (2023, Tz 39).

[37] Felten and Preiss (2020, Tz 11).

GDPR would ultimately lead to a coherent application of labour law and data protection law and would give space to collective bargaining also in the context of data processing and the protection of individual privacy rights.

## 9.6 CONCLUSION

The legal challenges linked to telework clearly highlight that one-dimensional solutions will in the future no longer be sufficient to guarantee adequate protection and appropriate working conditions for employees. This is particularly true when it comes to setting limits on extensive monitoring of teleworkers. The current labour law framework is increasingly proving inadequate on its own. Even the recognition of employees' rights as fundamental rights has had little effect on changing this. Due to the use of modern information and communication technologies, which inevitably involve the processing of employee data, data protection law must also be considered. While labour law and data protection law share structural similarities – both address a structural imbalance that must be mitigated through legal means – the tools and mechanisms used to achieve this goal differ significantly. In particular, the collective approach of labour law is alien to data protection law. However, as the example of teleworking shows, there are points of connection in existing law that make it possible to integrate the collective approach of labour law into data protection law, thereby closing existing protection gaps. This, however, currently requires significant interpretative effort, which entails a high degree of legal uncertainty for all parties involved, both employers and employees. It should, therefore, be the task of the European legislator to anchor data protection law more firmly to collective bargaining, as enshrined in the EU Charter of Fundamental Rights.

## REFERENCES


Aloisi, Antonio and De Stefano, Valerio, Essential jobs, remote work and digital surveillance: addressing the COVID-19 pandemic panopticon, *International Labour Review* Vol. 161, No. 2 (2022), pp. 289–315.

Aloisi, Antonio and Gramano, Elena, Artificial intelligence is watching you at work: digital surveillance, employee monitoring, and regulatory issues in the EU context comparative, *Labor Law & Policy Journal* Vol. 41, No. 1 (2019), pp. 95–122.

Auer-Mayer, Susanne, Dürfen Arbeitnehmer*innen im "Home-Office" überwacht werden?, CuRe 2020/88.

Felten, Elias and Preiss, Jochen, *§ 96a ArbVG*, in: Gahleitner, Sieglinde and Mosler, Rudolf (eds), *Arbeitsverfassungsrecht* $3^{6}$, ÖGB-Verlag: Wien, 2020, pp. 230–249.

Goricnik, Wolfgang, *Art 88 DSGVO*, in: Knyrim, Rainer (ed), *DatKomm*, Manz Verlag: Wien, 2023, pp. 1–63.

Goricnik, Wolfgang, Wider das "Trojanische Pferd" home-office im Dauerrecht, *DRdA-infas* Vol. 2 (2021), pp. 149–152.

Jervis, Claire E. M., Barbulescu v Romania: Why there is no room for complacency when it comes to privacy rights in the workplace. *Industrial Law Journal* Vol. 47, No. 3 (2018), pp. 440–453.

Kotschy, Waltraut, Article 6 Lawfulness of processing, in: Kuner, Christopher et al. (eds), *The EU General Data Protection Regulation (GDPR): A Commentary*, Oxford Academic: New York, 2020, pp. 321–344.

Krause, Rüdiger, Sozialverträgliche Arbeitnehmerüberwachung – Technikbasierte Beschäftigtenkontrolle als Gegenstand betrieblicher Mitbestimmung im digitalen Zeitalter, in: Gräfl, Edith, Lunk, Stefan, Oetker, Hartmund and Trebing, Yvonne (eds), *100 Jahre Betriebsverfassungsrecht*, CH Beck Verlag: München, 2020, pp. 353–369.

Molè, Michele and Mangan, David, 'Just more surveillance': The ECtHR and workplace monitoring. *European Labour Law Journal* Vol. 14, No. 4 (2023), pp. 694–700.

Nurse, Jason R. C., Williams, Nikki, Collins, Emily, Panteli, Niki, Blythe, John and Koppelman, Ben, Remote Working Pre- and Post-COVID-19: An Analysis of New Threats and Risks to Security and Privacy, in: 23[rd] *International Conference on Human-Computer Interaction*, 24–29 Jul 2021, pp. 1–8.

Van Eecke, Patrick and Šimkus, Anrijs, Article 88 Processing in the context of employment, in: Kuner, Christopher et al. (eds), *The EU General Data Protection Regulation (GDPR): A Commentary*. Oxford Academic: New York, 2020, pp. 1229–1239.

Vitak, Jessica and Zimmer, Michael, Surveillance and the future of work: exploring employees' attitudes toward monitoring in a post-COVID workplace. *Journal of Computer-Mediated Communication* Vol. 28, No. 4 (2023), pp 1–11.

WP29 2017: Article 29 Working Party, 'Opinion 02/2017 on Data Processing at Work' (WP 249, 8 June 2017).

# 10

# Remote Work and Artificial Intelligence

## *Threat or Chance for Worker's Rights?*

*Miguel Rodríguez-Piñero Royo and Eusebi Colàs-Neila*

### 10.1 INTRODUCTION: REMOTE WORK BETWEEN DIGITAL AND ALGORITHMIC LAW

Remote work is digital. Although traditional home-based work appeared well before the spread of digital technology, remote work in the way we perceive it in the twenty-first century developed in this technological context. It was digital technology that allowed remote work to develop and to become a widely prevalent form of employment. These media are extensively used not only to carry out the work but also to control it, making the teleworker a person who is especially monitored and supervised. The teleworker is a unique and distinctive employee, primarily due to their high dependence on technology.

Not only this. We could say that remote work through electronic devices, a category known as telework in Spanish law and other legal systems, is the quintessential manifestation of digital work, one whose very existence directly depends on the availability of these devices. It is technology that distinguishes it from other current forms of employment as well as from home-based work of past eras.

Remote work as we know it today became widespread in the twenty-first century due to technical developments, changes in the workforce, and the impact of the COVID-19 pandemic. In these early decades of the century, it is coexisting with another phenomenon that is shaping and characterizing social and economic evolution: the development of artificial intelligence (AI) systems, based on the use of algorithms for decision-making and the generation of texts, images, and content.

The Regulation of the European Parliament and of the Council laying down harmonized rules on artificial intelligence (the so-called Artificial Intelligence Act)[1] defines "artificial intelligence system" as any "*software that is developed with one or more of the techniques and approaches listed in Annex I and can, for a given set of*

[1] Regulation (EU) 2024/1689 of the European Parliament and of the Council of 13 June 2024.

*human-defined objectives, generate outputs such as content, predictions, recommendations, or decisions influencing the environments they interact with.*" These programs can be included in the decision-making process of companies (for example, to decide on hiring, firing, or rewarding; or be used in the development of the company's own activities, being available to its staff). In either case, they are already widespread and affecting the way people approach their work experience.

Remote work and AI have emerged simultaneously as two current manifestations of changes driven by rapid scientific advancements. Although they operate on different planes – remote work being a "physical" phenomenon as it pertains to the manner of conducting activities, and AI being "virtual" as it involves cutting-edge software – there are significant areas of intersection. Algorithmic management systems undoubtedly influence both the execution of telework and its prevalence in the market, potentially promoting and incentivizing it. In this context, and using a concept prevalent in AI studies, this form of employment is "highly exposed to AI," with substantial changes anticipated as these systems evolve and proliferate.

The AI revolution is being accompanied by the development of regulations aimed at organizing both its development and use, according to standards set by states and based on perceived or confirmed risks (Eurofound, 2023). The goal, as noted by the European Commission, is the ethical development of AI, which has led to the involvement of national and supranational legislators. Or, as the G7 Labour and Employment Ministers declared recently, a "*human-centred approach in seizing the opportunities and addressing the risks to the world of work.*"[2] Their regulations will also apply, as appropriate, to remote work, to the extent that such systems are used in it, as is foreseeable.

The starting hypothesis of this chapter is that a new branch is emerging in contemporary legal systems: Artificial Intelligence Law. This branch has a clear labor area, as these systems impact both work and the effectiveness of the regulations designed to govern it according to standards of rights, dignity, and justice. It has emerged as a specialization of Digital Labor Law, a spin-off, so to speak, sharing a common genetic code with it.

Remote work, when incorporating AI systems in its execution, is governed by this set of regulations, which are superimposed on the specific rules pertaining to this form of employment within digital labor law.

[2] G7, "Towards an inclusive human-centered approach for new challenges in the world of work", Ministerial Declaration of the G7 Labour and Employment Ministers' Meeting in Cagliari, 12–13 September 2024. To confront with the perspective of labour unions, see ETUC (2022), "Resolution calling for an EU Directive on Algorithmic Systems at Work"; https://etuc.org/sites/default/files/document/file/2023-01/Adopted%20ETUC%20Resolution%20calling%20for%20an%20EU%20Directive%20on%20Algorithmic%20Systems%20at%20Work%20.pdf; accessed: 05-06-2024.

## 10.2 REMOTE WORK UNDER DIGITAL LAW

As previously mentioned, remote work originated in a pre-electronic context, developed as analogical work and widespread as digital. The current regulations governing remote work are a central component of digital labor law, representing its most developed area and encompassing all relevant aspects of this regulation. However, this has not always been the case.

We can identify three generations in the legal regulation of remote work. Initially, outdated regulations on home-based work were generally applied. These regulations were designed in a completely different context and were intended more for domestic workshops than for services. The clear shortcomings of these solutions, which were not only obsolete but also brief and insufficient, required corrections and supplementation. This led to the emergence of primitive forms of collective regulation, such as the telework agreements signed in some companies to initiate the first experiences with this form of employment. Telework agreements became common in firms conducting pilot projects with this technical innovation, often being the only regulation available.

The generalization of this employment form rendered the situation both unsatisfactory and unsustainable, prompting the emergence of a second generation of regulations. At the EU level, the Framework Agreement on Telework (2002) played a pivotal role in both promoting this shift in the regulatory model and in disseminating a regulatory content model that national laws gradually adopted[3]. The legislation of this generation had a clear objective of protecting teleworkers and adopted a "contractual" approach, focusing on the balance of benefits between the parties affected by the fact that work is carried out away from the employer's premises on a regular basis using information technology (following the Framework Agreement's definition of telework).

Second-generation legislation emphasizes the voluntary nature of telework, guarantees the right to return to traditional employment, and ensures a general right to equal treatment. These regulations primarily focus on protecting privacy and personal data, along with fundamental issues related to work equipment, liability, and costs, rather than extensively addressing technical matters. Typically, this legislation is presented as a monographic regulation, which is not overly extensive, often found within a specific piece of legislation or, more commonly, in a dedicated article or section. In the Spanish context, this regulatory phase, although somewhat delayed, aligns with the drafting of Article 13 of the Revised Text of the Workers' Statute, introduced by the 2012 labor law reform.

[3] It is noteworthy that European social partners have played a significant role in the development of digital labor law. In 2020, they signed the European Framework Agreement on Digitalisation, which focuses on the impact of the digital transformation of the economy on workers. This agreement covers four areas, including AI and guaranteeing the human in control principle.

Later developments have radically transformed the legal approach to remote work. This shift is the result of a confluence of various factors, leading to a growing number of remote workers. Third-generation laws are significantly more comprehensive than their predecessors, typically taking the form of extensive, monographic pieces of legislation, often as stand-alone bills outside general labor codes or employment contract legislation. In terms of content, they build upon previous generation laws, ensuring contractual protections in areas such as voluntariness, reversibility, equal treatment, and compensation for expenses. Beyond these, legislative authorities have introduced a range of additional provisions, rights, and guarantees.

Substantial improvements are evident in two key areas: the recognition of rights for remote workers, which now extends well beyond the general principle of equal treatment found in previous regulations; and the attention given to technological issues, including surveillance devices, computers, communication tools, software, IT security, and BYOD (Bring Your Own Device).

In general terms, we can affirm that remote work is currently a highly regulated reality, with regulations increasingly oriented towards the protection of rights and a high degree of sophistication in addressing technical aspects. This fact is particularly relevant when dealing with AI, as it is generally easier to construct a normative framework for AI by building on existing regulations, which can then be adapted to meet the demands imposed by this technological innovation[4]. Regulating the impact of AI on remote work will involve identifying new requirements and assessing the effectiveness of existing rules, a task that, while not easy, is certainly more feasible than developing an entirely new set of regulations.

In the current landscape of digital law, there is a second element that can facilitate matters. In most cases, remote or telework is presented as a distinct form of employment, differentiated from other forms of dependent work, and recognized as an autonomous category with its own designation.

Related to this, third-generation laws tend to establish a comprehensive statute for these workers, addressing most aspects of their employment relationship. This approach also facilitates the introduction of new, specific legal solutions to potential issues arising from the impact of AI systems. These solutions will apply exclusively to remote workers *tout court*, those for whom remote working is so integral that it defines their status within the legal framework.

The third generation of remote working regulations has emerged in several European countries. According to a study commissioned by the European Union, Austria, Spain, Greece, Latvia, Portugal, Romania, and Slovakia have adopted new legislation since the beginning of the pandemic.[5]

[4] See Pasquale (2022, 42).

[5] Visionary Analytics (2024, p.8)

However, this example could be extended across the entire European Union, as the European Commission has expressed interest in developing a standard on this matter. In fact, it launched the first-stage consultation of European social partners, in accordance with Article 154(2) of the Treaty on the Functioning of the European Union, to gather their views on the possible direction of EU action on ensuring fair telework and the right to disconnect[6], following the European Parliament resolution of January 21, 2021, with recommendations to the Commission on the right to disconnect[7]. This initiative also addresses the European cross-industry social partners, who have initiated negotiations to update their 2002 Framework Agreement on telework. Additionally, the Council conclusions on telework, approved by the Council of the European Union (EPSCO) at its meeting held on June 14, 2021, support this initiative[8]. With this backing it is highly likely that a directive on this matter will be enacted in due course, triggering a wave of reforms in the national labor laws of member states.

## 10.3 THE CONSTRUCTION OF AI LAW

The starting point of this work is the existence of AI law, with a branch that addresses both the impact of these systems on human resources management and the consequences of their generalization in work environments, as well as their use by competent public authorities in the labor market. This is an emerging body of law that builds on digital law, differentiates itself as a spin-off, and gives rise to second-generation digital rights. Despite the recent nature of this phenomenon, it has already yielded significant results[9]. Not only have some far-reaching regulations been adopted, such as the European Data Protection Regulation (insofar as it addresses automated decisions) and notably the European Regulation on Artificial Intelligence, but a substantial array of potentially effective solutions is already available to tackle the issues that the proliferation of such systems in various fields may generate. The rules comprising this body of law apply a toolbox of original solutions, including transparency, accountability, human review, potential for discrimination, degree of exposure, and risk classification[10].

[6] EUROPEAN COMMISSION, "First-phase consultation of social partners under Article 154 TFEU on possible EU action in the area of telework and workers' right to disconnect", Brussels, 30.4.2024 C(2024) 2990 final. See the press release "Commission launches first-stage consultation of social partners on fair telework and the right to disconnect"; available at https://ec.europa.eu/commission/presscorner/detail/en/ip_24_1363; visited on September 8, 2024.

[7] Available at www.europarl.europa.eu/doceo/document/TA-9-2021-0021_EN.html; accessed: 08-09-2024.

[8] "Council conclusions on telework", Brussels, 15 June 2021 (OR. en) 9747/21

[9] For a complete overview of the current state-of-the-art see Joint Research Center (2022), "The algorithmic management of work: A basic compass"; Science for Policy Brief, Sevilla, European Commission.

[10] See Rodríguez-Piñero Royo(2024).

This is because this framework has been largely preemptive, initiated when concerns about the potential risks associated with AI first arose, before its widespread use across all domains. This is not to say that AI is not already in use, but rather that, unlike previous technological changes, solutions have been designed in advance, based on reasonable forecasts and expectations, rather than waiting for extensive use to generate problems. The differences observed from this perspective, compared to the regulation of work on digital platforms (to cite just one example), are notable. Regulation of digital platforms was only considered when this reality became a pressing issue in the labor market due to the erosion of labor rights it entailed. The perception is that action was taken reactively, rather than proactively, and that it was delayed until the damage had already been done, leaving platform workers to suffer an unacceptable level of precariousness.

Algorithmic law has not emerged as a "Law of Judges," unlike digital labor law. Instead, it is an academic and technocratic creation. Developed by experts from various disciplines who recognized its potential impacts, algorithmic law aims to anticipate these effects and facilitate the transition to a new technological environment that respects individuals and their rights. It is not surprising that the European Union has been at the forefront of its development, given its proactive stance on technological innovation.

For example, many rules of digital law codify preexisting solutions developed by international or national courts, notably constitutional courts. This is evident in areas such as privacy rights versus video surveillance or the monitoring of computer equipment. However, this is not the case with algorithmic law.

Another characteristic of algorithmic law is its technical complexity and sophistication. These rules govern intricate and demanding technological realities, developed through a deep understanding of these systems. They go beyond mere statements, general principles, or broad-spectrum solutions. Instead, their responses are concrete, precisely identifying both their factual assumptions and the legal consequences attached to them. They employ a specialized language, generated within the technological field.

There are also regulatory instruments that are not traditional in continental legal systems, such as those manifesting as soft law, including declarations and charters. This is particularly evident in digital law, where we encounter instruments like the European Declaration on Digital Rights and Principles. Additionally, the presence of specialized bodies, such as agencies and working groups, is noteworthy. Although these entities do not possess regulatory powers of their own, they significantly influence the development of this law through the interpretation of its rules and the drafting of guidelines and recommendations for its application.[11]

[11] Among others, the European Data Protection Board (EDPB), the High-Level Expert Group on Artificial Intelligence, the European Union Agency for Fundamental Rights, and the now-defunct Article 29 Working Party. Similar agencies are found in national administrations.

Algorithmic labor law adopts a multilevel framework, presenting itself as the sum, coexistence, and interaction of norms developed by various entities. This mirrors the broader trends observed in labor law in this century.

To date, the regulations governing the use of AI have primarily been incorporated into specific and monographic texts, rather than within the general frameworks of employment contracts and labor relations. This approach is logical, given their objective of regulating software use and their inherently technical nature. However, there are exceptions to this trend, such as the inclusion of algorithmic information rights in laws concerning worker representation in companies and in those addressing the conclusion and formalization of employment contracts.

Additionally, references to algorithmic instruments can be found in public law regulations that govern administrative intervention in labor relations. These regulations aim to manage various legal relationships arising from the public social protection system and enhance the efficiency of sanctioning law in labor matters. Acts regarding social security, labor inspection, and administrative procedures are beginning to permit and regulate the use of these mechanisms.

A unique aspect of algorithmic labor law is the existence of a dual regulatory framework. Alongside what can be considered "general" regulations applicable to all employment relationships, there is a specific set of rules tailored for a distinct group: platform workers. This form of employment, closely linked to the use of algorithms, has generated numerous problems and abuses, prompting the establishment of rules aimed at preventing such issues[12].

These regulations have particularly focused on the qualification of services, an area that general AI standards often overlook. The urgency of addressing these concerns for digital platforms has led to the development of standards that, in many cases, have been pioneering in the regulation of algorithms, effectively serving as a testing ground or sandbox for innovative solutions (Aloisi & Potocka-Sionek, 2022).

When progress has been made toward the adoption of general rules, especially at EU level, there has not been a unification of regulations, but they have remained separate. We have an Artificial Intelligence Regulation and a Directive for the improvement of working conditions on digital work platforms[13], and the same situation is found in other legal systems.

## 10.4 THE IMPACT OF AI ON REMOTE WORKING

AI is one of the main drivers of the new contemporary digital environment. Although it is still in the early stages of its evolution and we are only just glimpsing

[12] See International Labour Office, 2021, "The role of digital labour platforms in transforming the world of work"; World Employment and Social Outlook 2021; Geneva, Office of Publications of the ILO.

[13] For a first analysis, see Ponce Del Castillo (2023). Also, Rainone and Alosi (2024, 4).

what its impact is likely to be, there is no doubt that it is one of the most disruptive contemporary megatrends[14].

The introduction and progressive expansion of the use of AI systems in the world of work needs to be seen as part of the broader process of digital technological evolution that has been developing over the last decades. Considered from a diachronic perspective, some debates and issues are common, such as the potential for job creation/destruction or the renewed emphasis on fundamental rights. However, the ability of AI systems to automate decision-making and content generation, as a distinctive feature, poses new challenges.

Features of digital technology in general, and of AI in particular, make it difficult to analyze its impact on remote work. Firstly, its high level of technical complexity and its potential for development and change, which require prior knowledge (and continuous updating) of how it works. Moreover, its ambivalence, understood as the absence of technological determinism, means that its effects depend on its use, and can have either positive or negative implications for both parties in the employment relationship[15]. On the other hand, its ductile nature allows us to maintain, as a hypothesis, the lack of significant differences in its implementation regardless of the place where the work is performed, whether on-site or remotely. Particularities in the latter case may derive from an eventually greater intensity in its use, considering the physical absence of the workplace and the fact that digital technology is inherent to remote work, which may give rise to AI systems designed especially for these cases. Nevertheless, we can attempt to highlight a few potential areas where the effects of this combination are foreseeable[16].

Indeed, the algorithmization of remote work can be visible, with varying intensity, in areas such as the generation of remote jobs or their organization and management. The use of AI systems may be particularly beneficial in several aspects where traditional management tools may face challenges, such as the monitoring of work activity, communication and coordination between workers, and the control of compliance with labor legislation by the labor inspectorate; however, this improvement is not without risks, as some potential negative repercussions can also be foreseen.

[14] A more detailed analysis of the concept, its evolution, and manifestations in Mittelstaedt et al. (2014).

[15] According to Lucas Murillo, digital technology allows for a "dual, sometimes unconscious, use," and its "meaning, from a moral point of view" is a result of the purpose for which it is used (Lucas Murillo, 2003: 35). For Crawford, regarding AI, it "is not an objective, universal or neutral computational technique" since their form is given to them by human beings or institutions, and they reproduce and amplify hierarchies and situations of discrimination" (Crawford, 2021: 211). In addition, the dissemination management of Generative AI will determine its socioeconomic effects (Gmyrek et al., 2023).

[16] Baldwin and Okubo (2023) highlight, from a case study in Japan, that there is a complimentary relationship between software that facilitates telework and service task automation software. Thus, task automation can influence the ability to work from home in a number of ways.

As noted above, the traditional debate associated with the implementation of new technology in production processes about its capacity to create or destroy jobs can also be applied to AI, focusing mainly on the automation of tasks and the replacement of human labor by robots. One of the distinctive features of AI with respect to previous technologies is that the tasks subject to automation are not restricted to non-cognitive and routine tasks and, given its potential general use, any sector or occupation can be affected (OECD 2023, 14).

Focusing on remote working, digital technology and AI systems allow activities traditionally carried out in person to be performed remotely. AI makes it possible to broaden the spectrum of "teleworkable" jobs, adapting them to this end by providing effective tools to carry out the work, through virtual reality techniques or robot remote control[17], among others, and to monitor employees remotely[18]. Thus, the use of remote working depends to a large degree on the "teleworkability" of a job, that is, the extent to which it is feasible to work remotely. In addition, the development of work for digital platforms must be considered, a form of employment that encompasses a variety of cases that involve the use of an algorithm at some point in the production process.

Similarly, remote work is to digital law what platform work is to algorithmic law: its most striking manifestation. Both modalities require customized solutions due to the intensity of the technological component. In practice, there is a significant overlap between both categories, as a substantial part of platform work is done remotely. This overlap is particularly evident in self-employment, through various forms of service provision outside the traditional employment contract. By facilitating the meeting of supply and demand (acting as marketplaces), standardizing the services exchanged, providing payment security, and enabling crowdworking, these platforms have extended the phenomenon, allowing activities that were previously not 'teleworkable' to be performed remotely. In short, the ability of AI to reshape the nature (face-to-face or remote) of employment takes place not only in respect of subordinate employment but also in self-employment.

For these same reasons, digital platforms, which should indeed be labeled "algorithmic," enhance the transnational offer of remote work and digital nomadism. They make it easier for professionals to choose their place of residence and work, or the country in whose market they offer their services[19].

However, platform work comes at a cost, as it is associated with precariousness, the increase of the employer's powers and the unilateral determination of working

[17] Telesurgery, the possibility of remote surgery using robots, is taking its first successful steps. Recently, as part of the 21st Annual Meeting of the EAU Robotic Urology Section, a patient in Beijing underwent telesurgery from Bordeaux. See https://erus.uroweb.org/8264km-distance-historic-first-for-prof-breda-and-eau-event/.

[18] On the surveillance of teleworkers see Felten's contribution in this volume.

[19] On cross-border remote work and its regulatory implications, see the contribution by De le Court in this volume. See also Grušić (2023, 192).

conditions[20]. It is, therefore, not by chance that the regulation of this form of employment has been a pioneer in the development of AI labor law[21].

Work organization is characterized by algorithmic management, which makes it necessary to reexamine core labor law institutions such as working time, wages, health protection, or equality and nondiscrimination (Aloisi & De Stefano, 2022). Adams-Prassl (2022) highlights, among others, the following challenges: the potential lack of transparency of automated decisions, which can make it difficult for workers to understand decisions (in many cases integrated with "traditional" technological systems, such as video surveillance and biometrics); unpredictability or unstable working conditions, resulting from the automation of functions; or the perpetuation or worsening of discriminatory situations, insofar as decisions on labor issues taken by AI systems are a "potential source of discrimination" (Kullmann 2018), as a consequence of biases in the data and variables used by AI, relying on the difficulties of detection for various reasons (invisibility, technical complexity, mathematical authority of AI systems).

In remote work, AI systems can help to overcome problems arising from the ubiquity of performance. Firstly, organizing the work process with the employer and colleagues, through the tools such as Asana, Trello, or Microsoft Themes that use AI to optimize task management and collaboration[22], or the implementation of virtual workplaces or "metaverse offices" (Chen, 2024). These can also facilitate relations with workers' representatives, clients, or labor administrations.

The employer can carry out less intrusive monitoring of workers, without physical intrusion by the employer, to verify the fulfillment of employment obligations. This has always been an area plagued of difficulties. Video surveillance is not common in remote work, reasonably, because of its disproportionate impact on the privacy of workers and their families. However, there is a constant transmission of images through the remote communication tools commonly used in telework, especially in recent years, as the availability of these programs has increased, and their costs have decreased.

The integration of video surveillance with AI tools has led to the development of intelligent cameras, which adapt their monitoring based on algorithmic guidance, enabling advanced image analytics. These innovations have enhanced the effectiveness of monitoring, extending its utility to support decision-making and improve workplace environments. Intelligent video surveillance can serve multiple purposes:

[20] According to Crawford (2021, 211), "AI systems are expressions of power… created to increase profits and centralize control for those who wield them."

[21] The Spanish Rider Law was a pioneer in this field, by including in the Workers' Statute the presumption of the subordinate nature of the provision of services on delivery platforms (full version in Spanish available at www.boe.es/eli/es/l/2021/09/28/12/con). Subsequently, the Directive on improving working conditions in platform work regulates this area in great detail.

[22] See Ezpe (2024), who points to AI tools particularly useful for improving communication and productivity in remote work environments that allow for automatic translation (Slack), automatic transcription (Zoom), or noise cancellation in video conferences (Google Meet).

it can anticipate health issues for workers, verify compliance with occupational risk prevention measures, and monitor actual working hours, benefiting both parties in the employment relationship.

Nonetheless, it is considered a highly intrusive monitoring system, raising significant privacy concerns. One of the many advantages of intelligent cameras, though, is their ability to be adjusted to mitigate this intrusion. This can be achieved by limiting the collection of images, deleting images collected in specific areas or at certain times, or identifying non-employees to exclude them from monitoring.

Besides image-based monitoring, AI can verify workers' performance from the use of the devices provided to them (by detecting and drawing conclusions from keystrokes, for example). This allows the evaluation of productivity with a high level of objectivity, through 'digital exhaust'[23].

AI can also enable the company to fulfill its responsibilities as an employer. One area of particular interest relates to occupational risk prevention[24]. The use of AI can generally improve occupational health and safety monitoring, minimize exposure to some risk factors, and provide early warning of potential stress or fatigue[25]. At the same time, legal and ethical issues may arise that need to be properly analyzed (EU-OSHA, 2021). The EU's AI Regulation prohibits systems from inferring emotions in the workplace, except for medical or safety reasons. Recital 19 excludes from this prohibition the monitoring of physical states, such as pain or fatigue, including systems used to detect fatigue levels of professional pilots or drivers to prevent accidents. This allows the use of image analysis in the framework of workers' health and safety policies, as well as for the general physical and mental well-being of the workforce.

There are challenges in remote work, such as physical isolation, and technology can contribute to promoting emotional well-being of workers[26]. AI can not only identify or even anticipate this psychosocial risk factor but also generate interfaces that may help to reduce this feeling by simulating human interaction during certain tasks. It can also be useful to ensure full compliance with the right to digital disconnection by automatically disabling any communication mechanism[27]. However, specific risks related to this technology have been identified, such as

[23] "Digital exhaust" are records and metadata generated incidentally by employees' digital activities – through emails, video conferencing, and app use – which, when analyzed together, can provide a wealth of information about their behavior and productivity, particularly important in remote work. In this regard, Leonardi (2020) highlights that their transformation into "digital footprints" can, through AI, predict and shape work behavior.

[24] A detailed analysis of the impact of AI on occupational health in Llorens Espada (2023).

[25] Using sensors that measure heart rate, brain activity, or even through selfies (see www.rrhhpress.com/zona-tech/59395-lanzan-una-aplicacion-que-puede-detectar-fatiga-laboral-con-un-selfie).

[26] On the health and safety challenges posed by remote working, see the contribution by Goñi et al. in this volume.

[27] Other AI tools in this area include postural control tools, which allow proper posture to be maintained through real-time cameras and sensors (Bootsman et al., 2019).

technostress and anxiety linked to over-supervision. These risks are also present in remote work, potentially at a higher level.

The potential of AI to enable workers' representatives, the labor inspectorate, and other authorities to perform their functions and to monitor compliance with labor regulations in the case of remote workers, to detect possible fraud, which is more difficult due to geographical dispersion, may be considered. Some national experiences offer good examples that can be implemented in remote work[28].

A final impact that should be considered concerns regulatory instruments. As noted above, we are witnessing the emergence of an algorithmic law, with specific rules for the employment sphere. The use of AI systems in remote work implies their consideration in parallel to digital law, which is regulating this form of employment. The normative contents and logics of both legal bodies do not coincide, so it is important to analyze the normative consequences of this legal duality.

## 10.5 NEW RULES FOR A NEW REMOTE WORK

When remote work is facilitated, managed, or controlled by an AI system, it involves a combination of digital law and algorithmic law mandates, as both sectors of the legal system are applicable. In this section, we will analyze the legal consequences of this regulatory duality, based on a comparative study of the regulations governing this form of employment alongside the rules applicable to AI in the European Union. The idea is to explore the outcome of the combination of both normative areas.

It is important to note that legal systems are already beginning to respond to this convergence. Thus, recent legislation on remote work is increasingly addressing the issue of AI. The Sectoral Agreement on Digitalisation, signed on October 6, 2022, by the European Social Dialogue Committee for Central Government Administrations, encompasses provisions on various matters, including teleworking and AI. In Spain, Article 17.1 of Act No. 10/2021 on remote work contemplates the use of automated devices for monitoring the provision of labor services.

However, as will be discussed, both areas usually fail to converge in the same regulatory body, maintaining regulations with varying logics that interplay and must be considered jointly. Thus, while in telework, as a form of digital employment, the consideration of the digital instrument and the data it handles is crucial, when regulating AI systems, the logic of the potential risk which must be mitigated prevails. Telework regulation has in many cases developed outside the framework of the regulatory bodies governing subordinate employment, and has a different

[28] The Spanish Social Security General Treasury uses algorithms to detect possible infringements and automatically undertake different administrative actions, such as the issuing of infringement reports and the creation of proposals for the resolution of infringement proceedings. An analysis of how it operates, the regulatory framework, and the challenges posed to citizens' rights in Goerlich Pesset (2021).

profile due to technological impact, which is visible in some specific aspects, such as the recognition of a broader right to be informed and trained about this essential element of this type of employment. On the other hand, AI Regulation is technical and complex, with efficient and didactic rules for the various actors it addresses. Although it does not consider the remote worker in particular, some of the principles on which it is based (transparency, human control, risk mitigation), are very useful in teleworking.

There is thus a kind of transition between normative paradigms because of the impact of digital technology and AI systems, which is particularly evident in remote work involving AI. On the one hand, from the analogical labor law to the digital labor law, as an expression of the centripetal forces leading to "the decontractualisation of labour protection" – the expulsion of some types of workers from the common body of law to create new ones (López López, 2014). And on the other hand, from digital labor law to algorithmic labor law, as an expression of a process of "decoding" (Rodríguez-Piñero Royo, 2024), understood as a trend to relocate labor standards outside their specific regulatory corpus.

As a preliminary step, two determining factors must be identified that condition the application of the AI Regulation. The first involves the inclusion of systems to be used within one of the four categories outlined by the AI Regulation, as this will determine the legal obligations imposed on the companies employing them. According to the recitals of the EU Regulation itself, AI systems used in workforce management should be classified as high-risk, given their potential impact on workers' rights. Article 6 and Annex II support this categorization. This includes intelligent tools used for decision-making affecting the terms of employment relationships, promotion, and termination of employment contracts, task allocation based on individual behavior, personal traits or characteristics, and the monitoring or evaluation of individuals in employment relationships. AI systems used to monitor employee performance and behavior warrant this classification, as they may also infringe upon fundamental rights to data protection and privacy.

A second issue to be considered is the concept of "publicly accessible space," defined as "any publicly or privately owned physical place accessible to an undetermined number of natural persons, regardless of whether certain conditions for access may apply, and regardless of potential capacity restrictions" (Article 3). This notion applies irrespective of whether the space is privately or publicly owned or the activity for which the space may be used. Recital 19 clarifies that company and factory premises, as well as offices and workplaces, are not publicly accessible if they are intended to be accessed only by relevant employees and service providers. The challenge we face is that remote work, by definition, is performed outside the employer's premises. Nevertheless, since remote work is typically conducted at the workers' private residences, it is reasonable to exclude these working places from this classification and the associated obligations.

The primary obligation imposed upon employers is to implement appropriate technical and organizational measures to ensure the use of such systems in accordance with the accompanying instructions for use (Article 26.1 EU Regulation).

One of the areas to be explored is worker training, where the juxtaposition of regulatory areas results in the aggregation of differentiated training according to the objective pursued. The Framework Agreement on telework seeks to ensure that teleworkers have access to training, career development opportunities, and performance assessment mechanisms on the same terms as those working on-site. To that end, the employer is required to provide the necessary mechanisms, and to address training in the proper use of the equipment and the features of teleworking. This emphasis on ensuring a level playing field irrespective of the place of service provision is found in the implementation carried out in different countries[29]. The aim is to ensure that teleworkers are not disadvantaged by teleworking and to recognize their right to participate in ongoing training programs to improve their skills and abilities, in particular to enable them to make appropriate use of the technological tools required for their work.

The AI Act contains some provisions on training for all workers regardless of their place of work. For instance, related to the requirement for transparency and human control of AI systems used in the workplace, it is argued that employees should be informed about their use and adequately trained to interact with them safely and effectively. Specific training is required for workers interacting with high-risk AI systems (e.g., for performance evaluation or recruitment); the aim is to ensure that they have a clear understanding of the risks and any necessary risk mitigation measures. Companies should also provide training to employees on cybersecurity and data protection to ensure compliance with the relevant regulations.

Secondly, it is interesting to explore the information to be provided to workers which, as a consequence of the intersection of different rules, involves extending the catalogue of aspects that need to be known by workers, in particular on working conditions (tools provided, prevention of occupational hazards, automated activity management systems), privacy and data protection, or working tools (risks of the AI systems to be used).

In general terms, the Directive on Transparent and Predictable Working Conditions in the European Union mandates that employers provide workers with clear and comprehensive information regarding their working conditions[30]. This includes details such as the identity of the parties involved, the workplace location, the job description, the starting date, and, where applicable, the duration of the contract. Building on this foundation, the Framework Agreement outlines several specific aspects that are crucial for this type of employment. Additionally,

[29] See Eurofound (2022) for the details of the most significant recent regulatory frameworks and developments.

[30] Directive (EU) 2019/1152 of the European Parliament and of the Council of 20 June 2019.

concerning data protection and worker privacy, employers are required to inform employees about any potential restrictions on the use of equipment and the penalties for noncompliance. The use of digital equipment in teleworking makes it particularly relevant to consider data protection regulations for workers. This leads to consider the provisions of the General Data Protection Regulation (GDPR)[31], which also includes requirements for companies to provide individual and direct information on different aspects (Article 13)[32].

The same particular information contained in the Framework Agreement is common to the implementation rules of the European countries, and it is also usual to inform about security measures to be followed to protect sensitive information.

As noted above, the remote provision of work involves significant challenges for the protection of the occupational health of teleworkers. It is therefore also common for information to be provided to teleworkers to include how to maintain a safe working environment, with particular emphasis on ergonomic issues. It is also common to require that the terms and conditions for the development of telework must be set out in written form, including who is responsible for providing and maintaining the equipment for teleworking and the costs involved[33].

The AI Regulation imposes information obligations on employers to inform workers using or exposed to high-risk AI systems in the work environment. As an expression of the principle of transparency, they should be informed about the use of AI systems in the company and their interaction with them (their purpose, capabilities, technical characteristics, etc.) and share the results of impact assessments aimed at identifying and mitigating the risks associated with them. In addition, they should also receive information on the human supervision mechanisms in place. Information should also be provided about the handling of their data processed by AI systems and about their rights in relation to the use of AI, particularly the right to an explanation of automated decisions (as a precondition for being able to exercise the right to appeal against such decisions).

Accordingly, the information and participation of workers' representatives is being extended, and consequently greater demands are being placed on workers' representatives by the technical complexity of digital tools and AI systems[34]. Algorithmic labor law seeks to complement the provisions on information and consultation laid down in other rules. The Framework Agreement states that they must be informed

[31] Regulation (EU) 2016/679 on the protection of natural persons with regard to the processing of personal data and the free movement of such data.

[32] Purpose of collection and processing of employees' personal data, rights they have over them (access, rectification, cancellation, etc.), identity and contact details of the data controller and, if applicable, the data protection officer.

[33] The employer must provide the necessary equipment for teleworking, unless it is provided by the worker himself, compensating him for the expenses incurred (internet, electricity, etc.).

[34] Trade unions are making significant efforts to understand and manage the effects of AI systems. In this regard, see López López and Colàs-Neila (2023).

and consulted on the implementation of telework in the company (working conditions, data protection, health and safety, etc.), and must receive all the necessary data to be able to assess the impact of telework on working conditions and on employees' health and safety.

The AI Regulation also includes specific provisions to ensure that workers' representatives are adequately informed about the use of AI in the workplace, and the exposure of workers to high-risk AI systems, as another expression of the general principle of transparency that underpins the regulation. Thus, the company must inform workers' representatives about the use of AI systems that may affect working conditions, which are used for employment-related decision-making and performance evaluation, including the algorithms used and the data processed[35]; consultation and participation rights in the implementation of AI systems are also recognized, including the possibility to discuss and negotiate the conditions under which they will be used, with particular emphasis on high-risk AI systems, and human supervision[36].

Transparency is a vital mechanism for safeguarding rights in AI contexts. The AI Regulations impose transparency obligations on both providers and deployers, including employers who use AI systems to manage their remote workforce. Article 13 of the EU Regulation specifies that high-risk AI systems must be designed and developed to ensure their operation is sufficiently transparent, enabling deployers to interpret the system's output and use it appropriately[37]. In this context, employers must consider this aspect when acquiring management or intelligent control software for remote workers. They should be fully informed about the software's capabilities and limitations. Furthermore, it is essential to use these systems in a manner that allows for appropriate traceability and explainability, ensuring that individuals are aware when they are communicating or interacting with an AI system.

Specific obligations arise in certain cases. According to Article 50, if an employer deploys an emotion recognition system or a biometric categorization system, they must inform the individuals affected by the operation of the system. Furthermore, the employer is required to process personal data in compliance with applicable regulations.

[35] Here again, it is important to consider the information and consultation rights that the GDPR recognizes for workers' representatives in relation to the processing and protection of data within the scope of the employment relationship, such as the protection policies implemented, security incidents that may affect workers' data.

[36] The Spanish Rider Law was a pioneer in this field by introducing the obligation for companies to inform workers' representatives about the parameters, rules, and instructions on which AI algorithms or systems affecting decision-making in the workplace are based.

[37] This means that these programs shall be accompanied by instructions for use that include concise, complete, correct, and clear information that is relevant, accessible, and comprehensible to deployers.

A key aspect of algorithmic law is the right to AI literacy, which ensures that individuals have access to the necessary knowledge to make informed decisions regarding these systems. Remote workers affected by such technologies are certainly entitled to this right. The AI Regulation suggests that the widespread implementation of AI literacy measures could significantly enhance working conditions.

Article 4 of the AI Regulation places a responsibility on employers, as deployers of such systems, to ensure that their staff possesses a sufficient level of AI literacy. This entails providing the necessary knowledge to understand how AI-assisted decisions will affect them. This obligation extends beyond the traditional duty of information provision within the employment relationship. Employers must consider their employees' technical knowledge, experience, education, and training, as well as the context in which the AI system will be utilized and the individuals or groups it will impact.

Additionally, employers should ensure that those tasked with implementing the system's instructions and overseeing its use have the requisite competence, particularly a suitable level of AI literacy, training, and authority to effectively carry out these responsibilities.

Human oversight is a specific legal instrument within the AI Law framework, functioning both during the design phase and the utilization of high-risk systems. These systems must be designed and developed to allow natural persons to oversee their operation, ensuring they are used as intended and that their impacts are managed throughout the system's lifecycle (Article 14.1). To achieve this, appropriate human oversight measures should be identified by the system provider before the system is placed on the market or put into service.

According to Article 26, employers utilizing these systems must assign oversight responsibilities to individuals who possess the necessary competence, training, and authority, along with adequate support. This includes ensuring a sufficient level of AI literacy (Recital 93). In certain instances, the system should incorporate mechanisms to guide and inform the responsible person, enabling them to make informed decisions about when and how to intervene to prevent negative consequences or risks, or to halt the system if it fails to perform as intended (Recital 73).

Human oversight aims to prevent or minimize risks to health, safety, or fundamental rights that may arise when a high-risk AI system is used as intended or under conditions of reasonably foreseeable misuse (Article 14.2).

The system of sanctions applied to employees also requires significant reform. While collective agreements and internal codes of conduct already outline misconduct for remote workers – particularly regarding equipment use and communication duties – these measures should be updated to address potential misuse of AI systems provided to employees. This is especially relevant in cases where such programs are used without the employer's knowledge or authorization, a practice humorously dubbed "Bring Your Own AI."

It is important to recognize that algorithmic law is supported by a substantial sanctioning framework to ensure effective enforcement of its mandates. Consequently, noncompliance by employees can create obligations for companies.

Simultaneously, existing general sanctions in labor law and specific legislation on remote work will need to be reviewed to encompass all potential breaches of employer mandates under AI regulations when using intelligent tools and programs to manage remote workers.

Moreover, algorithms have significant potential to influence disciplinary procedures by identifying possible employee breaches through behavioral analysis, pattern recognition, and comparisons among workers. While this offers advantages in terms of efficiency and objectivity in oversight, it also raises concerns about algorithmic discrimination, erroneous conclusions, and over-surveillance. For employers, utilizing these intelligent tools to detect potential breaches is already a reality that aids in directing the attention of labor inspection. Therefore, it is logical to design systems that identify and prevent noncompliance with duties related to remote workers.

As a result, both legislation and, more importantly, collective agreements will need to evolve to identify all potential noncompliances and ensure a sanctioning system that is appropriate, proportional, and fair (OECD, 2023, 221).

## 10.6 FINAL REMARKS

Remote work is a form of employment that has reached an advanced and mature stage in its evolution, with a relevant presence in the labor market and a comprehensive regulatory framework, including third-generation laws in some cases. AI systems can and likely will be extensively utilized in telework environments, as this form of employment is highly susceptible to their impact due to its heavy reliance on technology.

AI systems can be extremely beneficial for remote work, helping to address structural challenges such as control, management, workflows, and psychosocial risk factors. They can enhance the monitoring of legal compliance by unions and labor administrations, making them a valuable tool for law enforcement. Additionally, technologies like digital platforms can expand telework opportunities and increase the number of tasks that can be performed remotely.

However, this progress comes with a price. Several risks for workers have been identified, such as algorithmic discrimination, excessive surveillance, technostress, and heavy workloads. Remote work exacerbates these risks compared to on-site work.

The widespread use of AI tools has prompted regulatory responses at all levels, leading to the emergence of a new branch of legal order known as "AI Law" or "Algorithmic Law." This includes significant mandates on their implementation by employers to manage employment relations. When remote work is facilitated, managed, or controlled by an AI system, both digital law and algorithmic law apply, resulting in an accumulation of rules and mandates for employers.

The analysis of the intersection between digital law and algorithmic law, arising from the use of AI systems in remote work, reveals that this accumulation generally does not pose significant problems. Both regulations include similar instruments, such as training and information dissemination. However, AI regulation extends further, introducing new requirements like transparency, human oversight, and digital literacy. This can be attributed to their common origin and shared objectives of protecting individuals. Nevertheless, increased coordination will undoubtedly be necessary.

## REFERENCES

Adams-Prassl, Jeremias. 2022. 'Regulating algorithms at work: Lessons for a «European approach to artificial intelligence»', *European Labour Law Journal* 13, 1: 30–50.

Aloisi, Antonio and De Stefano, Valerio. 2022. *Your Boss is an Algorithm. Artificial Intelligence, Platform Work and Labour.* Oxford: Hart Publishing.

Aloisi, Antonio and Potocka-Sionek, Nastazja. 2022. 'De-gigging the labour market? An analysis of the 'algorithmic management' provisions in the proposed Platform Work Directive', *Italian Labour Law e-Journal* 15, 1: 29–50.

Baiocco, Sara & Enrique, Fernández Macias (eds)., 2022. 'The algorithmic management of work: A basic compass', in *Science for Policy Brief*. Sevilla: Joint Research Center.

Baiocco, S., Fernández-Macías, E., Rani, U. and Pesole, A. 2022. *The Algorithmic Management of Work and Its Implications in Different Contexts*, Seville: European Commission.

Baldwin, Richard and Okubo, Toshihiro. 2023. 'Are Software Automation and Teleworkers Substitutes? Preliminary Evidence from Japan', *National Bureau of Economic Research*, Working Paper 31627.

Bootsman, Rik, Markopoulos, Panos, Qi, Qi, Wang, Qi and Timmermans, Annick. 2019. 'Wearable technology for posture monitoring at the workplace', *International Journal of Human-Computer Studies*, 132, 3: 99–111.

Chen, Zhisheng. 2024. 'Metaverse office: exploring future teleworking model', *Kybernetes*, 53, 6: 2029–2045

Crawford, Kate. 2021. *Atlas of AI*. New Haven: Yale University Press.

De Stefano, Valerio, 2019. 'Negotiating the algorithm: automation, artificial intelligence, and labor protection', *Comparative Labor Law & Policy Journal* 41, 1: 15–46.

EU-OSHA – European Agency for Safety and Health at Work. 2021. *Impact of Artificial Intelligence on Occupational Safety and Health.* Available at https://osha.europa.eu/en/publications/impact-artificial-intelligence-occupational-safety-and-health.

Eurofound. 2022a. *Telework in the EU: Regulatory Frameworks and Recent Updates.* Luxembourg: Publications Office of the European Union.

2022b. *The Rise in Telework: Impact on Working Conditions and Regulations.* Luxembourg: Publications Office of the European Union.

2023. *Ethical Digitalisation at Work: From Theory to Practice.* Luxembourg: Publications Office of the European Union.

Ezpe, Al. 2024. 'Navigating the Future: AI's Impact on Remote Works Dynamics and Innovation'. Available at www.unite.ai/navigating-the-future-ais-impact-on-remote-work-dynamics-innovation/.

Gmyrek, Pawel, Berg, Janine and Bescond, David. 2023. 'Generative AI and jobs: A global analysis of potential effects on job quantity and quality', in *ILO Working Paper* 96. Geneva: International Labour Office.

Goerlich Pesset, José María. 2021. 'Decisiones administrativas automatizadas en materia de social: algoritmos en la gestión de la Seguridad Social y en el procedimiento sancionador', *Labos* 2, 2: 22–42.

Grušić, Uglješa. 2023. 'Remote work in private international law', in Countouris, Nicolas, De Stefano, Valerio, Piasna, Agnieszka and Rainone, Silvia (eds), *The Future of Remote Work*. Brussels: ETUI, pp.185–199.

International Labour Office. 2021. 'The role of digital labour platforms in transforming the world of work', in *World Employment and Social Outlook 2021*. Geneve: Office of Publications of the ILO.

Kullmann, Miriam. 2018. 'Platform work, algorithmic decision-making, and EU gender equality law', *International Journal of Comparative Labour Law and Industrial Relations*, 1, 34: 1–21.

Leonardi, Paul M. 2020. 'COVID-19 and the new technologies of organizing: digital exhaust, digital footprints, and artificial intelligence in the wake of remote work', *Journal of Management Studies*, 58: 249–253.

Llorens Espada, Julen. 2023. *Límites al uso de la Inteligencia Artificial en el ámbito de la salud laboral*. Madrid: La Ley.

López López, Julia. 2014. 'Del Estatuto del Trabajador a los Estatutos de los Empleados: la des-contractualización laboral de la protección', in Julia López, dir., *Los Estatutos de los Trabajadores. Papel de las normas y la jurisprudencia en su formulación*. Valladolid: Lex Nova, pp. 21–47.

López López, Julia and Colàs-Neila, Eusebi. 2023. 'On social justice and artificial intelligence: Trade unions as instruments for the dissemination of transnational norms', in Brian Langille and Anne Trebilcock, eds., *Global Justice and the World of Work: Possible Global Futures. Essays in Honour of Francis Maupain*. Oxford: Hart Publishing, pp. 305–314.

Lucas Murillo, Pablo. 2003. 'Avances tecnológicos y derechos fundamentales. Los riesgos del progreso', in *Derechos fundamentales y nuevas tecnologías*. Vitoria-Gasteiz: Ararteko.

Mittelstaedt, John D., Shultz, Clifford J., Kilbourne, William E. & Peterson, Mark. 2014. 'Sustainability as megatrend: two schools of macromarketing thought', *Journal of Macromarketing*, 34, 3: 253–264.

OECD. 2023. *OECD Employment Outlook 2023: Artificial Intelligence and the Labour Market*. Paris: OECD Publishing.

Pasquale, Frank. 2022. *New Law of Robotics. Defending Human Experience in the Age of AI*. Cambridge: Harvard University Press.

Ponce Del Castillo, Aida, 2023. 'Regulating algorithmic management in the Platform Work Directive: correcting risky deviations'. Available at https://global-workplace-law-and-policy.kluwerlawonline.com/2023/11/22/regulating-algorithmic-management-in-the-plat form-work-directive-correcting-risky-deviations. visited on 01-06-2024.

2024. *The EU Platform Work Directive. What's New, What's Missing, What's Next?* Brussels: ETUI Policy Brief.

Rodríguez-Piñero Royo, Miguel. 2024. 'Derecho del Trabajo, Inteligencia Artificial y tutela de los trabajadores', *Teoría & Derechon°* 37: 120.

Todolí Signes, Adrián. 2023. *Algoritmos productivos y extractivos*. Pamplona: Aranzadi.

Visionary Analytics, 2024, 'Study exploring the social, economic and legal context and trends of telework and the right to disconnect, in the context of digitalisation and the future of work, during and beyond the COVID-19 pandemic', Luxembourg: Publications Office of the European Union, p.8.

Wood, A. J., 2021. *Algorithmic Management: Consequences for Work Organisation and Working Conditions*, JRC Working Papers on Labour, Education and Technology 2021-07, Seville: European Commission, JRC124874.

# 11

# Telework and Work–Life Balance

## *Best Practices Addressing Gender Inequalities*

*Nuria Pumar Beltrán*

### 11.1 INTRODUCTION: GENDER ISSUES AND TELEWORK

Women have traditionally been, and continue to be, the ones who have stayed at home engaged in 'industrial homework' (ILO, 2021)[1]. However, until relatively recently, in many countries it was men who engaged more regularly in 'telework' (Eurofound ILO, 2017; Eurofound 2020)[2] – a practice of organizing work that predominated among managers and workers in the technology industries and, more generally, in knowledge-based occupations – in what was a clear reflection of the gendered division of labour in the home and the job market. However, the predominance of male teleworkers might also be explained by masculine patterns of work time use and, indeed, teleworking is still conceived as a way of prolonging the working day at home (Figure 11.1).

Coinciding with the outbreak of the COVID-19 pandemic and fuelled by the development of new technologies, teleworking has expanded into other more traditional sectors[3], some of them heavily feminized, including financial services

[1] To employ ILO terminology in relation to working from home. ILO, *Working from Home: From Invisibility to Decent Work, International Labour Office* (Geneva: International Labour Organization, 2021).

[2] The 2015 European Working Conditions Survey (EWCS) showed that 54% of men teleworked while there was predominance of women engaged in home-based telework (57%). Eurofound and ILO, *Working Anytime, Anywhere: The Effects on the World of Work* (Luxembourg: Publications Office of the European Union, Geneva: International Labour Office, 2017), p. 18. Eurofound, *Regulations to Address Work–Life Balance in Digital Flexible Working Arrangements, New Forms of Employment Series* (Luxembourg: Publications Office of the European Union, 2020), p. 4.

[3] Based on the classification of jobs according to the impact of digitalization on them, we can speak of ICT-enhanced jobs, that is, activities supported by technology, but which could equally be carried out without it. This classification can be consulted in ILO, *Digitalization and Employment: A Review* (Geneva: International Labour Organization, 2022), p. 14. On the typology of teleworking linked to the development of new technologies see J.C. Messenger, 'Introduction: Telework in the 21st Century – An Evolutionary Perspective', in J.C. Messenger

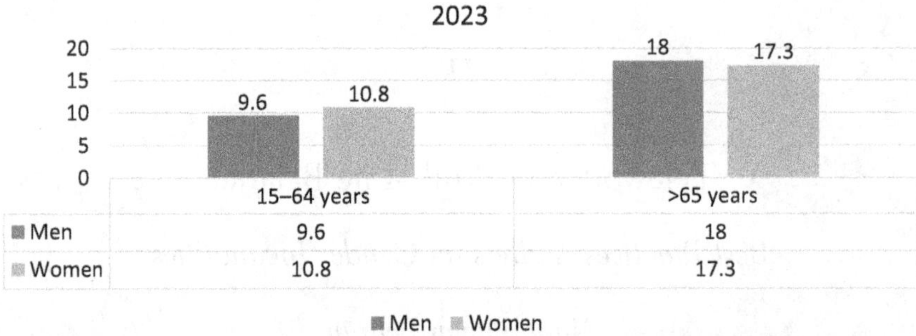


FIGURE 11.1 Employed persons working from home as a percentage of the total employment
Source: Eurostat (2024, https://ec.europa.eu/eurostat/databrowser/view/lfsa_ehomp__custom_12158505/default/table?lang=en).

and education, and, above all, the public sector[4]. Currently, in Europe, more women (24%) than men (21%) work from home (Eurofound 2022b[5]), with women tending to concentrate in potentially 'teleworkable' occupational sectors[6].

And yet, the gender divide in teleworking persists, with women teleworkers more likely to be engaged in home-based than in ICT-mobile work, where achieving work–life balance is usually more difficult (Eurofound and ILO 2017).

Telework presents two quite distinct faces as regards working time: in general, the statistics associate telework with the intensification of work and with longer, more irregular work schedules; yet, at the same time – and this particular characteristic is directly influenced by European regulations and the EU Framework Agreement on Telework – telework can constitute a working-time arrangement that facilitates a better reconciliation of work and family life, provided it is promoted in favour of workers' interests. Yet, when seeking to determine whether teleworking has a positive or negative impact on work–life balance (be it by means of statistics or qualitative studies), the outcomes are clearly ambivalent. Indeed, the extant literature examining the implications of teleworking for gender equality provides a

(ed), *Telework in the 21st Century – An Evolutionary Perspective* (Geneva: International Labour, 2019), pp. 1–34.

4 S. Kley, T. Reimer, 'Exploring the Gender Gap in Teleworking from Home. The Roles of Worker's Characteristics, Occupational Positions and Gender Equality in Europe' (2023) 168 *Social Indicators Research*, 185–206.

5 Data taken from the 2012 EWCS, Eurofound, *The Rise in Telework: Impact on Working Conditions and Regulations* (Luxembourg: Publications Office of the European Union, 2022b), p. 8.

6 Precisely because of the pandemic, teleworking has extended among 'mid-level clerical and administrative workers who previously had limited access'. M. Sostero, S. Milasi, J. Hurley, E. Fernández-Macías and M., Bisello, *Teleworkability and the COVID-19 Crisis: A New Digital Divide* (Seville: European Commission, 2020), p. 49. Also in Eurofound 'The rise in telework', p. 18.

somewhat surprising conclusion, but one that should be kept very much in mind: and, that is, that teleworking in itself is no guarantee of co-responsibility or the transformation of gender roles. On the contrary, due to the very nature of teleworking, but at the same time owing to business practices and prevailing social stereotypes, there is a risk that it is perceived as the more 'appropriate' working arrangement for women, in a way that perpetuates gender roles and, even, widens the labour gap. To address this danger, socio-economic and cultural alliances, policies and regulations must all row in the same direction and, in their wake, take steps to eliminate all patriarchal structures and systemic discrimination[7], in fulfilment of their gender duty[8].

This study is based on the premise that telework, in common with other forms of the flexible organization of working time, cannot be considered gender blind, given its very strong impact on women. Indeed, emerging from this same premise is the idea, upheld in other doctrinal works[9], that the greater autonomy in relation to working time offered by teleworking – and which might facilitate a better reconciliation of work and family life – has different ramifications for men and women. In general, for women teleworkers, the degree of interference – the porosity – of their working time on their personal lives is greater than it is for men[10]. Today, it can be argued that the vast majority of women who engage in telework – and this is something that was made more than evident during the pandemic – continue having to put in a double shift, but that this, instead of being something that is undertaken simultaneously, has become more episodic or intermittent in nature.

In what follows, I examine the impact that labour legislation and business practices of so-called 'indecent' working time have on women and explore the issues to which teleworking gives rise in relation to working time and work–life balance. Additionally, and with the focus more firmly on business practices, I address the opportunities afforded by telework as a working-time arrangement and the possible

[7] J. López, 'Systemic discrimination y políticas de igualdad efectiva de género' (2019) 1 *Revista del Ministerio de Empleo y Seguridad Social*, 35–50.

[8] See this concept as a way of combining legal,collective and voluntary measures in J. Rubery, A. Koukidiaki, 'Institutional Interactions in Gender Pay Equity: A Call for Inclusive, Equal and Transparent Labour Markets' (2018) 1 *University of Oxford Human Rights Hub Journal*, 138. C. Chacartegui, 'Gender Discrimination and Working Time: A Sustainable Approach', in Leal Filho, W. et al. (eds), *Gender Equality. Encyclopedia of the UN Sustainable Development Goals* (Springer, 2021) 423–431.

[9] C. Sullivan, S. Lewis, 'Home-based Telework, Gender, and the Synchronization of Work and Family: Perspectives of Teleworkers and their Co-residents' (2001) 8 *Gender, Work and Organization*, 2, 123–145. More recently, and in this same line, see, for example, J. Wajcman, E. Rose, 'Constant Connectivity: Rethinking Interruptions at Work' (2011) 32 *Organization Studies*, 7, 941–961; T. Carstensen, 'Orts- und zeitflexibles Arbeiten: Alte Geschlechterungle ichheiten und neue Muster der Arbeitsteilung durch Digitalisierung' (2020) 74 *Zeitschrift fur Arbeitswissenschaft*, 195–205.

[10] É. Genin, 'Technologies mobiles et travail à la maison: mise à disposition ou mode de Conciliation' (2015) 53 *Revue Interventions économiques*, 11.

penalties that women teleworkers may have to face. Finally, in an effort at preventing or reversing these inequalities, I undertake an assessment of the guarantees and protections provided by the European regulatory framework and of best practices in European transnational collective bargaining, where the lynchpins of these guarantees are the principles of voluntariness and non-discrimination, as well as respect for fundamental rights[11].

## 11.2 WORKING TIME FLEXIBILITY POLICIES AND GENDER EQUALITY

The social organization of working time is becoming less standardized, and the synchronicity of work and leisure has gradually disintegrated[12]. Today, various economic, technological and cultural factors influence the coexistence of more polarized, individualized patterns of working time that increasingly differ from those of the standard working model[13]. In keeping with this trend, telework makes it easier for firms to impose increasingly diverse, irregular and unpredictable working hours on their employees.

In response to the increasing gaps that have emerged in working time and which put workers' health at risk, there is a clear need to promote 'decent' working time, a model that is closely aligned with respect for human rights, gender equality and sustainable economic growth (ILO, 2007[14]).

The regulation of decent working time is essential for achieving real equality for women. But it is evident, even in the case of formal employment, that business practices are failing – to varying degrees depending on the sector and the legal and institutional framework of each country – to comply with working day regulations. At the same time as new reconciliation measures emerge in legislation and collective bargaining, labour reforms have increased the flexibility of working conditions to adapt to business interests, so that time reserved for personal and reproductive life is ignored, and the male breadwinner norm and gender-blindness prevail[15].

And this is because the standard regulation of the working day, while fixing limits on maximum hours of work and minimum rest periods and restricting the use of

[11] On these developments, concerning telework, J. López, 'Reconfiguring fundamental rights: the case of tele-workers', draft paper, *Pompeu Fabra University Seminar* (2023).

[12] J. Fudge, 'Control Over Working Time and Work-Life Balance: A Detailed Analysis of the Canada Labour Code Part III' (2007) Federal Labour Standards Review Commission, 4.

[13] J. Y. Boulin, M. Lallement, M., F. Michon, 'Decent working time in industrialized countries. Issues scopes and paradoxes', in J. Y. Boulin, M. Lallement, J. Messenger, and F. Michon (eds), *Decent Working Time: New Trends, New Issues* (Geneva: International Labour Organization, 2006), p. 15.

[14] ILO, Decent Working Time. Balancing Worker's Needs with Business Requirements (Geneva: International Labour Organization, 2007).

[15] J. Fudge, F. L. Vosko F. L., 'Gender, Segmentation and the Standard Employment Relationship in Canadian Labour Law' (2001) 22 *Legislation and Policy, Economic and Industrial Democracy*, 276.

overtime, offers firms multiple options for flexibility[16]. That is, specific norms serve to regulate certain groups and provide for notable elements of flexibility that give firms considerable leeway in determining work schedules and working hours. This is the case, for example, of Spanish regulation, which allows the irregular distribution of working hours throughout the year, their substantial modification at the behest of the employer, and the flexibilization of the overtime regime or the working hours of part-time workers. As Rubery et al. (1998) point out[17], different working-time regimes result in different working-time practices, since the norms act to 'limit or extend variations in working hours for full-timers, promote or discourage part-time work and unsocial hours working, and influence the terms and conditions under which overtime, unsocial hours or atypical work contracts are undertaken'. And, in turn, such norms impact the degree of gender inequality in labour relations.

Thus, European legislative policies have tended to push the general and collective reduction of working hours into the background, preferring to promote flexible solutions in the form, among others, of part-time work and reductions in working hours. Women more typically are in jobs with shorter working hours but at the expense of greater corporate control in the distribution of their working hours.

All these legislative policies and business practices end up imposing gender inequalities in the workplace, insofar as they facilitate the expulsion of women from those activities whose conditions are incompatible with work–life balance, aggravate psychosocial health problems derived from having to put in a double shift and, ultimately, increase gender labour segregation and widen the labour gap.

In general, doctrinal proposals in favour of decent working time from a gender perspective[18] agree in advocating the introduction of the 35-hour working week, limiting the recourse to overtime, ensuring greater compliance from firms with regulations governing working time, and granting workers greater power in how they wish to use their working time in terms, for example, of teleworking or other working-time arrangements.

## 11.3 EMERGING ISSUES IN WORKING TIME AND TELEWORK

As with traditional home work, in the case of telework – especially that which is carried out full time – only its results are visible, while the time spent in achieving these results goes largely ignored. Yet as work and its associated salary tend to be

[16] J. Fudge, Control over Working Time, p. 11.

[17] J. Rubery, M. Smith, C. Fagan, 'National working-time regimes and equal opportunities' (1998) 4 *Feminist Economics* 1, 71–101 at 71.

[18] In this sense, for instance, C. Chacartegui, 'Gender Discrimination and Working Time, p. 430, J. Rubery, C. Fagan,'National working-time regimes', p. 60.

measured in terms of results[19], actual working time is 'left out' or excluded from the employment contract and ceases to be an immediate object of that agreement[20].

When working time is deemed irrelevant in an employment contract, any request for a reduction in, or a redistribution of, working hours loses all relevance and the primary concern becomes the workload. This means that, more often than not, the worker has to put in more hours to achieve the expected results.

The greater potential for enhanced connectivity and mobility offered by new technologies means that the boundaries between the time dedicated to personal life and work are much fuzzier and more permeable. Moreover, the emergence of new technologies and hybrid ways of working trigger new debates about the organization, calculation and control of working time[21]. For example, the European Court of Justice[22] holds that the degree to which the employer's work demands affect the employee's private life should be assessed on a case-by-case basis, so as to determine whether so-called 'stand-by time' should be counted as working time. This way of measuring working time, outside of normal working hours, is novel because it takes into account a series of criteria to assess the true autonomy[23] of the employee to use the time dedicated to his or her own interests.

Indeed, as far as teleworking is concerned, not only do we need to consider the relative merits of physical and virtual work environments, but we also have to evaluate and establish limits on a worker's availability and connectivity, regulating working hours by exercising the so-called right to digital disconnection. And, at the same time, the ways of carrying out and organizing remote work have to take into consideration synchronous and asynchronous working time in virtual settings.

This overlapping of work and personal time, together with the intensification of work that results in the simultaneous conducting of multiple tasks and the possibility of the fragmentation of working time, can have a spillover effect on a teleworker's personal and work life but also on their health.

In this regard, it is worth stressing that the legal or conventional limits of general labour regulations should also be applied to teleworkers, in their capacity as wage-earners, since teleworking is a specific mode of work organization. Indeed,

[19] See the implications of this way of working for business control A, Perulli, A., *'Agile Work: a Paradigm for Hybrid Remote Working'*, draft paper, *Pompeu Fabra University Seminar* (2023).

[20] M. R. Alarcón Caracuel, 'La jornada ordinaria de trabajo y su distribución', in J. Aparicio, J. López-Gandía, *Tiempo de Trabajo* (Albacete: Bomarzo, 2008), pp. 33–55.

[21] Eurofound, *Hybrid work in Europe: Concept and practice* (Luxembourg: Publications Office of the European Union, 2023).

[22] Judgment of 9 March 2021, case Stadt Offenbach am Main, C-580/19; Judgment of 9 March 2021, case Radiotelevizija Slovenija, C-344/19. See more in deep on this case-law doctrine in European Commission (2023) Interpretative Communication on Directive 2003/88/EC, Official Journal C 143 of 26 April 2023 (2023/C 143/08).

[23] In this sense, on the relationship between autonomy and working time see S. Huybrechts, 'Working time and autonomy: Lessons for the new ways of working' (2023) 14 *European Labour Law Journal* 4, 570–587.

teleworking does not determine the type of employment contract signed by the teleworker or the legal regime applicable to the employment relationship.

What, however, amounts to a quite distinct issue is that, within the legal or conventional limits of the working day, those individuals that telework can enjoy complete freedom to organize their working schedules, as is expressly recognized, for example, by the Italian law on *lavoro agile*, literally, 'agile' or smart working[24]. Yet, teleworking cannot mean that workers forego their work breaks and relinquish their reconciliation rights since this would be tantamount to an illegal, if not discriminatory, waiver of rights.

Even so, the invisibility of working time increases the risk of a worker having to take on unpaid overtime, so to counter this it is important to establish two types of limits: those of an ex ante nature, that is, fixing, by means of collective bargaining or by way of the employment contract, the number of working and non-working hours and the right to digital disconnection; and, those of an a posteriori nature, that is, the obligation that firms have to control and record working hours. In this regard, regulatory frameworks are key in the working-time regime, influencing the degree of flexibility and autonomy that workers have with respect to their hours of work and the organization of their working schedules.

## 11.4 TELEWORK AND WORK–LIFE BALANCE

The adoption of telework has been both a curse and blessing for a worker's efforts to strike a good balance between work and personal life. In its favour, many teleworkers report that it means they are better able to organize their personal time. According to a Eurofound survey, two-thirds of European workers said they would like to adopt a hybrid form of teleworking[25].

Those who work from home save on commuting time and enjoy greater autonomy, being able to decide how, when and where they work. This advantage is especially evident in the management of their working time as it facilitates the adaptation of the working day to their personal needs. It is in this sense, as we shall see below, that the European Work-Life Balance Directive considers telework and the adaptation of the working schedule to a worker's personal needs and preferences the rights of all.

And yet, the implementation of telework is not without its drawbacks: numerous international reports associate telework with widespread practices of unpaid

[24] Legge 22 maggio 2017, n. 81.

[25] Eurofound, 'Telework in the EU: Regulatory frameworks and recent updates', (Luxembourg: Publications Office of the European Union, 2022a). Eurofound, 'The rise in telework: Impact on working conditions and regulations' (Luxembourg: Publications Office of the European Union, 2022b).

overtime and the blurring of boundaries between working hours and periods of rest[26] (Eurofound and ILO, 2017).

At the individual level, sociologists and labour economists have identified an '*autonomy paradox*' (Rodríguez Modroño and López-Igual, 2021;[27] Tomei, 2021[28]; Eurofound, 2020): workers dispose of greater flexibility to organize themselves but, at the same time, teleworking can lead to greater work demands, an intensification of working hours and, in general, to the greater *immediacy* or constant availability of workers that blurs the separation between personal life and work. Thus, workers are presented with an informal or unstructured flexibility[29] which can lead to greater family–work conflicts, as well as stress-related health problems and greater exposure to psychosocial risks.

This trend is, in part, attributable to those technologies that today facilitate more flexible working schedules and workdays, but the weight of the regulatory framework, employment status and the culture of the specific business/sector concerned cannot be ignored. Thus, overtime is more common in labour sectors with poorly regulated working conditions and unstructured working hours.[30] In contrast, in professional sectors or occupations where working conditions are strictly regulated, both by legislation and by collective bargaining, the advantages of the autonomy afforded by teleworking are more evident.

And yet, long working hours are often the result of the fact that among teleworkers there is a preponderance of professionals and managers who prolong their hours outside the agreed work schedule. Another common practice, in this case among women, is that of working during their periods of personal rest because in this way they are better able to reconcile their family and work responsibilities.

Finally, a gender perspective reveals the possible penalties associated with telework as far as women are concerned. The experience of the pandemic highlighted the fact that enforced teleworking contributed to perpetuating traditional gender roles, insofar as it was women who had to shoulder most of the domestic work and childcare duties during lockdown. Yet, clearly, the origin of these inequalities can be found in the patriarchal organization of society, and they are not solely attributable to telework.

[26] Eurofound and ILO, 2017, Working anytime, anywhere. p. 22 *ff*.

[27] See, in this sense, P. Rodríguez-Modroño, P. López-Igual, 'Job Quality and Work–Life Balance of Teleworkers' (2021) 18 *International Journal of Environmental Research and Public Health* 18 (6), 1–13.

[28] M. Tomei, 'Teleworking: A Curse or a Blessing for Gender Equality and Work-Life Balance?' (2021) 56 *Intereconomics* 260–264.

[29] I employ Colette Fagan's classification of flexibility types. C. Fagan, 'Gender and Working-time in Industrialized Countries: Practices and Preferences', in J. Messenger, *Working-time and Workers' Preferences in Industrialized Countries: Finding the Balance* (Geneva: International Labour Organization, 2004), pp. 108–114.

[30] J. Kim et al., 'Workplace Flexibility and Worker Well-Being by Gender' (2020) 82 *Journal of Marriage and Family* 892–910.

In studies of the impact of teleworking on work–life balance, such as that conducted more than two decades ago by Sullivan and Lewis[31], it was concluded that this work practice can simultaneously lead to results that are mutually exclusive. Thus, telework may equally be an opportunity to involve both parents more in family responsibilities or these responsibilities may fall even more heavily on women teleworkers, reinforcing traditional roles. Indeed, some studies identify different uses of unpaid time by women and men teleworkers: the latter are reported to dedicate more time to childcare activities, while the former dedicate more time to domestic duties[32]. It is found that women with children tend to fragment their working time more so as to be better able to combine their work with their family responsibilities. In this way, however, their working time ends up interfering more in their personal lives[33]. These qualitative studies show, therefore, that the traditional double shifts – most often assumed by women – persist in teleworking relationships, but that they have now become more intermittent, taking place within the home, and more often than not occurring at times that coincide with those of social rest.

Leaving to one side the teleworking that emerged during the pandemic – given its exceptional and enforced nature – this practice can be considered neither a neutral nor a gender-blind form of organization: it is not neutral because it brings paid work into the domestic sphere, a traditionally feminine domain where productive and reproductive spaces overlap, and because those who work from home are invisible to the firm, and so they run the risk that their labour rights (as regards occupational health and the right to rest) and their professional rights (as regards training and promotion) are ignored. Likewise, the gender dimension of the mental health risks associated with teleworking should not be overlooked. More specifically, the situations of stress and isolation experienced by women teleworkers, attributable to the difficulties they face in disconnecting from work and the overload of intermittent double shifts, need to be carefully assessed.

Finally, as far as psychosocial and gender risks are concerned, it is worth mentioning the need to prevent harassment, including that of a sexual nature, in digital media spaces, and to protect female workers from gender violence.

## 11.5 TELEWORK AS A GENDERED WORKING-TIME ARRANGEMENT

In the business environment, flexible work agreements should seek to emphasize the promotion of worker autonomy as far as the organization of their work is concerned, giving them greater leeway to take decisions about how they use their time. In fact,

[31] C. Sullivan, S. Lewis, S., 'Home-based Telework", pp.123–145.

[32] See for further details, N. Chesley, 'Blurring Boundaries? Linking Technology Use, Spillover, Individual Distress, and Family Satisfaction' (2005) 67 *Journal of Marriage and Family* 5, 1237–1248.

[33] É. Genin, 'Technologies mobiles et travail à la maison : mise à disposition ou mode de Conciliation' (2015) 53 *Revue Interventions économiques*', 11.

many companies, which in the wake of the pandemic adopted hybrid teleworking, report lower rates of absenteeism and a fall in requests form employees to reduce the number of hours worked and to work part-time[34]. Although these data have yet to be studied in greater depth, they seem to indicate that remote working promotes a better work–life balance and can facilitate the employment transitions of older workers towards retirement[35].

Unlike other options for achieving reconciliation that imply a reduction in working time or taking a leave of absence, the adoption of teleworking does not mean working fewer hours nor does it increase the possibilities of job abandonment. Teleworking, compared to other modes of conciliation, is not based on leave of absence rights and can serve as a suitable alternative to other modes that tend to penalize the worker more.

In principle, opting for telework should not mean that the worker has to waive any part of their salary, at least not immediately. For example, some studies show that being able to opt for a combination of flexitime and telework has allowed women who work part-time to increase their hours of dedication[36]. It has also allowed workers, who have recently become mothers, to avoid the labour penalties typically associated with motherhood[37].

However, as with other measures of workplace conciliation, certain business practices and associated stereotypes can lead to teleworking becoming seen as the 'mommy track'[38], *chosen* above all by women, so that it becomes another manifestation of the so-called flexibility stigma[39], linked to the exercise of motherhood and childcare.

This flexibility stigma can be especially evident when companies do not opt to implement systems of teleworking across the board and make them accessible to all workers, but rather they only authorize them on justified grounds and, only then, in exceptional cases[40]. Such decisions serve to promote gender gaps within a company,

34 El País, 'Los efectos del teletrabajo: bajan las reducciones de jornada' (7 March 2022), https://elpais.com/economia/negocios/2022-03-07/los-efectos-del-teletrabajo-bajan-las-reducciones-de-jornada.html.

35 J. López, N. Pumar, E. Colàs, 'Telework, Sustainability of Pensions and Synergies with Market Institutions: Constructing a Theory of Fundamental Rights', in M. Rönnmar, J. J. Votinius (eds), *Older Workers, Active Ageing, and the Future of Work*, (Alphen aan den Rijn: Kluwer Law International, forthcoming).

36 T. Carstensen, 'Orts- und zeitflexibles Arbeiten', p. 201.

37 H. Chung, M. Van der Host, Women's employment patterns after childbirth and the perceived access to and use of flexitime and teleworking (2018) 71 *Human Relations* 1, 47–72.

38 J. Rubery, J., C. Fagan, 'How to Combat Segregation in the Labour Market for both low- and high-qualified women', in N. Crowley, S. Sansonetti (eds), *New Visions for Gender Equality* (Brussels: European Commission, 2019), p. 59.

39 H. Chung, 'Gender, Flexibility Stigma and the Perceived Negative Consequences of Flexible Working in the UK' (2020) 151 *Social Indicators Research*, 521–545.

40 For instance, big companies such as Amazon and Twitter have eliminated the teleworking arrangements that had been in place since the pandemic and now oblige their employees to work in-person full-time, with teleworking only being authorized in exceptional cases.

in response to which, it is best to collectively negotiate a series of best practices for the regulation of telework. This is discussed in detail in the section that follows.

## 11.6 REGULATORY FRAMEWORKS GUARANTEEING RIGHTS AND BEST PRACTICES IN THE EUROPEAN SOCIAL DIALOGUE

With the emergence of new technologies and the strengthening of the digital economy, new norms governing the workplace are needed that guarantee decent work and which respect fundamental rights. However, the solution does not necessarily involve the creation of specific regulations for new categories of workers, but rather the application of labour rights that recognize these new realities and offer guarantees that address emerging issues in the digital field that have a direct impact on fundamental rights[41].

As discussed earlier, teleworkers are not in any danger of falling into a legal vacuum given that they are protected by general labour regulations. This is the case for example of their rights with regard to working time and their right to equality and non-discrimination as recognized in European directives. The Working Time Directive 2003/88/EC which, in addition to limiting the length of the working day and establishing minimum daily rest periods, regulates two aspects of particular relevance for telework: first, the consideration of effective working time, outside the firm's facilities, when the teleworker is available and reachable by their employer;[42] and, second, following the judgment of the European Court of Justice in 2019[43], the requirement that firms set up a system enabling the duration of time worked each day by each worker to be measured.

Indeed, from the beginning of the employment relationship, Directive 2019/1152, on Transparent and Predictable Working Conditions, recognizes the right of workers to know in advance and in detail their working conditions, including the length of their standard working day or week, even in those labour relations where the work patterns are 'entirely or mostly unpredictable' (Art. 4)[44]. However, regulation at the European level of the right to digital disconnection, as proposed by the European Parliament and as negotiated by the social agents in their revision of the EU Framework Agreement, remains pending.

[41] V. De Stefano, *The Rise of the 'Just-in-Time Workforce: On-Demand Work, Crowd Work, and Labour Protection in the 'Gig-Economy* (Geneva: International Labour Organisation, 2016), p. 21.

[42] Judgment of 9 March 2021, case Stadt Offenbach am Main, C-580/19; Judgment of 9 March 2021, case Radiotelevizija Slovenija, C-344/19.

[43] Judgment of 14 May 2019, case CCOO vs. Deutsche Bank, C-155/18.

[44] On the main improvements in workers' rights introduced by this Directive, see S. Canalda Criado, 'The new directive on transparent and predictable working conditions in the European Union' (2019) 440 *Revista de Trabajo y Seguridad Social*, 161–184.

As far as conciliation is concerned, the Work-Life Balance Directive 2019/1158 recognizes the individual right of workers 'to request flexible working arrangements for caring purposes', arrangements that include remote work (Art. 9).

EU directives concerning equality and discrimination on grounds of gender and other factors, in addition to prohibiting discrimination and establishing measures to guarantee the effectiveness of rights, call on different stakeholders to implement preventive policies. One of the advantages of teleworking is that it can be a resource for the adoption of business diversity policies, facilitating access to employment for the disabled or those with mobility problems due to health, age, etc. Although the latter opt in the main for remote working, firms are obliged, in accordance with international and European regulations, to guarantee access for the disabled to the workplace, making reasonable modifications to their physical spaces and, in the same vein, they are required to evaluate all job posts in accordance with the personal characteristics of their workers.

Moreover, the transfer of the principles of voluntariness and non-discrimination in teleworking to the regulatory frameworks of European countries – by means of the European Framework Agreement on Telework – is critical in defending fundamental labour rights. Thus, the principle of voluntariness prohibits employers from unilaterally imposing telework or, equally, from prohibiting it, and this voluntariness is required at the individual level, and is compatible with its collective implementation. However, the principle of voluntariness becomes somewhat blurred when telework forms part of the initial job description.

The principle of non-discrimination between workers who work remotely and those that work onsite is a basic guarantee of compliance with the rest of a worker's rights. Based on this principle, firms are required to employ objective and transparent criteria for offering access to telework and it is prohibited to establish conditions that are more detrimental or which give a less favourable treatment to remote workers.

Collective bargaining is critical for the implementation of teleworking, even in those countries where specific regulations govern the practice. In what follows, I provide a summary of proposals regarding best practices as identified by the European Trade Union Confederation (ETUC) and as contained in European cross-sectoral and sectoral agreements on telework[45], focusing specifically on matters of working time and gender equality.

[45] The European sectoral agreements cited in this contribution are: ETNO and UNI Europa, the EU Telecom Social Partner's Guidelines on Remote Work, 2023; Eurocommerce and UNI, Europa, European agreement on guidelines on Telework and ICT-mobile work in commerce, 2018; EACB, EBF-FBE, ESBG and UNI Global Union, Declaration on Telework in the European Banking Sector, 2017. Available at: Social dialogue texts database - Employment, Social Affairs & Inclusion - European Commission (europa.eu).

Although organization of work is considered a classic managerial prerogative[46], European sectoral agreements insist on the importance of its negotiated implementation in firms. In this sense, telework is part of the firm's culture as far as its labour relations are concerned and, as such, firms are advised to understand it as an inclusive, co-responsible formula, and as one that is compatible with other measures for reconciling family and work life.

The recommendations insist on the negotiated implementation of hybrid forms of teleworking. For this reason, it is important to establish the frequency and the proportion of the working time that is to be completed remotely and, above all, what jobs are to be carried out in this mode and who has the possibility of working from home and – if it is a temporary option – what situations justify telework. As the EU Telecom Social Partners' Guidelines on Remote Work point out, to avoid gender-based segregation, it is essential to negotiate inclusive access to teleworking for all workers, whenever this is technically possible and to ensure that it is not only certain groups of workers that are able to engage in remote working.

In terms of working time, as we have seen, the autonomy of teleworkers should be facilitated, respecting at all times their work days and working schedules, as well as their right to digital disconnection. A key aspect to take into account here, especially when work is results-driven, is to reach an agreement on workloads, 'which need to be identified and evaluated jointly'[47].

In addition, the calculation of overtime has to be agreed to, on the understanding that remuneration for these extra hours should be the same as for the overtime performed in the physical working environment. Moreover, time spent on-call or standby should be treated as working time. An example of this is provided by the EU Telecom Social Partners' Guidelines on Remote Work, which states that 'remote on-call duty will be governed by the same rules as if performed by employees using office workplaces, including a possible on-call or standby allowance'. Likewise, teleworkers that have requested a leave of absence should be substituted by other workers, in the same circumstances as worksite-based employees.

The role of worker's representatives to ensure the equality of teleworkers is critical and, in this regard, a firm's equality plan, as a negotiated instrument, makes it possible to detect, prevent and cease gender-based segregation in telework, including any possible disparities in matters of remuneration, training or promotion, as well as any possible penalties resulting from remote working. An additional aspect that needs to be taken into consideration is the incorporation in harassment protocols of steps to prevent digital violence, as well as the provision of support and the

[46] See on managerial prerogative and the role of collective bargaining and telework in M. Rönnmar, *Telework, Managerial Prerogative, Collective Bargaining and Health and Safety at Work*, draft paper, *Pompeu Fabra University Seminar* (2023).

[47] European Social Partners Framework Agreement on Digitalisation (2020).

obligation to guarantee a safe work environment for victims of gender violence, taking into account the particular circumstances of teleworking[48].

In short, the implementation of teleworking, as a mode that is respectful of decent work and of a worker's fundamental rights, needs to be firmly anchored in regulatory and institutional frameworks and in collective bargaining at a range of levels, which seek to promote equality and diversity in firms in a transversal and transparent fashion and in adherence with the principle of co-responsibility.

## REFERENCES

Alarcón Caracuel, M.R., 'La jornada ordinaria de trabajo y su distribución', in J. Aparicio, J. López-Gandía (eds), *Tiempo de Trabajo* (Albacete: Bomarzo, 2008), pp. 33–55.

Boulin, J.Y., Lallement, M., Michon, F., 'Decent working time in industrialized countries: Issues, scopes and paradoxes', in Jean-Yves Boulin, Michel Lallement, J.C. Messenger, F. Michon (eds), *Decent Working Time: New Trends, New Issues* (Geneva: International Labour Organization, 2006).

Canalda Criado, S., 'The New Directive on Transparent and Predictable Working Conditions in the European Union' (2019) 440 *Revista de Trabajo y Seguridad Social*, 161–184.

Carstensen, T., 'Orts- und zeitflexibles Arbeiten: Alte Geschlechterungleichheiten und neue Muster der Arbeitsteilung durch Digitalisierung' (2020) 74 *Zeitschrift fur Arbeitswissenschaft*, 195–205.

Chacartegui, C., 'Gender Discrimination and Working Time: A Sustainable Approach., in W. Leal Filho et al. (eds), *Gender Equality. Encyclopedia of the UN Sustainable Development Goals* (Springer 2021), pp. 423–431.

Chesley, N., 'Blurring Boundaries? Linking Technology Use, Spillover, Individual Distress, and Family Satisfaction' (2005) 67 *Journal of Marriage and Family*, 5, 1237–1248.

Chung, H., 'Gender, Flexibility Stigma and the Perceived Negative Consequences of Flexible Working in the UK' (2020) 151 *Social Indicators Research*, 521–545.

Chung, H., Van der Host, M., 'Women's Employment Patterns after Childbirth and the Perceived Access to and Use of Flexitime and Teleworking' (2018), 71 *Human Relations*, 1, 47–72.

De Stefano, V., *The Rise of the Just-in-Time Workforce: On-Demand Work, Crowdwork, and Labour Protection in the Gig-Economy* (Geneva: International Labour Organisation, 2016).

Eurofound and ILO, *Working Anytime, Anywhere: The Effects on the World of Work (Luxembourg: Publications Office of the European Union* (Geneva: International Labour Office, 2017).

Eurofound, *Hybrid Work in Europe: Concept and Practice* (Luxembourg: Publications Office of the European Union, 2023).

*Regulations to Address Work–Life Balance in Digital Flexible Working Arrangements, New Forms of Employment Series* (Luxembourg: Publications Office of the European Union, 2020).

*Telework in the EU: Regulatory Frameworks and Recent Updates*, (Luxembourg: Publications Office of the European Union, 2022a).

[48] See, in this regard, EU Cross-Sectoral Guidelines on Violence and Harassment at Work (2021).

*The Rise in Telework: Impact on Working Conditions and Regulations* (Luxembourg: Publications Office of the European Union, 2022b).

European Commission, Interpretative Communication on Directive 2003/88/EC, Official Journal C 143 of 26 April 2023 (2023/C 143/08).

Fagan, C., 'Gender and Working-time in Industrialized Countries: Practices and Preferences' in J. Messenger (ed), *Working-Time and Workers' Preferences in Industrialized Countries: Finding the Balance* (Geneva: International Labour Organization, 2004), pp. 108–114.

Fudge, J., 'Control Over Working Time and Work-Life Balance: A Detailed Analysis of the Canada Labour Code Part III' (2007) *Federal Labour Standards Review Commission.* https://papers.ssrn.com/sol3/papers.cfm?abstract_id = 974920.

Fudge, J., Vosko F.L., 'Gender, Segmentation and the Standard Employment Relationship in Canadian Labour Law' (2001) 22 *Legislation and Policy, Economic and Industrial Democracy*, 276, 271–310.

Genin, É., 'Technologies mobiles et travail à la Maison: mise à disposition ou mode de Conciliation' (2015) 53 *Revue Interventions Économiques*, 1–15.

Huybrechts, S., 'Working Time and Autonomy: Lessons for the New Ways of Working' (2023) 14 *European Labour Law Journal*, 4, 570–587.

ILO, *Decent Working Time. Balancing Worker's Needs with Business Requirements* (Geneva: International Labour Organization, 2007).

*Digitalization and Employment: A Review* (Geneva: International Labour Organization, 2022).

*Working from Home: From Invisibility to Decent Work, International Labour Office* (Geneva: International Labour Organization, 2021).

Kim, J. et al., Workplace Flexibility and Worker Well-Being by Gender (2020) 82 *Journal of Marriage and Family*, 892–910.

Kley, S., Reimer, T., 'Exploring the Gender Gap in Teleworking from Home. The Roles of Worker's Characteristics' (2023) 168 *Occupational Positions and Gender Equality in Europe, Social Indicators Research*, 185–206.

López, J., 'Reconfiguring Fundamental Rights: The Case of Tele-Workers', draft paper, Pompeu Fabra University Seminar (2023).

'Systemic discrimination y políticas de igualdad efectiva de género' (2019) 1 *Revista del Ministerio de Empleo y Seguridad Social*, 35–50.

López, J., Pumar, N., Colàs, E. (2023), 'Telework, Sustainability of Pensions and Synergies with Markets Institutions: Constructing a Theory of Fundamental Rights' in M. Rönnmar, J.J. Votinius (eds) *Older Workers, Active Ageing, and the Future of Work*, (Alphen aan den Rijn: Kluwer Law International, forthcoming).

Messenger, J.C., 'Introduction: Telework in the 21st Century – An Evolutionary Perspective', in J.C. Messenger (ed), *Telework in the 21st Century- An Evolutionary Perspective* (Geneva: International Labour Organization, 2019), pp. 1–34.

Perulli, A., 'Agile Work': A Paradigm for Hybrid Remote Working', draft paper, Pompeu Fabra University Seminar (2023).

Rodríguez-Modroño, P., López-Igual, P., 'Job Quality and Work Life Balance of Teleworkers' (2021) 18 *International Journal of Environmental Research and Public Health*, 18 (6), 1–13.

Rönnmar, M., Telework, Managerial Prerogative, Collective Bargaining and Health and Safety at Work, draft paper, Pompeu Fabra University Seminar (2023).

Rubery, J., Fagan, C., 'How to combat segregation in the labour market for both low- and high-qualified women', in N. Crowley, S. Sansonetti (eds), *New Vision for Gender Equality* (Brussels: European Commission, 2019), pp. 58–62.

Rubery, J., Koukidiaki, A., 'Institutional Interactions in Gender Pay Equity: A Call for Inclusive, Equal and Transparent Labour Markets' (2018) 1 *University of Oxford Human Rights Hub Journal*, 115–142.

Rubery J., Smith M., Fagan C., 'National Working Time Regimes and Equal Opportunities' (1998) 4 *Feminist Economics*, 1, 71–101.

Sostero M., Milasi S., Hurley J., Fernández-Macías E., Bisello M., *Teleworkability and the COVID-19 Crisis: A New Digital Divide?* (Seville: European Commission, 2020).

Sullivan, C., Lewis, S., 'Home-Based Telework, Gender, and the Synchronization of Work and Family: Perspectives of Teleworkers and their Co-Residents' (2001) 8 *Gender, Work and Organization*, 2, 123–145.

Tomei, M.,'Teleworking: A Curse or a Blessing for Gender Equality and Work-Life Balance?' (2021) 56 *Intereconomics*, 56, 260–264.

Wajcman, Judy, Rose, Emily, 'Constant Connectivity: Rethinking Interruptions at Work' (2011) 32 *Organization Studies*, 7, 941–961.

# 12

# An International Perspective on Occupational Health and Safety Challenges for Remote Workers

*José Luis Goñi Sein, Beatriz Rodríguez Sanz de Galdeano, Julen Llorens Espada, and Uxue Del Río Ilincheta*

## 12.1 REMOTE WORKING: DELIMITATION OF THE CONCEPTUAL FRAMEWORK AND APPLICABLE OCCUPATIONAL SAFETY AND HEALTH LEGISLATION

The possibilities opened up by telecommuting have raised important challenges for labour law, affecting some of its essential institutions. In general, the provision of work as an employee has been attached to a certain place of work which, from time to time, could change, but served as a fundamental basis for determining the applicable legislation and the rest of the working conditions. This certainty provided by the existence of a regular, physical place of work has been challenged by the possibilities opened up by technology and the spread of teleworking. The lack of a more or less stable physical place of work highlights the difficulty of adapting legislation designed to provide a response to regular work, attached to a fixed workplace. In addition, in the international nature of the service, the very bases of international conflict rules are overwhelmed by the need to respond to a reality that until recently was unimaginable.

On the other hand, transnational remote work can take many different forms, and there is a wide range of remote working practices, not always homogeneous (V.A. 2021; Garicano & Alonso De Armiño Rodríguez 2021).

In an effort to summarise, the following forms of remote work can be identified according to their duration, whether they are voluntary, whether to its original or supervening nature or whether there is certainty as to where services are provided:

- A worker could initially be recruited in one company is posted on a temporary basis to provide services in another country and that a large part of the service is provided by remote means in the country of posting.
- It is the employee himself who may decide to work remotely and asks the employer, on either a temporary or a permanent basis, to provide services remotely in a third country.

- The case could also be that the service is provided in different countries and that even the country and the time from which the service is to be provided is not known precisely. In this case, it could be that the choice for mobility is made by the worker himself or that it responds to the needs of the company.

As far as we are concerned here, the question that arises is what the protection in terms of occupational risk prevention should be for these workers who provide their services remotely and with an element of internationality. In order to address this question, it is essential to first determine which legislation is applicable to the contract, unless a common legislative framework on the matter is adopted at European or international level, as will be seen later.

To determine the law applicable to the contract, the starting point is the Rome I Regulation[1], which in Article 8 sets out the conflict rules to be applied to employment contracts and begins by referring to the general rule laid down in Article 3, according to which the contract is governed by the law freely chosen by the parties. However, the Regulation then qualifies that the application of the chosen law cannot deprive the employee of the application of the rules '*which cannot be excluded by agreement*' and which would have been applicable in the absence of an agreement.

The following paragraphs of Art. 8 set out the rules applicable in the absence of an agreement. Firstly, according to Art. 8(2), the following shall apply: '*the law of the place in the country in which or, failing that, from which the worker, in performance of the contract, habitually carries out his work*'. The application of the *lex loci laboris* is thus enshrined as a general rule. With regard to the habitual place of provision of services, the Regulation states that the temporary provision of services in another country does not imply a change of the habitual place of provision of services, as will be seen later. However, there are cases in which it will be difficult to determine the habitual place of work.

For those cases in which the habitual place of provision of services cannot be determined, Article 8.3 of the Regulation states that the law of the establishment through which the worker has been recruited shall apply. The *lex loci* delegation is therefore introduced as a subsidiary criterion.

However, the regulation is completed by a final escape clause, contained in Art. 8.4, according to which, when it is clear from all the circumstances that the contract is more closely connected with a law other than the place of provision of services or the place of establishment, the law of that other country more directly related to the contract shall apply.

The principle of territoriality is at the heart of the Rome Regulation. The aim is to identify a place to which the provision of services can be assigned, giving priority to

[1] Regulation (EC) No. 593/2008 of the European Parliament and of the Council of 17 June 2008.

the place where the services are habitually provided and using other additional rules. However, there are occasions, beyond remote working, where it is not easy to identify the place of the habitual place of provision of services, such as in cases of multi-location contracts. When the European Court of Justice has had to clarify these conflicting cases concerning the place of provision of services, the CJEU, by all means, tries to seek a habitual place of provision of services in which to locate the provision of services and which prevents the next connecting factor, that of the establishment of the contract, from coming into play. It is not clear, however, what the criteria should be for determining this habitual place of supply of services. Thus, in the judgment of 15 March 2011, *Heiko Koelzsch and État du Grand-Duché de Luxembourg*, Case C-29/10, the Court seems to focus primarily on the place where most of the work is carried out, but in the judgment of 15 December 2011, *Jan Voogsgeerd v Navimer* SA, Case C-384/10, seems to grant greater importance to other qualitative elements, such as the place where the activity is mainly carried out. The situation becomes even more complicated when it comes to differentiating between the usual place of provision of services and the place with which the work is most closely connected (Fontinopoulou Basurko 2006).

These difficulties in determining the applicable law have led to solutions being proposed specifically for international remote work, which seek to delimit the place of provision of services for the purpose of identifying the applicable social security system.

Thus, the European Commission, through its Administrative Commission for the Coordination of Social Security Systems, has issued a guidance note for the application of the regulations on social security coordination No 883/2004 and No 987/2009. The note, which is not binding, provides for certain exceptions to the application of the law of the place of the habitual provision of services in cases of international telework[2].

In the domestic sphere, Law 28/2022, of 21 December, on the promotion of the start-up ecosystem, for the first time contemplates the situation and residence of international teleworkers, who work in Spain for companies based abroad.

These are, as can be seen, laudable initiatives which attempt to respond to imminent problems, but which may not be sufficient to provide a full response to the challenges posed by international telework. On the other hand, efforts seem to be focused on trying to find also in international remote work a usual place of provision of services; although, as some scholars have warned, the very characterisation of international telework may clash with such a strict conception of the place of provision of services and its consequent effects on the determination of the applicable law (Moreno Márquez 2005).

[2] Note dated 13 May 2022: Guidance Note on telework. Available at: htps://everfive.es/wp-content/uploads/2022/10/125-22REV2en.pdf.

It is perhaps for this reason that it is necessary to remove the classic schemes of defining working conditions after choosing the applicable law, especially in the most extreme cases of absolute lack of definition of the place of work and, even more so, in those cases in which the place of provision of services may be indifferent.

However, if a possible regulatory review of the conflict rules is undertaken, the various interests at stake and the workers' protection needs must be taken into account. Sometimes transnational service provision is a response to a company's need to meet a particular demand abroad, but it should also be borne in mind that these forms of nomadic work are sometimes used in order to avoid the application of stricter national rules, known as social dumping. Apart from this, it should be taken into account that the protection of workers in terms of prevention is one of the basic conditions for ensuring decent work. In fact, both at EU level and in the framework of the ILO, occupational safety and health has been a subject on which it has been possible to agree a common regulatory framework.

The question at this point is whether, perhaps, from a substantive point of view, the preventive regulation of remote workers within an international context could be susceptible to a minimum regulation that would specifically attend to the peculiarities of this type of provision and to some conditioning factors, which will be referred to later, that may make it difficult to apply the existing preventive regulations, since they also start from a model based on the physical workplace as the place of provision.

Two basic conclusions can be drawn from the foregoing: the first is that the rules of conflict for the determination of the applicable law need to be revised to try to respond to the problems raised by international telework, especially in those cases where the place of provision of services is completely undefined; the second conclusion is that perhaps, also from a substantive point of view, a revision of the preventive obligations is necessary, in order to take into account the particularities of this type of work and to accommodate to this new virtual obligations that have traditionally been based on the workplace as the physical place.

On the basis of this briefly described reality, the options that could be considered are the following

1. To make a conceptual approach to the different forms of international remote service provision, in order to differentiate those in which, despite the fact that the work is provided remotely, there is a clear and stable element to determine the applicable law. In this sense, for example, where temporary service provision is envisaged, or where a minimum of physical presence at a particular workplace is required, the classic conflict rules could still apply. In cases where there are no elements that clearly allow for the identification of the applicable law, a reform of the Rome I Regulation could be considered, in order to clarify what may be the decisive elements for identifying the law applicable to remote working.

2. In keeping with the basic outline of the first option, it could be decided that, in any case, despite being able to identify a law applicable to the contract, the maximum safety standards provided in the rules applicable the maximum standards should always be required to be respected (V.A. 2021).
3. At EU level, it might be advisable to undertake specific legislation harmonising the employer's preventive obligations with regard to workers providing remote services. Such legislation would provide a homogeneous level of safety for all EU countries and would also make it possible to accommodate current preventive regulations which, as will be seen, still rely on the physical workplace as a key element.

## 12.2 THE TIME FACTOR AS AN OCCUPATIONAL HAZARD IN REMOTE WORKING

### 12.2.1 *Introduction*

One of the main characteristics of remote work is that it allows *working anytime, anywhere* (Eurofound and the International Labour Office 2017), generating a resizing of the temporal and spatial element of work provision. Within the broad concept of 'remote work', new forms of work provision appear, such as *telework, home-based work* and *work based on online platforms*. But all of them show a common need to adapt the concepts of 'working time' that are currently provided for, in our case, in European and national law, as well as to create new time categories in accordance with the peculiarities of the time of provision of these forms of employment (Martín Rivera 2022).

The central element of the whole conceptual disruption derives from the fact that working time is provided outside the workplace, either from a fixed post or in an itinerant manner.

### 12.2.2 *Is There a Need for a Reconceptualisation of Working and Resting Times?*

The first innovative and problematic element of remote working is the availability of the worker. The fact that rendering of the service can be required at any time, with a high degree of unpredictability, means that the worker is, for long periods of their daily working time, under the anticipation of having to connect and commence the actual working day, if required to do so.

The conceptual classification of these times is not an easy question to answer within the conceptual binomial between working time and rest time. The concept of working time used in Europe is determined by Directive 2003/88/EC of the European Parliament and of the Council of 4 November 2003 concerning certain aspects of the organisation of working time, which lays down minimum safety and health requirements for the organisation of working time. The Directive does not provide for time arrangements that fall outside either concept, so that waiting time for activation of remote workers will have to be counted as working time or rest time, and thus be subject to the maximum working time limits in the former case or become part of the mandatory minimum rest periods in the latter.

According to the Directive, working time is considered to be 'any period during which the worker is at work, at the employer's disposal and carrying out his activity or duties'.

This conceptualisation is constructed on the basis of work performed at a workplace on the premises of the company. However, other indicators appear, such as availability in favour of the employer and the exercise of the activity or functions, which go beyond the spatial anchorage to the workplace, and pay greater attention to the functional element, that is, the possibility that during this time the worker is required to perform the functions inherent to his or her employment contract.

On this basis, European case law has gradually defined when these times on the borderline between actual working time and rest time fall into one or the other concept. In the case of non-face-to-face time off, the CJEU has focused its decision on whether the times in question affect the employee's freedom to move around freely and the freedom to use the time to pursue his or her private life or interests[3].

If the times in question do not generate a limitation in their capacity to freely manage the time dedicated to their personal and social life, this time of availability will be considered as rest time, and if they do generate it, on the contrary, it will be considered as effective working time. The key elements to determine whether or not this free availability is affected are whether or not the company obliges the worker to remain in a certain, localised place, and the reaction time that the company gives the worker so that, once his or her services have been requested, the worker can start the work activity[4].

The problem with transferring this doctrine to the case of remote workers is that it is designed for situations in which the worker is required to travel to an on-site workstation for the start of the activity, once his or her services have been requested. However, for remote workers, the start of work after the call can take place from any location. At a national level, the Spanish Supreme Court has considered, in these cases, decisive the reaction time that the company allows the worker to make the connection[5], and has considered as excluded from the concept of working time the times of availability in which the requested services can be resolved remotely (via telephone call) and would need only exceptionally need to travel to an specific workplace.

3 CJEU of 9 March 2021 (Case C-344/19), ECLI:EU:C:2021:182.

4 CJEU of 21 February 2018 (Case C-518/15).

5 STS of 18 June 2020 (rec 242/2018) and SAN 20 September 2018 (rec. 125/2018).

From all of the above, it is considered necessary to regulate a special working day for remote workers that regulates which times of availability will be counted as effective working time or rest time, as well as the maximum limits that a remote worker can be employed under these times. However, when giving a regulatory response, it should be borne in mind that the European Committee of Social Rights has already expressed its opposition to the view that on-call time should be regarded as ordinary rest periods, since during this time the worker does not have an absolute guarantee that there will be no business interference, thus diminishing the right to rest (Salcedo Beltrán 2019).

In turn, this state of disposition and its disproportionate duration are occupational risk factors that must be taken into consideration in the corresponding occupational risk assessment, like any other occupational risk. Within the assessment of psychosocial risk factors, working time, 'taking into account the rest periods allowed by the activity, their quantity and quality and the effect of working time on social life', and the workload, both quantitatively and qualitatively (NTP 926 2012), are factors that must be assessed and to which the relevant measures to eliminate or reduce the intensity of exposure must be applied.

Among the psychosocial risk factors, the Spanish Labour and Social Security Inspectorate (ITSS) has identified workload and work rhythm as excessive or insufficient workload, time pressure and fixed deadlines, within the psychosocial factors of workload and work rhythm; and as psychosocial risk factors associated with working time, very long or unpredictable working hours, continuous connection to work, shift work and night work (ITSS 2021). Poor management of these factors will lead to occupational risks such as (techno)stress at work, burnout syndrome, substance abuse or difficulties in reconciling work and family life (Llorens Espada 2020).

In this sense, the company will become responsible for incorrect assessment and preventive planning, and will be civilly liable for damages and losses that may arise in the form of work-related accidents or occupational illnesses.

### 12.2.3 *Invasion of Working Time into Private Time*

Another problem, in connection with the previous one, is the exhausting working hours that remote workers may have. Firstly, due to an inadequate conceptualisation of the limits of the working day itself, as mentioned in the previous section in relation to availability times; secondly, due to the lengthening of the actual working day.

Among the activities that can be carried out remotely, it is common to find sectors in which work is eminently measured by results, to the detriment of actual hours of work, such as graphic or web design, translation, software development, social media management and digital marketing.

This means that, faced with an excessive burden of productive objectives, workers have to invest an inordinate number of hours in order to meet business requirements, in detriment of the hours dedicated to their private lives.

The right to digital disconnection appears as a buffer against these overflows of the working day, in order to protect those spaces free of work-related demands or communications related to professional activity. Through digital disconnection, the aim is to guarantee rest times, by preserving temporary spaces in which the worker is kept free of digital communications from the company and from the use of the smart devices used to carry out their functions.

In our opinion, the right to digital disconnection, as a key element in guaranteeing the health and safety of remote workers, has a special impact on this type of production, and would require specific legislative development for these workers. On 21 January 2021, the European Parliament passed a resolution in favour of the right to disconnect, calling on the Commission to prepare a directive 'that enables those who work digitally to disconnect outside their working hours'. As it was said, the Directive 'should also establish minimum requirements for remote working and clarify working conditions, hours and rest periods'. This legislation has been regarded as vital 'to protect their physical and mental health and well-being and to protect them from psychological risks' (Eurofound 2021).

### 12.2.4 *Controlling Working Time in Remote Work*

This problem is linked to a third problem, which is how to control the number of hours actually worked during the working day when working remotely. New systems are appearing to comply with legal requirements, such as keeping a record of the working day via telematic systems to measure working time, but they are easily malleable.

Malleable in a double sense. Firstly, because they mean delegating to the good faith of the worker the accurate recording of data on when work is done and when rest is taken, which can lead to the worker being coerced into working shorter hours in situations of overload, for fear of reprisals from the company. But it can also happen the other way around and additional hours may be reported as worked when they have not actually been worked. These increases or decreases in the reporting of working hours have a direct correlation with the salary to be received by the worker, which can generate a high level of conflict in the company. It is usual that, in the absence of an express agreement, working longer hours than those agreed requires an express agreement between the parties, so problems can arise when the worker reports working longer hours than those previously agreed and the company refuses to pay them (Llorens Espada 2022).

Secondly, there may be a need for the company to verify that the person who is carrying out the activity in front of the computer is really the worker who has been hired and not a third person. For this purpose, some companies introduce biometric recognition or verification systems, such as the use of fingerprints or facial or voice recognition. However, it is worth warning about the possible illegality of many of these systems, as they generate the processing of workers' personal data, often without any legitimate basis for it, as they go beyond what would be considered 'necessary' practices for the execution of the employment contract, with the processing of particularly sensitive data (art. 6.1 b and 9.2 b of the General Data Protection Regulation).

From the perspective of the Labour Authority's inspection of working time, it is not easy to control due compliance with these records when workers are dispersed and relocated. In this sense, it seems necessary to set up registers of remote workers in which, by means of digital systems, the competent labour authority can obtain a digital measurement of the working times carried out by the company and maintain a direct contact channel with these workers.

A multitude of work performance evaluation techniques are appearing on the market aimed at monitoring the activity of remote workers, whether based on geolocation systems, digital cameras, biometric sensors, performance monitoring using software capable of detecting emotions or counting keystrokes and scrolling time, and so on.

From the perspective of occupational risk prevention, these techniques that the company installs, whether for time supervision or monitoring the activity of remote workers, increase the psychosocial occupational risks of the worker. These risks are accentuated when an algorithm intervenes in the data collection and management of the employment relationship. In fact, the empirical analysis confirms that the use of surveillance technologies and algorithmic management practices increases psychosocial risk and negative health outcomes (EU-OSHA 2023).

These risks are accentuated when an algorithm intervenes in the data collection and management of the employment relationship. As noted by EU-OSHA, 'the amplified use of surveillance and the constant feel of monitoring also have wide repercussions for job quality, leading to reduced work autonomy, work intensification, increased level of stress and anxiety, and reciprocal mistrust between workers and management with serious consequences for the wellbeing of workers' (EU-OSHA 2023).

In this respect, the involvement of trade union actors in the governance of the algorithms introduced in the company is essential.

### 12.2.5 *High Rate of Unpredictability of the Work Activity*

Another characteristic of remote work is its great dependence on the variability of the working hours, which means that these workers have very high rates of irregular distribution of the working day, subject to constant changes. The very modality of work tends to be accompanied by a requirement for flexibility in terms of working hours, which can lead to high concentrations of workload in short periods of time, which would be counteracted by subsequent periods of low demand.

This factor of unpredictability of the service, combined with excessive availability times, can lead to a direct reduction in the psychophysical health conditions of workers.

The establishment of new specific break times for these remote workers should be reconsidered, taking into account their specific digital connectivity. For this purpose, collective bargaining plays a key role, as it allows working time regulation to be adapted to the specificities of each sector and company. This makes it possible to establish specific break times and maximum availability times, but also something as important as the remuneration or monetary compensation of those spaces which, being breaks, generate a need for activation or action when there is a call from the company. Likewise, collective bargaining is the ideal source of rules to regulate the reaction times available to each worker in the event of a call-out.

However, although collective bargaining is called upon to complement regulation in each sector, this does not prevent the legislator from introducing the necessary safeguards to ensure that remote workers enjoy the same guarantees as other workers in matters such as rest, working hours, overtime regulation, vacations, night or shift work and work–life balance (García Quiñones 2018).

### 12.2.6 *The Delimitation of Working Time for the Purposes of Occupational Classification of the Contingency*

It is also important to define which time periods fall under the concept of 'working time', as this has legal consequences for other important occupational health and safety institutions. The fact that the worker is within the effective working time not only means that he or she is dependent on the company and that reciprocal rights and obligations arise in terms of prevention, but also that the occurrence of an accident at work or occupational disease within these areas is subject to special protection under the umbrella of the social security, and may give rise to company liability arising from non-compliance with occupational health and safety regulations during that part of time.

Each national regulation has constructed a specific concept of occupational accident, occupational disease and occupational illness, but the time element of the contingency will always be an important factor to determine when a person is entitled to access that benefit.

An interesting debate is the creation of a specific type of presumption of being at work for digital workers. In the same way that social security protection has included specific cases of protection, such as accidents '*in itinere*', in which coverage has been extended to temporary periods of commuting to the workplace, consideration should be given to the possibility of including digital roaming times in protection. Otherwise, in addition, the worker may encounter problems in obtaining adequate proof of events or situations that have occurred in private spaces or where there has been no interaction with third parties.

## 12.3 ICT, REMOTE WORKING AND ACTIVITY MANAGEMENT: CRITICAL ASPECTS

### 12.3.1 *The Management of Preventive Activity in Teleworking*

Business management of preventive activity in telework is one of the most controversial areas, as new risk factors emerge with the introduction of new elements.

The use of ICTs affects the health of workers, yet the regulatory protection at both EU and national levels is insufficient, and it is necessary to strengthen legislation towards a digitalisation of labour relations (Arangüez Valenzuela 2019). The use of technology in labour relations must be considered as a risk-generating factor, so it is essential that both the risk assessment and the subsequent planning of preventive activity consider all the digital devices used by workers to provide services, since excessive use of these devices can lead to occupational pathologies (Trujillo Pons 2022). Despite the advantages of using digital tools in terms of flexibility, autonomy and work organisation and management, their use can lead to an increase in the duration, intensity and volume of work (Gil Pérez 2023), resulting in psychosocial symptoms such as stress or anxiety, as well as physical ailments such as eyestrain, musculoskeletal disorders or headaches.

It is therefore essential that the management of preventive activity takes into account the remote location of the company's workplace and the use of ICT in the provision of services, so that the risk assessment considers all the risks faced by teleworkers, both the traditional risks arising from the use of display screens and the new risks arising from the provision of services with the exclusive use of ICT in a place reserved for the privacy of the worker, and then to plan preventive activity by implementing the most appropriate measures to eliminate or reduce these risks.

### 12.3.2 *Risk Assessment after the Distance Working Act 10/2021*

Law 10/2021 on teleworking introduces nuances about risk assessment in teleworking with the intention of maintaining a balance between the employer's obligations and the worker's rights, specifying in Article 16 that the assessment must only cover the area set aside for teleworking, without extending to the rest of the home or place chosen for the development of teleworking. The duty of prevention imposes that the risks must be known and for this, the person in charge of the prevention service must have all the information about the risks to which the worker is exposed[6], so that the decentralisation of the workplace in remote work can be an obstacle to obtaining the necessary information. Here, the right to privacy (art. 18.1 EC) and the right to inviolability of the home (art. 18.2 EC) become important, which may be affected by the employer's preventive obligations, and the question arises as to how far the

[6] SAN 44/2022, of 22 de March 2022.

employer's managerial and organisational powers extend. The LTD, in accordance with the provisions of the 'European Framework Agreement on Telework' of 16 July 2002, resolves the doubt by pointing out the possibility of the competent authority in preventive matters visiting the teleworker's home, provided that two requirements are met: a report justifying the visit must be drawn up and the worker's permission to enter his or her home must be obtained.

The regulation is generic in relation to access authorisation, as it does not specify whether it must be given for all access relating to the development of prevention activities, that is, both for the initial assessment and for periodic checks of the working conditions and activity of workers in the provision of services. In this respect, the Audiencia Nacional in Ruling 44/2022 of 22 March confirms the nullity of prior, generic and unconditional authorisation clauses in individual teleworking agreements that authorise entry to the home, so that each access by the prevention service must have the permission of the teleworker.

In the case of mobile teleworkers, that is, those who combine remote work with tourism, the flexibility provided by their form of remote work allows them to frequently change their place of residence and even the physical space from which they provide their services, making it difficult for them to carry out their preventive activity.

Leaving aside the problem posed by the number of physical spaces from which they can provide their services, the requirement for permission to access the teleworker's home or that of a third natural person for risk assessment purposes makes it necessary to determine the concept of home, since the areas enabled for remote working may consist of hotel rooms, hostels or co-working spaces. The Constitutional Court[7] affirms that for a space to be considered a domicile for the purposes of the protection of art. 18.2 EC, it is essential that it has the capacity to develop private life, and this classification is not prevented by the lack of habitual use or enjoyment. It follows that the hotel room from which the digital nomad carries out his work and private life, being his 'home' during the time he stays there, is protected by Art. 18.2 EC and is therefore considered to be a home, so that in these cases the prevention service must also request permission from the worker to access the room and assess the risks in the area set aside for the work to be carried out.

When the two requirements do not coexist, or when the first requirement has been fulfilled and the second is lacking, in order to provide a methodology that offers confidence in the results, the Remote Work Act provides that the risk assessment can be carried out by the worker himself by means of a self-assessment system consisting of filling in a questionnaire and following the instructions of the prevention service. This procedure, as confirmed by the National High Court in Ruling 44/2022 of 22 March, does not affect the right to effective health and safety

7 STC 10/2022, of 17 January.

protection at work, nor does it imply the transfer of the employer's obligation to the worker.

However, part of the doctrine (Gonzalez Cobaleda 2022) warns of the new and significant risk factors that emerge in teleworking, the assessment of which may be affected, thus not guaranteeing effective protection of health and safety at work. Although, according to the preventive regulations, the risk assessment should only cover the area set aside for teleworking, the Courts[8] have been pointing out that the workplace is not only the workstation consisting of a chair, desk and computer, but also other spaces in the home in which the teleworker can carry out activities or a working life similar to that which he/she would carry out if he/she worked in person. Accordingly, self-assessments, irrespective of whether or not they are considered a suitable environment, should refer to those other spaces in the home where the teleworker would normally carry out his/her working life, such as the bathroom or kitchen.

Moreover, the implementation of prevention measures in remote work following a self-assessment may be laxer than in an ordinary environment and given that a workplace is in a space reserved for the worker's privacy, the possibilities for company control over the worker's compliance with these measures are limited (Rodríguez Cardo 2023).

In short, the regulations require the use of a method that offers confidence in the results, but, in accordance with the above, the emergence of new forms of work organisation, of new risk factors in a digitalised working environment and the generic regulations on the subject, together with the worker's lack of knowledge of prevention or his or her lack of collaboration, can have undesirable results for the worker, as well as consequences for the employer's liability.

### 12.3.3 *Planning of Preventive Activity: Preventive Training and Distance Work*

When the assessment reveals the existence of risks, the employer will plan the preventive activity, in which he will refer to the human and material resources necessary to avoid and reduce the risks, the emergency and health surveillance measures to be implemented and the process of informing and training workers in preventive matters, among others. Correct planning requires a risk assessment carried out using the most reliable methodology and which allows sufficient information to be obtained to implement the necessary preventive measures, so that if the self-assessment method is questioned, subsequent preventive planning will not be effective.

[8] SSJS Cáceres of 26 October 2022 (Rec. 273/2022) y TSJ Madrid of 11 November 2022 (Rec. 526/2022).

Given the inherent characteristics of remote service provision, one of the most critical aspects of basic preventive activities is training. In accordance with art. 19 of the LPRL, it is an obligation of the employer to provide both theoretical and practical training, sufficient and appropriate, in preventive matters, and it becomes important when implementing basic corrective preventive measures under the instructions of the prevention service (Orofino Vega & Notario González 2021)[9]. Training must serve to ensure that workers obtain knowledge that helps to eliminate or reduce occupational risks, and that involves the modification of behaviour and the acquisition of the value of occupational health and safety, and teleworking should not be an impediment to this.

However, the regulations do not introduce specific requirements to help ensure sufficient and appropriate training, as this will depend on the level of risk of each job. This requires a prior risk assessment to be carried out which, if it does not exist, makes it impossible to plan preventive activity and to develop specific training for the worker's job and function (Fernández Collados 2018), as will be the case when the self-assessment of risks is called into question, both in terms of form and substance.

Leaving aside the assessment and even though the content of the training is not specified in the legislation, the Courts establish that it must be correlated with the work that is carried out, generic, abstract and indiscriminate training not being sufficient for the fulfilment of the obligation[10].

The absence of the teleworker's presence in the company centre raises controversy regarding the content and the way in which the training is given, and it is questioned whether the regulation requires the presence of the teleworker for the practical training to be sufficient (Estardid Colom 2023). The LPRL does not expressly state that prevention training must be face-to-face, however, the Social Court of the Balearic Islands (Palma)[11] understands that practical training acts as a complement to theoretical training and helps the understanding, mastery and application of theoretical knowledge to the reality of the company, so that theoretical training can be given at a distance, but on the other hand, to ensure the effectiveness of practical training, it must be face-to-face. Along the same lines, there are judicial pronouncements by High Courts of Justice that consider the obligation of Article 19 LPRL to have been infringed when, without proof of having received the practical training, there is only the signature of a receipt of delivery of a

9 Along these lines, the ILO and the WHO have expressed their views on the interest and value of training in occupational risk prevention in teleworking for both workers and managers. Healthy and safe telework: technical brief. Geneva: World Health Organization and the International Labour Organization, 2021. Available at: www.ilo.org/wcmsp5/groups/public/—ed_dialogue/—lab_admin/documents/publication/wcms_836250.pdf.

10 STSJ Andalucía 249/2009 de 22 enero (Rec. 4247/2007).

11 SJS de Islas Baleares (Palma), of 28 May 2019 (Proce. 442/2018).

prevention manual seven years before the occupational accident occurred[12], as well as when the preventive training on the handling of machinery has been carried out at a distance[13].

Therefore, judicial doctrine has been mostly inclined to reject online practical training, however, it has done so because in most cases the use of techniques whose effectiveness surpasses classroom training is not guaranteed, thus considering it insufficient and in cases where it is understood that the employment relationship is based on presence and therefore, an application of theoretical knowledge to the practical reality of the company is required, as well as in physical work where the handling of machinery is required. Likewise, the practical classroom training must also be adequate for the worker to be able to face the risks derived from their job, without the classroom nature per se being sufficient for this (Pérez Capitán 2023).

Due to the generality with which the LPRL regulates training in preventive matters, collective bargaining becomes a way to regulate and impose limits on the form and substance. Several collective agreements introduce references to preventive training[14], indicating that it must be specifically focused on the specific job or function of each worker, but without being more specific than the LPRL about the content of the training. As regards the way in which training is provided, not many agreements regulate the type of training, but as an example we can cite the 4th State Collective Bargaining Agreement for Industry, New Technologies and Services in the Metal Sector, Annex V of which allows managers to provide face-to-face or blended training, that is, training that combines face-to-face and e-learning, but does not allow fully online training. Thus, the generality and lack of specification in the regulations on the subject and the lack of doctrinal unanimity may represent a limit when it comes to regulating practical online training through collective bargaining, which leads companies to opt for the mixed mode for remote workers.

Given the delocalisation of teleworking, the requirement of being present in person interferes with the characteristic element of teleworking, which allows work to be carried out without the need to go to the company's workplace, although a solution is found in the teleworking agreement, in which the workplace to which the worker is assigned must be detailed, so that nuances and limits can be introduced to the absence of presence.

However, the development of ICT and the digitalisation of the working environment require that in order for training in preventive matters to be carried out in

[12] STSJ de Islas Canarias (Las Palmas), of 19 April 2012 (Rec. 2448/2009).

[13] STSJ Castilla y León, of 31 October 2007(Rec. 1595/2007).

[14] Examples of this are the Resolution of 19 August 2021, of the Directorate General of Labour, which registers and publishes the III Collective Bargaining Agreement of Ilunion Seguridad, SA; Resolution of 29 January 2021, of the Directorate General of Labour, which registers and publishes the II Collective Bargaining Agreement of the Vodafone Spain Group and Resolution of 11 February 2023, of the Directorate General of Labour, which registers and publishes the X Framework Agreement of the Repsol Group.

accordance with the defining elements of teleworking, and even more so when it is mobile teleworking, companies have to develop plans that guarantee theoretical and practical training that is entirely online, in which a preventive culture is acquired and which is appropriate for the job, going beyond the effectiveness of face-to-face training.

### 12.3.4 *Cyber-Bullying as an Occupational Hazard*

Harassment at work is not a new phenomenon, however, the rise of information and communication technologies in the work environment has become a new way of materialising harassment behaviours (López Rodríguez 2018), thus, the publication of false information about the victim on websites or the sending of defamatory emails are examples of the use of new technologies as a means for the development of behaviours constituting types of harassment: sexual harassment, harassment on grounds of sex, discriminatory harassment and moral harassment (Pérez Agulla 2022) or *mobbing*[15]. It is important to detail that harassment is an act that always affects the dignity of the worker, in some cases having a discriminatory motive, and in others not, and that when the company consents without preventing situations of harassment or establishing a protocol for prevention, management, control and resolution, the general obligation of art. 14 LRPR to protect the health and safety of workers is breached (Fabregat Monfort 2023).

Although there is no internationally accepted definition of digital harassment at work or cyberbullying at work (Pérez Agulla 2022), from the existing doctrinal definitions it can be defined as any psychological violence produced through ICTs that generates a humiliating or degrading work environment for people who provide their services in an organisation, whatever the legal nature of the employment relationship (Álvarez Del Cuvillo 2021). The implementation of new and emerging forms of work organisation that do not require being present in the company's premises is not an obstacle to the development of harassment situations and conduct, as the incorporation of ICTs has shown that it is not essential to share the same physical space (Pérez Agulla 2022). As teleworkers also have the right to health and safety at work, the employer maintains preventive obligations against violence and harassment, including cyberbullying.

In this respect, ILO Convention No. 190 on violence and harassment includes in its scope of protection 'violence and harassment in the world of work occurring during, in connection with or as a result of work' (Art. 3), so that the scope of application, and therefore of protection of health and safety, cannot be limited to the

[15] A term used by Heinz Leymann, a German psychologist who pioneered the study of harassment in the workplace and is responsible for the main research on the subject, to describe hostile and unethical behaviour directed systematically by one person or group against another, who is placed in a situation of indefinition and neglect.

limits of the physical space of the workplace. The precept adds a series of cases far from the business centre to which protection is extended, including the workplace located in a public or private space and those that occur 'in the context of work-related communications, including those made by means of information and communication technologies', and in which, of course, there must be a work-related link or connection between the victim and the perpetrator or perpetrators (Fabregat Monfort 2023).

Harassment at work is considered a psychosocial risk that causes psychological harm, such as stress or depression, and physical harm, such as hypertension or headaches (INSS 2018). This is the basis for ILO Convention 190, which considers violence and harassment as conduct which, regardless of its frequency, 'is intended to cause or is likely to cause physical, psychological, sexual or economic harm' (Art. 1) and which aims to eradicate violence and harassment in the workplace and with the aim of eradicating them in order to achieve a working environment free of violence and harassment, obliges member states to adopt legislation requiring employers to take measures to prevent violence and harassment in the workplace and in particular to assess the risks of violence and harassment, with the participation of workers and their representatives, and to provide them with information and training on the risks identified as well as the corresponding prevention and protection measures.

## REFERENCES

Álvarez Del Cuvillo, A. (2021) El ciberacoso en el trabajo como categoría jurídica. *Temas laborales: Revista andaluza de trabajo y bienestar social* 157.

Arangüez, Valenzuela L. (2019) *Relación laboral digitalizada: colaboración y control en un contexto tecnológico. Cizur Menor: Editorial Thomson Reuters.*

Carrillo Pozo, L.F. (2011) La ley aplicable al contrato de trabajo en el Reglamento Roma I. *Civitas. Revista Española de Derecho del Trabajo* 152.

Estardid Colom, F. (2023) La formación en prevención de riesgos laborales ante el impacto tecnológico. *Lan Harremanak - Revista de Relaciones Laborales* 49.

EU-OSHA (2023) *Surveillance and monitoring of remote workers: implications for occupational safety and health.* Luxembourg: European Agency for Safety and Health at Work.

Eurofound (2021) *Right to disconnect.* Dublin: European Industrial Relations Dictionary.

(2023) *Ethical digitalisation at work: From theory to practice.* Luxembourg: Publications Office of the European Union.

Eurofound and the International Labour Office (2017) *Working anytime, anywhere: The effects on the world of work.* Geneva: Publications Office of the European Union, Luxembourg, and the International Labour Office.

Fabregat Monfort, G. (2023) *Compliance Laboral en acoso y otras conductas contrarias a la libertad sexual e integridad moral. La responsabilidad empresarial.* Madrid: Francis Lefebvre,

Fernández Collados, M.B. (2018) La responsabilidad empresarial en materia de seguridad y salud laboral: Especial referencia a la obligación de formación de los trabajadores. *Revista de Trabajo y Seguridad Social. CEF* 418.

FEEX (2021) *Libro Blanco Teletrabajo Internacional.* FEEX. Asociación Española De Movilidad Laboral Internacional.

Fontinopoulou Basurko, O. (2006) *La determinación de la ley aplicable al contrato de trabajo internacional. Estudio del Convenio de 19 de junio de 1980, hecho en Roma, sobre ley aplicable a las obligaciones contractuales*. Pamplona: Aranzadi.

García Quiñones, J. C. (2018) La organización del tiempo de trabajo y descanso y la conciliación en el teletrabajo. In Mella Méndez L. (dir.) & Villalba Sánchez A. (cord.), *La revolución tecnológica y sus efectos en el mercado laboral: un reto del siglo XXI*. Madrid: Wolters Kluwer.

Garicano, A., Alonso De Armiño Rodríguez, J. (2021) Retos legales del teletrabajo internacional. *Documentación laboral* 124.

Gil Pérez, M.E. (2023) El teletrabajo y el impacto de las nuevas tecnologías en la salud y seguridad laboral. Albacete: Editorial Bomarzo.

Gonzalez Cobaleda, E. (2022) Evaluación de riesgos laborales, teletrabajo y desconexión digital: una lectura judicial garantista. Comentario a la Sentencia de la Audiencia Nacional 44/2022, de 22 de marzo. *Revista de Trabajo y Seguridad Social*. CEF 469.

INSS (2018) *El efecto sobre la salud de los riesgos psicosociales en el trabajo: una visión general*. Madrid: Instituto Nacional de Seguridad y Salud en el Trabajo (INSST).

ITSS (2021) *Criterio Técnico 104/2021, sobre actuaciones de la Inspección de Trabajo y Seguridad Social en Riesgos Psicosociales*. Madrid: Ministry of Labour and Social Economy.

Llorens Espada, J. (2020) Tiempo de Conexión y Trabajo, Tiempo de Conexión y Trabajo. In Todolí Signes, A. (dir.), *Riesgos Laborales Específicos del Trabajo en Plataformas Digitales*. Barakaldo: Osalan.

(2022) Application programs (app) for the daily working time register. *Conditions of Legality*. Labos, 3 1.

López Rodríguez, J. (2018) Caracterización jurídica del ciberacoso moral laboral. In Mella Méndez L. (dir.) & Villalba Sánchez A. (cord.), *La revolución tecnológica y sus efectos en el mercado laboral: un reto del siglo XXI*. Las Rozas (Madrid): Wolters Kluwer.

Martín Rivera, L. (2022) Tendencias recientes en la ordenación del tiempo de trabajo. *Revista Española de Derecho del Trabajo* 250.

Moreno Márquez, A. (2005) Ley aplicable al teletrabajo transnacional: problemas existentes y posibles soluciones. *Revista de la contratación electrónica* 58.

NTP 926 (2012) *Psychosocial factors: assessment methodology*, Instituto Nacional de Seguridad e Higiene en el Trabajo.

Orofino Vega, P. & Notario González, I. (2021) Telework: criterios para su integración en el sistema de gestión de la seguridad y salud en el trabajo. Madrid: INSST.

Pérez Agulla, S. (2022) Los riesgos psicosociales en un mercado laboral digitalizado: el ciberacoso en el trabajo. *Nueva revista española de derecho del trabajo* 255.

Pérez Capitán, L. (2023) Use of new technologies for preventive management purposes. Posibilidades a la luz de la normativa en materia de seguridad y salud laboral. In Egusquiza Balmaseda, M.A. & Rodríguez Sanz De Galdeano, B. (dir.), *Inteligencia artificial y prevención de riesgos laborales: obligaciones y responsabilidades*. Valencia: Tirant lo Blanch.

Rodríguez Cardo, I.A. (2023) Accidente de trabajo y teletrabajo: una relación difícil. *Temas Laborales: Revista Andaluza de Trabajo y Bienestar Social* 166.

Salcedo Beltrán, C. (2019) Tiempo de trabajo en la sociedad digital: jornada de trabajo y “conexión” en los períodos de guardia localizada. In García González, G. & Regina Redinha, M. (dir.), *Relaciones contractuales en la economía colaborativa y en la sociedad digital*. Madrid: Dykinson.

Trujillo Pons, F. (2022) *La fatiga informática en el trabajo. Albacete: Editorial Bomarzo.*

# Index


2011 smart work guideline, 137
2030 Agenda, 3, 26–28, 33, 36

access to information, 68, 109
accumulation of capital, 104
Administrative Commission for the Coordination of Social Security Systems (EU), 61, 120, 201
agile work, 99–100, 107–108, 111–114
AI, 8–10, 162–164
AI Act, 9, 162, 175
AI driven tools of worker control, 5, 59
AI law, 166–168
AI regulation, 168, 174–179
AI tools, 8, 171, 179
AI-driven systems, 155
Alarcón, M. R., 188
algorithmic information rights, 168
algorithmic law, 173, 179
algorithmic management, 5, 9, 31, 59, 67, 70, 171, 207
algorithmic management systems, 163
algorithmic system, 99–100, 163
alienation, 110, 135
antidiscrimination law, 48
appeal courts, 124
applicable law
  determination of, 11, 129–131, 201–203
  in cross-border situations, 116–120, 130
applicable law shopping, 124
Artificial Intelligence. *See* AI
assessment of interests, 154
associations
  labour, 69
  workplace, 45, 47
Australia, 82
Austria, 17, 19, 156, 165

authority, 178
  administrative, 103, 137
  employer's direct, 150
  hierarchical, 104
  managerial, 150
  principle of, 104, 110
  public, 141
authority transfer, 87, 91
automated decisions, 166, 171, 176
autonomy, 23
  and trust, 99, 108
  collective, 65–66, 71–72, 76, 139, 145
  flexibility and, 29, 102, 113, 189
  of movement, 32
  of workers organisations, 69
autonomy paradox, 190

balancing of interests, 159
Barbulescu, 152
Belgium, 17, 20
beneficial ownership, 126–127
Better Life Index, 93
biometric categorization system, 177
biometric recognition, 207
Bismarck model (for social security), 142
BPR (Business process reengineering), 84–85
bridging ties, 47–48, 52
burden of proof, 140–143
business practices, 10, 185–187, 192

Canada, 118, 122, 125, 186
capabilities approach, 113, 136–138
capitalist neofeudalism, 65
CFREU, 20–21, 69–72, 155–160
Charter of Fundamental Rights of the European Union. *See* CFREU

child labour, 32, 35
childcare, 84, 87, 92, 134, 142, 190, 192
China, 93
choice of law, 121, 123, 129–130
Chung, Heejung, 192
civil society, 33, 45–48
CJEU, 121–123, 127–128, 156–159, 193, 201–204
  Heiko Koelzsch and État du Grand-Duché de Luxembourg, Case C-29/10, 201
  Jan Voogsgeerd v Navimer SA, Case C-384/10, 201
collective action, 46, 70
  problem, 53
  tactics, 5, 60, 72
  unconventional modes of, 73
collective agreements, 36, 72, 136–138, 145, 157–159, 179, 213
  at company level, 106
  at the European Union level, 17
  for the financial sector, 22
  Italian, 102
  national, 21
  of the Benetton Group, 102
  universally applicable, 119
collective autonomy, 65–66, 71–72, 76, 139, 145
collective bargaining
  multinational, 145
  transnational, 70, 186
collective dismissal, 18
collective institutions, 53, 55
collective labour law, 60, 66, 72, 156, 159
collective labour rights, 60, 65–68, 76
collective organisation, 32, 69, 73, 75
  and action, 5
  EU transnational, 71
collective participation, 69
collective power, 49, 54
collective representation, 50, 155, 157
collective voice, 54
command-and-control model, 99, 110
command-and-control paradigm, 109
communal values, 66
communication, 133, 144
  and collaboration technology, 150
  and cooperation, 104
  and coordination between workers, 169
  and interaction between coworkers, 64
  between digital workers, 70, 72
  digital networks of, 75
  health consultation system and, 88
  means of, 125
  of teleworkers, 63
  online, 5, 60, 86
communication channels, 68
communication devices, 137–138, 141
communication mechanism, 172
communication right, 69
communication technologies, 136, 149, *See also* ICT
communication tools, 165, 171
Community Charter (CC), 69
compliance
  by unions and labour administrations, 179
  from firms with regulations governing working time, 187
  with a rigidly predetermined working time, 113
  with applicable regulations, 177
  with labour legislation, 169
  with labour regulations, 173
  with labour rights, 32
  with occupational health and safety regulations, 208
  with occupational risk prevention measures, 172
  with sustainability, 33
  with the labour contract, 150, 154
  with the relevant regulations, 175
  with the rest of a worker's rights, 194
  with the right to digital disconnection, 172
  worker's, 211
communication
  unmediated and unmonitored, 67
conciliation, 113, 194, *See also* reconciliation
  apply for, 156
  objective of, 113
  workplace, 10, 192
conciliation between life and work, 2, 21, 108
conciliation measures, 112
conditions
  decent, 102
  health, 92, 208
  labour, 3, 37, 118
  living, 9, 32
constitutional court, 143, 167, 210
consultation rights, 67–69, 76, 177
contact hypothesis, 47
contract of employment, 99, 110, 117, 120, 122–123, 130
contractual distancing, 99, 118
contractual rights, 142
cooperation, 4
  intergroup, 48
  interpersonal, 47, 49
co-responsibility, 10–11, 185, 196
corporate social responsibility (CSR), 15, 19, 21, 26
Countouris, Nicola, 98, 100, 117–118, 124, 140, 144
Court of Justice of the European Union. *See* *CJEU*

courts of the location of the employer, 124, 127
courts of the Member States of the EU, 120
COVID-19 pandemic, 4–6, 19, 28, 31, 34–35, 44, 61–63, 66, 81–84, 89–90, 92–94, 98, 102, 124, 148, 162, 183
co-worker interactions, 4, 45, 54
cross-border crowdworkers, 120
cross-border remote work, 6–7, 118–119, 122, 124–125, 129–131, 170
cross-cutting social ties, 45
cyberbullying, 22, 214

data breach, 151
data controller, 151, 153, 176
data protection, 62, 148, 177
data protection law, 153–155, 160
  European, 151
  labour and, 8, 156–159
data protection rights, 151
De Stefano, Valerio, 14, 27, 31, 36, 98, 100, 105, 118, 140, 144, 171
decent conditions, 102
dehumanisation, 66
delocalisation, 59, 75, 118, 120, 127, 213
democracy, 23
democracy at work, 15, 53
democratic governance, 47
demutualisation, 117–118
depersonalisation, 66
digital communities, 69
digital connection, 61
digital disconnection, 11, 22
digital education, 22
digital hardware, 30, 32
digital law, 165–167, 170, 173, 179
digital market, 65–66, 70
digital nomadism, 170
digital nomads, 6, 120–123, 210
digital platforms, 167–171, 179
digital rights, 22, 166
digital spaces, 33
digital sphere, 12, 38, 46
digital surveillance, 8, 31, 148, 153
digital tools, 52, 67, 176, 209
Digital Transformation. *See* DX
digital violence, 195
digitalization, 7–8, 35, 39, 98, 183
dignity, 23, 163, 214
dignity and privacy, 21
Directive for the improvement of working conditions on digital work platforms (EU), 168
Directive on part-time work, 19
Directive on reconciliation 2019/1158, 18
Directive on Transparent and Predictable Working Conditions (EU), 175, 193
Directives on equality, 18
disconnection from their colleagues, 62
discretionary work, 86–87, 89, 137
domestic work, 16, 164, 190
double shifts, 191
Durkheim, Émile, 46
DX, 84–85

EC, 9, 209–210
ECHR, 70, 152–153, 155–156
economic, social and governance (ESG), 37
ECtHR, 69, 154–155
education and training, 90
EFAs
  2002 Framework Agreement on Telework, 18, 164
  2006 Framework Agreement on Telework, 66
  2020 Framework Agreement on Digitalisation, 164, 195
  2022 Framework Agreement on habitual cross-border telework, 60–61, 66
emotion recognition system, 177
employee participation, 157, 159
employment
  lifetime, 83
  membership-based, 83, 85, 91
  status of, 118, 124, 129
employment contract, 99
  legislation, 165
  or relationship, 149
employment contracts, 5, 8, 83, 135, 144–145, 151, 188, 204
  at the time of entering into the, 153
  conflict rules to be applied to, 200
  general frameworks of, 168
  law rules concerning, 120
  necessary practices fo r the execution of the, 207
  or relationship, 19, 60
  or work rules, 139
  promotion and termination of, 174
  signed by the teleworker, 189
  to order telework, 91–92
  traditional, 141, 170
  with a cross-border element, 130
employment management, 90
employment practices, 81–82
employment regulation system, 15
employment status, 15, 31, 36, 118, 124, 129–130, 190
Employment, Social Policy, Health and Consumer Affairs Council configuration (EPSCO), 166
environmental protection, 84, 101

equal respect, 23
Equal Treatment Framework Directive (2000/78/EC), 95
equality and non-discrimination, 18
equality plan, 195
ESC, 69–70
escape clause, 121, 127, 200
Estlund, Cynthia, 119
EU common market, 66
EU Directive on Algorithmic Systems at Work, 163
EU law, 20, 70, 76
EU regulations, 17–18
EU Telecom Social Partners' Guidelines on Remote Work, 195
European Association of Craft, Small and Medium-Sized Enterprises (UEAPME), 17
European Centre of Enterprises with Public Participation (CEEP), 17, 60
European Commission, 163, 166, 201, *See* EC
European Committee of Social Rights, 69, 71, 205
European Convention of Human Rights. *See* ECHR
European Court of Human Rights. *See* ECtHR
European Data Protection Regulation, 166
European Framework Agreement on Telework, 111, 194, 210
European Parliament, 21, 60, 67, 89, 118, 162, 166, 175, 193, 200, 203, 206
European Parliament's draft Directive on the right to disconnect (2021), 89
European Regulation on Artificial Intelligence, 166
European Social Charter. *See* ESC
European Social Dialogue, 173, 193
European Trade Union Confederation (ETUC), 15, 17, 60, 194
e-work, 27
exclusivity, 141
exploitation, 99, 119

face-time, 50–51
face-to-face interactions, 52, 85
family-work conflicts, 190
fertility rate, 134, 142
Flexible Work Act (Netherlands), 92
flexible working laws, 82
flexicurity model, 2, 18
forced labour, 32, 37
forum of establishment, 126, 129
fragmentation
  multifaceted, 64
  of working time, 188
  organisational, 64
  social, 74
  spatial, 4, 59, 68
  technological, 64
  workplace, 5, 60
Framework Agreement on habitual cross-border telework (2022), 60–61, 66
Framework Agreement on Telework (2006), 66
Framework Agreement on Telework (EU), 10, 90, 92, 164, 184
France, 17, 20, 91, 102, 119
  Labor Code amendment (2016), 89
freedom from work, 101
freedom of action, 107
freedom of association, 32–33, 35–37, 69
freedom of self-determination, 93
freedom of speech, 32–33
freedom of workers to work remotely from other jurisdictions, 130
freely given consent, 153
Fudge, Judy, 31, 186
fundamental rights, 33, 100, 109, 129, 152–153, 169, 178, 186, 193
  equality and non-discrimination, 18, *See also* right to equality and non-discrimination
  of remote workers, 14
  privacy and dignity, 21, 23
  to data protection and privacy, 174

GDPR, 9, 176, 207
gender blind, 185
gender duty, 185
gender equality, 10, 17, 20, 28, 51, 184, 186, 194
gender gaps, 192
gender roles, 10, 185, 190
generational gap, 84
geolocation data, 153
geo-tracking, 154
Germany, 17, 91, 93, 102, 156
  short time working arrangements system (Kurzarbeit), 124
gig economy, 99
Gizmodo, 73
governance of remote work, 17
Greece, 17, 165
  SETEP (Union of Workers in Teleperformance), 73
  teleperformance workers, 73–75

Hamaguchi, Keiichiro, 83
health and safety, 18
  at work, 11, 67, 211, 214
  regulations, 88, 208
health conditions, 92, 208
health consultations, 88
hetero-direction, 103

hierarchy, 45, 103–105, 108
HLPF, 34
home office, 62–63, 124, 155
home working, 35
home-based telework, 84, 183
home-based work, 1–2, 14, 23, 88, 91, 162, 164, 203
HR management guidelines, 106
HR strategies, 99
human control, 23, 174
human dignity, 156–159
human rights, 37, 148, 186
hybrid instruments, 17
hybrid labour, 59
hybrid teleworking, 73, 192
hybrid work, 50, 84
  arrangement, 82
  digitised, 5, 60, 63
  inclusive, 102
  models, 90
  strategies, 29
hybridization, 3, 5, 12, 23

ICT, 4, 8, 14, 59, 62, 81, 156, 160, 214–215
ICT devices and tools, 63
ICT infrastructure, 90
ICT tools, 64, 67, 84–85
ICT-mobile work, 184, 194
ILO Guidelines on Just Transitions, 36, 39
ILO Tripartite Declaration, 38
India, 122
industrial accident, 136–137, 140–143
industrial action, 72–74
industrial democracy, 109
industrial relations, 52, 71
industrial relations systems, 52
Industrial Revolution, 49, 105
informal sociability, 47
information
  access to, 68, 109
  right to, 68
  subject specific, 67
Information and Communication Technology. *See* ICT
information technologies, 148, 155–156
in-office work, 30, 82
in-person working, 50, 55
institutional interaction, 6
intelligent cameras, 171–172
intergroup conflict, 48
intergroup relations at work, 47
international institutions, 3, 26, 28, 33
International Labour Organization. *See* ILO
interpersonal bonds, 4, 63–64
interstitial sociability, 48
inviolability of the home, 91
isolation, 63, 66–68, 74, 90, 172, 191
IT companies, 134
IT industry, 133
IT security, 165
Italy, 17, 19
  Inter-confederal Agreement on agile working for artisan businesses and SMEs, 106
  law on agile working, 99–100, 111–114

Japan
  2013 Act on Employment Promotion of Persons with Disabilities, 95
  Child Care and Family Care Leave Act, 92, 95
  deaths from overwork (Karoshi), 88
  Industrial Safety and Health Act, 87–88
  Labor Standards Act, 86, 92
  labor unions, 93
  Lifetime Employment, 83
  Ministry of Internal Affairs and Communications (MIC), 84
  Telework Promotion Council, 82
  traditional employment system, 5, 82
job precariousness, 99
job satisfaction, 49, 108, 135
job security, 74, 83, 108

Korea
  Comprehensive Manual on Work at home, 138
  KAKAO (Company), 133
  labor unions, 143
  LSA, 136–139
  MOEL (Ministry of Employment and Labor), 134–138, 142
  Occupational Safety and Health Act, 138, 142
  traditional labour law, 8, 134

Labor Standards Act (Japan), 86, 92
Labor Standards Act (Korea). *See* LSA (Korea)
labor unions. *See also* trade unions
  Japan, 93
  Korea, 143
labour and employment law, 4, 45, 140
labour associations, 69
labour conditions, 3, 37, 118
labour consciousness, 64
labour gap, 10, 185, 187
labour inspectorate, 31, 169
labour law
  traditional, 54, 82, 93–94, 140
  traditional (Korea), 8, 134
labour law institutions, 4–6, 12, 18, 131, 171
labour law protections, 23, 35
labour rights

labour rights (cont.)
 application of, 193
 basic, 129
 erosion of, 167
 fundamental, 194
 legislative, 109
 principles of, 15
labour standards, 7, 9, 23, 37, 39, 137, 174
Latvia, 165
legitimate interests, 152–154, 157–159
lifetime employment, 83
litigation, 120, 125
López, Julia, 14, 21, 174, 176, 185, 192, 214
loyalty, 46, 82, 102, 104, 107
LPRL (Spanish Labour Risk Prevention Law), 212
Luxembourg, 18, 20, 201

managerial compulsion, 47
managerial prerogatives, 98, 100, 110
mandatory provisions, 121, 127–128, 130–131
membership-based employment, 83, 85, 91
mental health, 88, 191, 206
misclassification, 99, 141
mobbing, 214
mobile office, 62–63
mobile work, 14, 62, 81, 102
monitoring measures, 8, 150
monitoring of computer equipment, 167
monitoring software, 63, 150
monitoring systems, 100, 112, 158, 172
monitoring technologies, 53
monitoring tools, 150
motherhood, 11, 192
multi-jobs, 140
multi-location contracts, 201
multinational corporate governance, 38
mutual aid, 64–66

neo-republicanism, 109
Netherlands, 82, 92, 122
 Flexible Work Act, 92
new technologies, 67, 100, 105, 117–123, 125, 155, 183, 193
 and hybrid ways of working, 188
 development of, 183
 on privacy and dignity, 8
 use of, 214
non-face-to-face industries, 136
normative values, 70
North-Eastern Asia, 122

occupational hazard, 175
occupational risk, 205, 212
occupational risk prevention, 11, 172, 200, 207

OECD, 38, 93, 134
office
 mobile, 62–63
 virtual, 62, 64
office work, 84, 92
offshoring, 27
offshoring countries, 119
offshoring work, 118
off-site work, 86–87, 89, 149
Organisation for Economic Co-operation and Development. *See* OECD
organization model
 non-hierarchical, 105
organizational model, 98
outsourcing, 7, 27, 74, 99, 140

participation
 collective, 69
 employee, 157, 159
 worker, 20, 103–104
participation rights, 22, 177
Part-Time Agreement (1997), 18
part-time work, 15, 18, 92, 95, 187
performance evaluation, 138, 175, 177
performance evaluation techniques, 207
performance evaluation tools, 149
personal data
 access to, 151
 protection of, 157, 159
personal rights, 91, 152–153, 155–156, 159
personal trust, 100, 105, 107
platform work, 27, 33–34, 36, 59, 64–65, 67–68, 99, 170–171
Platform Work Directive. *See* PWD
porosity, 185
Portugal, 19, 165
power imbalance, 66–67, 76
presumed working hour system, 86–87
principle of inclusive solidarity, 21
principles of participation and proportionality, 16
principles of voluntariness
 and non-discrimination, 11, 186, 194
 and reversibility, 18–20, 165
privacy and dignity, 23
privacy concerns, 141, 172
privacy protection, 87
private international law, 144–145
private law, 71
 international (Korea), 144
production
 cycle, 99
 means of, 103–104, 108, 116–117, 155
 process(es), 73, 104, 114, 140, 170
 responsible consumption and, 28

psychosocial risks, 11–12, 172, 179, 190, 205, 207, 215
public goods, 4, 45, 53
public order, 139–141
public spaces, 30, 39
Putnam, Robert, 45–47
PWD, 67–69, 72, 118, 130

Quebec, 125–126

reasonable accommodation, 82, 92–94
reciprocity, 45, 48
reconciliation, 192
reconciliation measures, 186
reconciliation of life and working time, 111, 114
reconciliation of work and family life, 10, 22, 184–185
reconciliation rights, 189
redistribution, 7, 136, 145, 188
regulation of remote work, 2–3, 17–18, 24, 39, 164
regulatory tools typical of labour law, 101
remotization of work, 98
responsible business conduct (RBC), 37
right of participation, 21
right to collective bargaining, 32, 35, 72, 155, 159
right to data protection and privacy, 174
right to digital disconnection, 3, 172, 188–189, 193, 206
right to disconnect, 89, 99, 166, 206
right to equality, 21
right to equality and non-discrimination, 9, 15, 21–23, 193
right to information, 68
right to inviolability of the home, 209
right to order telework, 90
right to organise, 37, 69
right to privacy, 21, 209
right to private communication between workers, 68
right to refuse home-based work, 91
right to request flexible working arrangements, 92, 95
right to request telework, 90, 92, 95
right to respect for private life, 91, 152–153
right to strike, 32, 72
rights
  algorithmic information, 168
  at work, 35
  communication, 69
  consultation, 67–69, 76, 177
  contractual, 142
  data protection, 151
  digital, 22, 166
  information, 18, 68
  participation, 22, 177
  personal, 91, 152–153, 155–156, 159
  reconciliation, 189
  social, 18, 20, 99
  transnational association, 69
  working time, 193
rights to collective organisation and action, 60
risk mitigation, 174–175
risk of isolation, 62
Rogers, Brishen, 53
Romania, 152, 165
Rome I Regulation, 200
  Article 8 of the, 120–124
  Article 9 of the, 127–128
Rubery, Jill, 187

safety and health education, 88
satellite office work, 81
satellite office-based telework, 84
satellite offices, 84, 134
SDGs, 26–29, 32–38, 75, 185
second-generation laws, 164–165, 179
Sectoral Agreement on Digitalisation (EU), 173
self-determination, 141
self-employed, 61, 86, 123–124, 144
self-employed telework, 86
self-employment, 86, 99, 104, 111, 123, 170
sense of community with co-workers, 49
sexual harassment, 214
Slovakia, 165
sociability, 4, 44
social capital, 45, 49
social dialogue, 21, 23, 35–36, 70–72, 102, 106
social distancing, 98, 135
social dumping, 7, 118–119, 127–129, 202
social integration, 46, 54
social justice, 23, 37
social market economy, 70
social partners, 60, 63, 71–72, 98, 106–107, 149, 159, 166
social protection, 32, 35, 117, 128, 168
social rights, 18, 20, 99
social security protection, 17, 34, 208
social security system, 120, 201
  coordination of, 60
  German, 124
social ties, 45–46, 48–49
social well-being, 31
solidaristic ties, 54–55
solidarity, 4, 46–47
  between workers, 119
  mechanisms of, 63
  social, 48, 66

solidarity (cont.)
  substantive and formal, 64
  values of, 104
  worker, 52–55
sources of regulation, 15, 17, 23
Spain, 17, 19, 165, 173, 201
  Labour and Social Security Inspectorate (ITSS), 205
  LPRL (Spanish Labour Risk Prevention Law), 212
  Organic Law 3/2018, of December 5, on the Protection of Personal Data and guarantee of digital rights, 21
spillover, 13–15, 52, 188
spillover benefits, 4, 45, 48
stakeholders, 61, 101, 140, 194
state regulatory compulsion, 48
strike, 69
strike action, 73
structural imbalance, 153, 156, 160
subordinate work, 98–99
subordination, 6, 12, 45, 86, 100, 103, 105–111, 118
subsidiarity principle, 13, 16–17, 19
supreme court, 142, 204
sustainable cities, 28, 32
sustainable democratic society, 45
Sustainable Development Goals. *See* SDGs

Taylor-Fordism, 106
teamwork-oriented employment practices, 83
technological tools, 4, 59, 61, 111, 175
technologies
  remote work, 50, 52
  telematic, 98
technostress, 173, 179, 205
telecommuting, 134–136, 139, 143, 199
telematic technologies, 98
telemigration, 118
teleperformance, 62, 73–75
telework
  home-based, 84, 183
  satellite office-based, 84
territoriality principle, 124
TEU, 70
TFEU, 69–72, 166
ties
  among wo-workers, 46
  bridging, 47–48, 52
  social, 45–46, 48–49
  solidaristic, 54–55
  workplace, 4, 46–48, 50, 54–55
Tocqueville, Alexis de, 45–46
Togo, 122
trade unions, 8–10, 32, 36–37, 68–69, 73, 101, 129, 133, 158, 179
transparency, 67, 158, 166, 171, 174, 176–177, 180
travel time, 84
Treaty on European Union. *See* TEU
Treaty on the Functioning of the European Union. *See* TFEU
tripartism, 35

UK, 69, 82, 92, 119, 122
UN, 3, 26–27, 33
UN Global Compact, 38
UN Guiding Principles on Business and Human Rights, 38
UN High Level Political Forum on Sustainable Development. *See* HLPF
UN Secretary-General, 34
Union of Industrial and Employers' Confederations of Europe (UNICE), 17
unionization, 52–54, *See also trade unions*
United Kingdom. *See* UK
United Nations. *See* UN
United States. *See* US
universal protection, 82, 94–96
US, 50–53, 73, 84, 95, 118, 125
  GMG Union, 73

voluntary associations, 45–48
voluntary national review (VNR), 34
voluntary status, 18, 20
vulnerability, 3, 12, 18, 23, 120, 131

well-being, 82, 84, 93, 206
  of workers, 81, 96, 172
  worker satisfaction and, 112
WHO, 27, 32, 212
work
  discretionary, 86–87, 89, 137
  from home, 4, 44, 51, 54, 81, 87, 92, 94, 110, 136, 149, 184, 189, 191, 195
  ICT-mobile, 184, 194
  mobile, 14, 62, 81, 102
  offshoring, 118
  off-site, 86–87, 89, 149
  part-time, 15, 18, 92, 95, 187, 192
  platform, 27, 33–34, 36, 59, 64–65, 67–68, 99, 170–171
  social dimension of, 4, 44–45, 52
  subordinate, 98–99
work commodification, 66, 76
work digitization, 4–5
work rules, 136, 138
work styles, 86–87, 94
  compatible with the telework environment, 90
  flexible, 85
  teamwork-oriented, 81

worker mobilisation, 72–73
worker representatives, 39, 63, 68, 129
workers
  agile, 107, *See also* agile work
  crowd, 6
  in-demand, 51
  in-office, 52
  low-wage, 51
  platform, 6, 68, 72, 118, 120, 124, 167–168
working conditions, 8, 46, 51, 54–55, 118, 137–138, 141, 175, 193, 202, 210
  applicable legislation and the rest of, 199
  appropriate, 160
  changes affecting, 68
  decision-making power about the, 144
  fair, 155
  flexibility of, 186
  hours and rest periods, 206
  impact of telework on, 177
  labour sectors with poorly regulated, 190
  minimum, 93, 139
  of remote workers, 10
  potential adverse effects on, 67
  unilateral determination of, 171
  unsatisfactory, 103
  working hours and, 74
working poverty, 35
working time, 10, 22, 112, 118, 135, 194
  and rest time, 11, 203–204
  decent, 186–187
  employers' power to extend, 23
  unregulated, 29
Working Time Directive 2003/88/EC, 193
working time management, 87
working time regulation, 87, 141, 208
working time rights, 193
work-life balance, 4, 6, 44, 51, 54–55, 87, 112, 116, 135, 208
Work-Life Balance Directive 2019/1158, 149, 189, 193
workplace
  in-person, 52
  office, 195
  traditional, 82
  virtual, 61, 68, 70, 171
workplace associations, 45, 47
workplace conciliation, 10, 192
workplace connectedness, 49, 52–53
workplace technology, 4, 45, 52–53, 55
work-related spaces, 32
work-related stress, 32
works council, 156–158
World Health Organization. *See* WHO

Printed by Integrated Books International,
United States of America